# The Modern Soul

*Harvard Dissertations in Religion*

Editors

Margaret R. Miles
and
Bernadette J. Brooten

*Number 21*

*The Modern Soul:*
*Michel Foucault*
*and the Theological Discourse*
*of Gordon Kaufman and David Tracy*

S. Alan Ray

# The Modern Soul

## Michel Foucault
## and the Theological Discourse
## of Gordon Kaufman and David Tracy

S. Alan Ray

Fortress Press                    Philadelphia

Copyright © 1987

The President and Fellows of Harvard College

------------

**Library of Congress Cataloging-in-Publication Data**

Ray, Stephen Alan.
  The modern soul.

    (Harvard dissertations in religion; no. 21)
    1. Theology—Methodology—History—20th century.
  2. Foucault, Michel. 3. Kaufman, Gordon D.
  4. Tracy, David. I. Title. II. Series.
BR118.R38 1987    230'.01    87–21094
ISBN 0–8006–7073–6

------------

3233H87  Printed in the United States of America  1–7073

To The Reverend and Mrs. Thompson Gene Hodges

and

Jeff Taylor Abbott

# Contents

# Acknowledgments

The following individuals and institutions have contributed to the realization of this dissertation. I am pleased to acknowledge their support and cooperation.

I trace the "descent" of this project to a seminar on Foucault and critical theories of history offered by Marilyn Massey in 1982 at Harvard Divinity School. I am grateful to her for later assisting in the preparation of my prospectus, and for her continued interest in my thesis research and writing. Hilary Putnam of the Harvard Philosophy Department also was instrumental in the formation of that prospectus, and went on to assist me as thesis advisor. I very much appreciate his critical and consistently useful comments on early drafts of this dissertation. His own reading of Foucault has been an incentive for reflection on my part. In the nine years of our acquaintance, Margaret Miles and Gordon Kaufman of Harvard Divinity School have helped me understand better the history of theology and the theology of history, and I thank them both for the generosity of their conversation, scholarly advice, and encouragement at each step in the development of this work.

During the academic year 1984–85 it was my pleasure to study with Hubert Dreyfus and Paul Rabinow of the University of California, Berkeley. I gladly acknowledge my debt to them and the University of California for their hospitality, collegiality, and sharing of resources. Special thanks are due Hubert Dreyfus for enhancing my appreciation of social practices as the unpredictable basis for human-scientific theorizing.

I am also pleased to acknowledge American Indian Scholarships, Inc., and Harvard Graduate School of Arts and Sciences for providing the financial assistance which has made the timely completion of this dissertation possible.

The present form of *The Modern Soul* results from the labors of several persons. First and foremost, I wish to thank Marsha Takayanagi, who keyboarded the initial manuscript, for her technical expertise and willingness to make changes as we went along. She skillfully handled every challenge the production of my dissertation entailed. Pamela Chance, as liaison between the Harvard Dissertations in Religion series and Fortress Press, has my sincere gratitude for her highly professional service on behalf of this work. My thanks, also, to Joe Snowden, whose excellent editorial judgment likewise deserves and readily receives my appreciation.

Finally, of the many whose good humor, criticism, and patient friendship have been of benefit to me, I especially want to recognize the Reverend and Mrs. Thompson Gene Hodges, and Jeff Taylor Abbott. They are my stepfather, mother, and partner in life. To them this dissertation is respectfully dedicated.

# Abbreviations

| | |
|---|---|
| *AI* | David Tracy, *The Analogical Imagination* (New York: Crossroad, 1981). |
| *AK* | Michel Foucault, *The Archaeology of Knowledge* (New York: Pantheon, 1972). |
| *BC* | Michel Foucault, *The Birth of the Clinic* (New York: Vintage, 1973). |
| *BRO* | David Tracy, *Blessed Rage for Order* (New York: Crossroad, 1978). |
| *BT* | Martin Heidegger, *Being and Time* (New York/Evanston: Harper & Row, 1962). |
| *DP* | Michel Foucault, *Discipline and Punish* (New York: Vintage, 1977). |
| *ETM* | Gordon D. Kaufman, *An Essay on Theological Method* (rev. ed.; Missoula, MT: Scholars Press, 1979). |
| *GP* | Gordon D. Kaufman, *God the Problem* (Cambridge, MA: Harvard University Press, 1972). |
| *HS* | Michel Foucault, *The History of Sexuality*, vol. 1: *An Introduction* (New York: Vintage, 1978). |
| *HTR* | *Harvard Theological Review* |
| *I & C* | *Ideology and Consciousness* |
| *JAAR* | *Journal of the American Academy of Religion* |
| *JR* | *Journal of Religion* |
| *MC* | Michel Foucault, *Madness and Civilization* (New York: Vintage, 1965). |
| *NGH* | Michel Foucault, "Nietzsche, Genealogy, History," *Language, Counter-Memory, Practice* (Ithaca: Cornell University Press, 1977) 139–64. |

NI        David Tracy, "The Necessity and Insufficiency of Funda-
          mental Theology," in René Latourelle and Gerald
          O'Collins, eds., *Problems and Perspectives of Fundamen-
          tal Theology* (New York/Ramsey, NJ:
          Paulist, 1982) 23–36.

OT        Michel Foucault, *The Order of Things* (New York:
          Vintage, 1970).

PK        Michel Foucault, *Power/Knowledge* (New York:
          Pantheon, 1980).

RelS      *Religious Studies*

RKF       Gordon D. Kaufman, *Relativism, Knowledge, and Faith*
          (Chicago: University of Chicago Press, 1960).

SP        Michel Foucault, "The Subject and Power," Afterword to
          Hubert L. Dreyfus and Paul Rabinow, eds., *Michel
          Foucault* (2d. ed.; Chicago: University of Chicago Press,
          1983) 208–26.

ST        Gordon D. Kaufman, *Systematic Theology* (New York:
          Scribner's Sons, 1978).

TI        Gordon D. Kaufman, *The Theological Imagination*
          (Philadelphia: Westminster, 1981).

TNA       Gordon D. Kaufman, *Theology for a Nuclear Age*
          (Manchester: Manchester University Press; Philadelphia:
          Westminster, 1985).

TToday    *Theology Today*

USQR      *Union Seminary Quarterly Review*

WIE       Michel Foucault, "What is Enlightenment?" *The Foucault
          Reader* (New York: Pantheon, 1984) 32–50.

# Short Titles

Information appears here for frequently used works which are cited by short title. A few short titles do not appear in this list, but in each instance full bibliography is given on the page(s) preceding such references.

Dreyfus and Rabinow, *Michel Foucault*
> Dreyfus, Hubert L., and Paul Rabinow, *Michel Foucault* (2d. ed.; Chicago: University of Chicago Press, 1983).

Foucault, *Language*
> Michel Foucault, *Language, Counter-Memory, Practice* (Ithaca: Cornell University Press, 1977).

Gadamer, *Truth and Method*
> Gadamer, Hans-Georg, *Truth and Method* (New York: Seabury, 1975).

Habermas, *Knowledge*
> Habermas, Jürgen, *Knowledge and Human Interests* (Boston: Beacon, 1971).

Harvey, *Historian*
> Harvey, Van A., *The Historian and the Believer* (Philadelphia: Westminster, 1966).

Hoy, *Foucault*
> David Couzens Hoy, ed., *Foucault: A Critical Reader* (Oxford: Blackwell, 1986).

Kant, *Critique*
> Kant, Immanuel, *Critique of Pure Reason* (New York: St. Martin's, 1929).

Putnam, *Reason*
> Putnam, Hilary, *Reason, Truth and History* (Cambridge: Cambridge University Press, 1981).

Rabinow and Sullivan, *Interpretive Social Science*
> Rabinow, Paul and William M. Sullivan, eds.
> *Interpretive Social Science*
> (Berkeley: University of California Press, 1979).

Rorty, *Consequences*
> Rorty, Richard, *Consequences of Pragmatism*
> (Minneapolis: University of Minnesota Press, 1982).

Rorty, *Philosophy*
> Rorty, Richard, *Philosophy and the Mirror of Nature*
> (Princeton: Princeton University Press, 1979).

Tillich, *Systematic Theology*
> Tillich, Paul, *Systematic Theology*
> ( 3 vols.; Chicago: University of Chicago Press,
> 1951 – 1963).

Tracy, "Defending the Public Character of Theology"
> Tracy, David, "Defending the Public Character
> of Theology," *Christian Century* 98 (1981) 350 – 56.

But let there be no misunderstanding: it is not that a real man, the object of knowledge, philosophical reflection or technical intervention, has been substituted for the soul, the illusion of the theologians. The man described for us, whom we are invited to free, is already in himself the effect of a subjection much more profound than himself. A "soul" inhabits him and brings him to existence, which is itself a factor in the mastery that power exercises over the body. The soul is the effect and instrument of a political anatomy; the soul is the prison of the body.

Michel Foucault, Discipline and Punish

# Introduction

Edward Farley claims that the present debate concerning method in theology is the inheritance of a four-hundred year transformation of Christian self-understanding, inaugurated by the Protestant and Catholic Reformations, and significantly influenced by the rise of the historical-critical method in the late eighteenth and nineteenth centuries. In this Introduction I shall look briefly at both of these important shifts in order to understand better the antecedents of the current "problem beneath the problem of theological method," namely, the problem of the reality of the referents of traditional and demythologized discourse about God, the soul, and salvation history.[1]

I

Prior to the sixteenth century, the institutional Christian community was virtually united in its agreement on three broad subjects: the reality of that toward which its faith, liturgy, and tradition inclined; how these realities manifested themselves (revelation and reason); and how to settle disputes over the interpretation of scripture and tradition (appeal to scripture's "fourfold" sense; citation of precedential interpretations by the magisterium, and sometimes secular authorities). Patristic and medieval theologians, as they began their treatises, alluded to scripture or the teachings of the church. No

---

[1] Edward Farley, *Ecclesial Man* (Philadelphia: Fortress, 1975) 3. Farley's synopsis of the history of the problem of theological method orients parts I and II of the Introduction.

elaborate defense of the authority of these sources, nor of the reality of their (supernatural) referents was expected.[2]

The breakdown of this consensus during and after the Reformations was felt in two directions: one, in the appearance of rival conceptions of the nature of Christianity itself, its ideas of law, freedom, justification, sanctification and faith; and two, in the dispute over the relation of scripture to tradition as the material norms of faith. As Protestants endeavored to establish scripture's autonomy from tradition as a legitimate theological source, and to argue (against the magisterium) for scripture's power to interpret itself and the tradition, the proper method of theological reflection became for the first time a problem within the mind of the Christian community. The result was the birth of theological prolegomena:

> In post-tridentine Catholic thought, inclusive treatises in sacred doctrine were introduced by expositions of revelation as it is contained in the apostolic deposit of tradition and presided over by the magisterium. In Protestant theology, these treatises were introduced by exposition of revelation as it is deposited in Scripture.[3]

The debate over the relative authority of scripture and tradition within the Christian church was itself relativized, though by no means concluded, as Protestant and Catholic communities began first to react against and then to assimilate the techniques and results of historical criticism. The advent of critical scholarship in historiography and philology contributed to the second major shift in the problem of theological method since the Middle Ages: the relativization of classical Christian authorities (self-interpreting scripture and magisterial pronouncements on tradition and scripture) by the authority of

---

[2] Farley argues that the unity of patristic and medieval theological discourse relied on authoritarian methodological presuppositions which were carried over into the debates of the Reformations, and continue to inform much recent theology. See Edward Farley, *Ecclesial Reflection* (Philadelphia: Fortress, 1982) esp. 1 – 168. On the history of hermeneutics from the primitive church to Luther, cf. E. C. Blackman, *Biblical Interpretation* (London: Independent, 1957) 65 – 115; Robert M. Grant with David Tracy, *A Short History of the Interpretation of the Bible* (2d. ed.; Philadelphia: Fortress, 1984) 8 – 91; and James D. Wood, *The Interpretation of the Bible* (London: Duckworth, 1958) 30 – 84.

[3] Farley, *Ecclesial Man*, 4. On scripture and tradition at Trent, cf. Josef Rupert Geiselmann, *Die Heilige Schrift und die Tradition* (Freiburg: Herder, 1962) esp. 91 – 107, 161 – 65; and Karl Rahner, "Scripture and Tradition," *Encyclopedia of Theology* (New York: Crossroad, 1982) 1549 – 54. On the hermeneutics of the Protestant Reformers, cf. Hans Frei, *The Eclipse of Biblical Narrative* (New Haven/London: Yale University Press, 1974) 18 – 37; and James S. Preus, *From Shadow to Promise* (Cambridge, MA: Belknap, 1969) 176 – 99, 226 – 65.

reason reflecting within the new "morality of historical knowledge."[4]

Theologians of the nineteenth century used the historical-critical method to address the Enlightenment's polarization of reason and revelation.[5] They were challenged to defend the truth of traditional Christian claims before an increasingly secular public, whose morality of knowledge and respect for the achievements of science they shared. This required them to define new problematics for theology like the quest for the historical Jesus and the search for an essence of Christianity, whose resolutions would require the application of critical techniques but produce results conducive to faith, and to the prosperity of its institutions. The overriding concern for both Catholic and Protestant theology in and since the nineteenth century has been called the search for a unitary method, a method uniting the claims of faith and the limits of reason.[6]

One effect of theology's assimilation of the historical-critical method was the gradual diminishment of the necessary contents of faith. Ernst Troeltsch,

---

[4] The morality of historical knowledge imposes a moral obligation on all serious speakers to make only those claims which can be justified by reference to prevailing disciplinary standards for truth. As Van Harvey states: "The revolution in historical method occurred only when integrity was identified with loyalty to the methodological procedures of the intellectual community, when historians agreed on general canons of inquiry" (Harvey, *The Historian and the Believer* [Philadelphia: Westminster, 1966] 103).

[5] Frei argues that the immediate effect of the Enlightenment on Christians was not the conversion of believers to atheism, but the polarization of Christians between belief in the miraculous (consistent with the older view of revelation) and belief in a religion of reason:

> Theologically, the centrifugal pressure of modernity in the late eighteenth century (when outright religious skepticism was still a rare thing) was toward complete polarization between those who, equating revelation with unique, salvific, miraculous occurrence qua occurrence, affirmed it, and those who denied positive revelation altogether and opted instead for . . . a straightforward theism or "natural religion." (Frei, *Eclipse*, 62–63)

Cf. Ernst Cassirer (*The Philosophy of the Enlightenment* [Princeton: Princeton University Press, 1951] 134–96), who agrees with Frei that the English and German Enlightenments do not conform to the stereotype of scepticist crusades against religion, but argues that the French movement does. Consequences of the Enlightenment's separation of reason and revelation for piety are definitively drawn in Immanuel Kant, *Religion within the Limits of Reason Alone* (New York: Harper & Row, 1960) 139–90.

[6] On the efforts of the Catholic Tübingen School to develop a post-Kantian theology, and the neoscholastic reaction at midcentury, see Gerald A. McCool, *Catholic Theology in the Nineteenth Century* (New York: Seabury, 1977) esp. 1–36, 129–44; and T. Mark Schoof, *A Survey of Catholic Theology: 1800–1970* (Glen Rock, NJ: Paulist Newman, 1970) esp. 14–44, 165–79. On the rise of critical biblical theology, cf. Charles C. Anderson, *Critical Quests for Jesus* (Grand Rapids: Eerdmans, 1969); Frei, *Eclipse*, 86 and passim; Stephen Neill, *The Interpretation of the New Testament:1861–1961* (London: Oxford University Press, 1964) esp. 1–32; and Claude Welch, *Protestant Thought in the Nineteenth Century, Volume 2: 1870–1914* (New Haven/London: Yale University Press, 1985).

writing in 1898, stated three principles which epitomized the historiographic norms of his day. Troeltsch's principles have influenced theological reflection since. They are the principle of criticism (historical judgments are always merely probable and are subject to revision); the principle of analogy (judgments of probability presuppose the congruity of all events, past and present), and the principle of correlation (the interdependence of all historical events excludes the explanation of any event apart from its spatiotemporal conditions).[7] Together, these principles function to diminish the contents of faith whenever the propositions of faith are formulated in discourse abnormal to the principles of serious reflection. The apodictic historical judgment, the incongruous event, and the unique occurrence—comprehensible in some interpretive communities even through the eighteenth century—were no longer the referents of responsible discourse after the nineteenth century. For contemporary theology, this implies that many if not most of its key doctrines are framed in propositions that are no longer credible:

> In some instances, classical motifs are simply excised such as the resurrection of the body, the determination of each individual's ultimate destiny prior to death and eternal punishment. In most cases, classical motifs were retained in an ambiguous rhetoric which still spoke of Jesus as the Word, God's mighty acts, the resurrection, and the trinity but in such revised senses that few could understand what was really retained.[8]

Until recently, however, theological reflection according to the historical morality of knowledge had this much in common: an unquestioned belief that theological discourse, despite its lack of a unitary method and no matter which of the available problematics it took as its point of departure, was nonetheless discourse about some reality beyond the theological conversation itself. Theology referred to entities "out there" in the "real world," even when the scope of that reference was reduced by historical criticism to pertain to a very small set of objects: a transcendent creator-God, human beings with specific religious potentials, and the historical event and person of Jesus. Theological communities assumed that faith ultimately witnessed to "distinctive transcendent, human, and historical realities."[9]

---

[7] Ernst Troeltsch, "Ueber historische und dogmatische Methode in der Theologie," *Gesammelte Schriften* [4 vols.; Tübingen: Mohr-Siebeck, 1911–1925] 2. 729–53); see also idem, "Historiography," *Encyclopaedia of Religion and Ethics*, (13 vols.; New York: Scribner's Sons, 1951) 6. 716–23.

[8] Farley, *Ecclesial Man*, 5–6.

[9] Ibid., 6.

Taking stock, we see that nineteenth-century theology relativized the Reformers' quarrels over the interpretation of scripture and tradition (how their respective "weights" should inform the rules of textual exegesis). Theology since the Enlightenment has, under the influence of the historical-critical imagination, gone on to question how the supernatural realities indicated in pious conversation can be morally brought to language. For much of the present century, the problem of theological method has been the problem of selecting critieria appropriate to the clarification of human relations with these realities (however diversely conceived), bearing in mind the morality of historical knowledge. It was the assumption of the reality of the referents of theological discourse that linked both liberal and neoorthodox projects with the intraecclesial disputes of the Reformations, and with the medieval and patristic consensus before them.

## II

In the early 1960s Protestant theologians began entertaining what Farley calls the "nasty suspicion" that theological assertions about the nature of reality were, in fact, empty and that the traditional referents of religious language did not exist.[10] This suspicion was in part the result of what Langdon Gilkey describes as the "breakup on an intellectual level" of an "uneasy dualism" effected by neoorthodoxy, when it attempted in the early decades of the twentieth century to "ingraft" traditional biblical notions of God, the human, and salvation history onto the post-Enlightenment, secular cosmology and self-understanding.[11] Two reasons for this breakup deserve notice.

The first is the relativization of the uniqueness of received formulations of Christian doctrine by theologians influenced by the anthropological categories of existentialism. Rudolf Bultmann attempted to isolate a "kerygma" or message from the (obsolete) mythological biblical picture which would be acceptable to his enlightened contemporaries, but beyond the principles of verification then employed by science. Bultmann flatly states, "the historical problem is not of interest to Christian belief in the resurrection," adding that the apostles "may be regarded merely as figures of past history, and the Church as a sociological and historical phenomenon."[12] Bultmann wanted the tenets of faith to conform to the ontology of human existence developed by the early Heidegger in *Being and Time.* The Word of God, for its part, was to be indebted to the findings of phenomenology for its possible (existential) meaning, and to the free response of faith for its concrete

---

[10] Ibid., 6–7.

[11] Langdon Gilkey, *Naming the Whirlwind* (New York: Bobbs-Merrill, 1969) 91–92.

[12] Rudolf Bultmann, *Kerygma and Myth* (New York: Harper & Row, 1961) 42, 44.

(existentielle) significance. By systematically deriving the possibility of faith from an analytic of existence, Bultmann, like his contemporaries Paul Tillich and Karl Rahner, distinguished his position from the neoorthodox dialecticism of Karl Barth. The transcendence of *Dasein* joined the transcendence of God "beyond the visible world and beyond rational thinking."[13] Together the overtly existentialist theologies stood together like an inverted pyramid, balanced precariously on Heidegger's analytic of *Dasein* as their apex.

The surface on which this pyramid would rest, however, was property claimed by critics of transcendence, and it was not long before interpreters of Karl Marx, Friedrich Nietzsche, and Sigmund Freud began to challenge, now from within theology, the reality of God, the soul, and salvation history which traditional and demythologized theological discourse had presupposed. The reality of God as Ground of Being, of Jesus as the New Being, of the human as hearer-of-the-Word, and of history as the medium of God's proclamation of freedom was fundamentally challenged. The conclusions of the "masters of suspicion" (Ricoeur) went straight to the heart of theology's claim to be talking about more than the resentment of the strong by the weak (Nietzsche), the rationalization of economic oppression (Marx), or the sublimation of desire (Freud).[14]

Theological hermeneutics was deemed insufficient to grasp the underlying reality of its own discourse. What is needed, so it has been claimed, is the application of anthropologically critical theories to unmask resentment, ideology, and infantile distress for what they are. Paul Ricoeur, who is in sympathy with this aim, has declared that the conclusions of Freud, Marx, and Nietzsche "are hereafter the views through which any kind of mediation of faith must pass."[15] The existentialist pyramid was beginning to tumble.

---

[13] Rudolf Bultmann, *Jesus Christ and Mythology* (New York: Scribner's Sons, 1958) 40.

[14] Cf. Sigmund Freud, *Civilization and its Discontents* (New York: Norton, 1961); idem, *The Future of an Illusion* (New York: Norton, 1961); idem, *Moses and Monotheism* (New York: Vintage, 1967); idem, *Totem and Taboo* (New York: Vintage, 1946); Karl Marx, "Contribution to the Critique of Hegel's *Philosophy of Right*: Introduction," "Economic and Philosophic Manuscripts of 1844: Selections," "Theses on Feuerbach," "The German Ideology: Part I," in Robert C. Tucker, ed., *The Marx-Engels Reader* (New York: Norton, 1972) 11–23, 52–103, 107–9, 110–64; Karl Marx and Friedrich Engels, *On Religion*, (New York: Schocken, 1964); Friedrich Nietzsche, *Beyond Good and Evil* (New York: Vintage, 1966) 57–76; Friedrich Nietzsche, "The Gay Science," "Thus Spoke Zarathustra," "Twilight of the Idols," "The Antichrist," in Walter Kaufmann, ed., *The Portable Nietzsche* (New York: Viking, 1968) 93–102, 112–439, 463–563, 568–656.

[15] Paul Ricoeur, "The Critique of Religion," *USQR* 28 (1973) 209. See idem, *Freud and Philosophy* (New Haven/London: Yale University Press, 1970); and Hans Küng (*Does God Exist?* [Garden City, NY: Doubleday, 1980] esp. 189–424) on post-Enlightenment critiques of religion.

In the hands of political and other liberation theologians, the critique of religion proceeded alongside or within the criticism of society. Dorothee Soelle, a pupil of Bultmann, joined other students of existential theology in attacking the abstract separation of the conditions of freedom from the lived reality of oppression. She asks:

> Why has the concern for demythologizing, if it is after all a part of an enlightened movement, gnawed away exclusively at mythology? Who made the prior decision that mythology would be our essential and sole problem?[16]

She asserts that "the verification principle of every theological statement is the praxis that it enables for the future. Theological statements contain as much truth as they deliver practically in transforming reality."[17] Johannes Metz, a former student of Rahner, states in agreement:

> Any existential and personal theology that claims to understand human existence, but not as a political problem in the widest sense, is an abstract theology with regard to the existential situation of the individual.[18]

In summary, the "uneasy dualism" of ancient and post-Enlightenment worldviews proposed by neoorthodoxy failed to sustain a unitary theological discourse because (1) the existentialist interpretations of traditional Christian concepts and doctrines relativized the authority of particular, historical faith claims to the "comportment" of some version of *Dasein* so that accepting the biblically announced kerygma meant accepting a correlative ontological addressee. This was followed in the 1960s by (2) a growing dissatisfaction with transcendence as a theological point of departure, manifested since approximately 1970 in the theologies of liberation, whose methods have been influenced by the hermeneutics of suspicion and the critique of culture.[19]

---

[16] Dorothee Soelle, *Political Theology* (Philadelphia: Fortress, 1974) 49–50.

[17] Ibid., 77.

[18] Johannes B. Metz, *Faith in History and Society* (New York: Crossroad, 1980) 62–63. See idem, *Theology of the World* (New York: Herder and Herder, 1969). See Elisabeth Schüssler Fiorenza, *In Memory of Her* (New York: Crossroad, 1983) 3–95, presenting a feminist critical method for the theological reconstruction of Christian origins, and its application (pp. 99–351); also, cf. two political theologies influenced by Jürgen Habermas's critique of communicative competence. Helmut Peukert, *Science, Action, and Fundamental Theology* (Cambridge, MA: MIT Press, 1984), and Rudolf J. Siebert, *From Critical Theory of Society to Theology of Communicative Praxis* (Lanham, MD: University Press of America, 1979).

[19] The Death of God movement's attack on obejctified theism in the early 1960s, inasmuch as general observations can be offered, was an endorsement of radical transcendence in the form of an eschatological faith in the imminent negation of time by eternity. As Thomas J. J. Altizer

Where critical hermeneutics has been consistently performed, the result has been the eclipse of the problem of theological criteria by the subproblem of the reality of the referents of theological discourse. There is now, for the first time, a fear within many theological circles that those things which were previously visible from a religious frame of reference are, and were always, unreal, the mirages of *ressentiment*, economic oppression, or frustrated desire.

### III

This dissertation is not an attempt to allay these fears. It is an argument claiming that in two cases, the problem of the reality of the referents of theological discourse is a logical consequence of the anthropological assumptions held by the speakers of that discourse. The two cases are the positions of Gordon Kaufman and David Tracy. To support this thesis I develop a structural and historical perspective on philosophical anthropology based on the work of the late Michel Foucault. Foucault's researches make the reader keenly aware of the historicity of anthropological discourse, its contingency upon specific social practices and institutions, and its possibility of demise. His studies offer an informed perspective on existentialism and critical theories which can assist in understanding the problem of the reality of the referents of theological discourse neither as an inevitable implication of the clash of intrinsic determinations toward facticity and self-transcendence, nor as a vestige of false consciousness or an illusion, nor as a false problem for "real faith" which holds its object by "grace alone."

Foucault's historico-criticism of the human sciences offers an interpretive grid through which the theological anthropologies of Kaufman and Tracy can be viewed. I argue that these two positions see the human as a self-transcending entity whose language and experiences provide (for Tracy) access points to depth knowledge of reality, or (for Kaufman) raw material for the increasingly comprehensive organization of life. For both, language is an instrument at the disposal of a self-transcending subject.

---

paradoxically asserts: "Theology must learn of an eschatological faith that can liberate the contemporary believer from the inescapable reality of history. (Altizer and William Hamilton, *Radical Theology and the Death of God* [Indianapolis/New York: Bobbs-Merrill, 1966] 110). The failure of the dialectical method advocated by Altizer and Hamilton to include as one of its moments a political critique of the theologians' situation, confined its credibility to that assigned to neoorthodox positions before it (p. 109). More indicative of the trend toward theologies of liberation *within* history is Harvey Cox, *The Secular City* (rev. ed.; New York: Macmillan, 1966) esp. 91 – 142.

The relationship of the subject to self-knowledge is explored in terms of the two theologians' methodological integrations of the human sciences. For Tracy, they are indispensable therapies for distorted consciousness and necessary means of acquiring true knowledge about the world. The revisionist theologian is morally bound to observe the authority of their conclusions. For Kaufman, the human sciences have either a limited authority as preparatories for theological reflection, or, as his most recent work indicates, they have no intrinsic authority over theological thinking. The self-transcending subject is obligated in its construction to observe purely formal norms derived from analysis of the God-concept. To the extent that each position incorporates the human sciences into its theological method, Foucault's criticism of these sciences serves as an interpretive device for assessing possible consequences within theological discourse.

The particular consequence for which I argue is the position that the problem of the reality of God will remain unsolved for these theologies inasmuch as they share the human sciences' vision of an anthropological subject of experience knowable only through the critique of its objective experiences. Foucault calls this anthropological subject/object, "man." The problem of God's reality cannot be overcome within anthropologically oriented theology because "man" is morally obligated to discover the deep truth of his nature by critical reflection on his manifold ways of appearing, and cannot posit their foundation (God) outside the self. Foucault's work enables me to argue that this is something human-scientific and contemporary theological reflection cannot do. The figure addressed and assumed by the discourse of philosophical anthropology, the "Modern soul," remains a stranger to itself and to its foundations.

# 1

# Philosophical Debates
# on the Human Sciences

This chapter offers a sketch of recent thought by selected philosophers on the scientific study of human beings. My aim is orientational: to alert the reader to contemporary issues in reflection on the human sciences (anthropology, economics, linguistics, political science, psychology, and sociology, inter alia); and to illustrate how these issues have been treated by divergent philosophical orientations (Rorty and Habermas) and perspectives of some similarity (Taylor and Dreyfus). My intention is orientational in a second sense: to provide a context where, in Chapters 2 and 3, Foucault's texts can be read for insight into the philosophical problems framed below.

## Background: Dilthey's Historicism

A touchstone for current discussion of the object, method, and status of the human sciences remains Wilhelm Dilthey's distinction between sciences of mind or "spirit" (*Geisteswissenschaften*) and sciences of matter or "nature" (*Naturwissenschaften*). Dilthey argued that artifacts and history are unlike natural objects and events in so far as the former are objective manifestations of individual and collective "life" (*Leben*).[1] The study of

---

[1] By "life" Dilthey does not mean exclusively the biological features of existence, but on the contrary, "the whole sphere of human life . . . the life of mankind with its social organizations and cultural achievements" (*Pattern and Meaning in History* [New York: Harper & Row, 1961] 64). Dilthey's *Geisteswissenschaften* include not only the sciences of anthropology, economics,

history and other meaningful human expressions is possible because "these systems have sprung from the same human nature as I experience in myself and others":[2]

> The interrelation of life, expression and understanding, embraces gestures, facial expressions and words ... permanent mental creations ... and permanent objectifications of the mind in social structures in which human nature is surely and for ever manifest.[3]

Retrieving the meaning of these life-expressions cannot be achieved by imposing heteronomous laws according to hypothesis and deduction, since their order springs from the peculiar concerns of historically situated actors whose intentions cannot be formalized. Instead, the human sciences rely on the empathetic powers of the interpreter to reconstruct imaginatively the significance underlying an expression of life. As Dilthey explains,

> Life, experience of life and the human studies are, thus, constantly related and interacting. It is not conceptual procedure which forms the foundation of the human studies but the becoming aware of a mental state in its totality and the rediscovering of it by empathy. Here life grasps life and the power with which these two basic procedures of the human studies are carried out preconditions their adequacy in all other branches.[4]

Dilthey's historicism placed his followers in a bind. On the one hand, the study of *human* capacities should not attempt to apply the hypothetico-deductive model to its objects. On the other, this same study can and should aspire to the status of *science* :

> In every science as such the demand for general validity is implied. If the human studies are to be sciences in the strict sense of the word they must aim at validity more consciously and more critically.[5]

Anglo-American philosophy, after a generation of logical empiricism and its quest for a unified science, has turned with new interest in the last twenty-

---

etc., listed above, but include history, law, philosophy, architecture, and the humanities: study of religion, literature, poetry, and music, et al. (p. 68).

[2] Ibid., 66.

[3] Ibid., 71.

[4] Ibid., 79.

[5] Ibid., 81.

five years to the problematic defined by Dilthey and others at the turn of the last century.[6] In 1980 Hubert Dreyfus wrote:

Of the many issues surrounding the new interest in hermeneutics, current debate has converged upon two:
1. Is there any difference between the natural and the human sciences?
2. If there were such a difference, what personal and political difference would it make?[7]

Dreyfus's questions will orient the following.

# Hermeneutics and Critical Theory

*Richard Rorty*

Richard Rorty admits a difference has existed in the past between human and natural sciences but argues that today it is "uninteresting": the *historical* distinction philosophers have drawn between the *Geistes-* and *Naturwissenschaften* mirrors no *ontological* distinction between people and natural objects.[8] It is only a case in which the natural sciences have been successful in articulating the conditions under which agreement could be reached on any controversial point. Natural sciences' discourses have been "commensurable," by which Rorty means they are "able to be brought under a set of rules which will tell us how rational agreement can be reached on what

---

[6] This time, however, Dilthey's faith in an historical substrate of common human nature, his assumption of a possible contemporaneity with the spirit of others, and his hermeneutic progressivism ("we understand Goethe better than he understood himself")—in short, those positions that allow us to call him a romanticist—have been seriously challenged by Hans-Georg Gadamer's argument for the radically linguistic character of our being-in-the-world. In addition to Gadamer, *Truth and Method* (New York: Seabury, 1975), see also his related essays, "The Universality of the Hermeneutical Problem" (1966) and "Man and Language" (1966), in idem, *Philosophical Hermeneutics* (Berkeley: University of California Press, 1976) 3–17, 59–68. Other bibliographic resources on romanticist and contemporary hermeneutics are found at Chapter 7, n. 8, below.

On the career of logical empiricism and its engagement with philosophy of language and the human sciences, cf. Richard Rorty, "Introduction: Metaphilosophical Difficulties of Linguistic Philosophy," in idem, ed., *The Linguistic Turn* (Chicago: University of Chicago Press, 1967) 1–39; Karl-Otto Apel, *Analytic Philosophy of Language and the Geisteswissenschaften* (Dordrecht: Reidel, 1967); Paul Rabinow and William M. Sullivan, "The Interpretive Turn: Emergence of an Approach," in idem, eds., *Interpretive Social Science* (Berkeley: University of California Press, 1979) 1–21.

[7] Hubert L. Dreyfus, "Holism and Hermeneutics," *The Review of Metaphysics* 34 (1980) 3.

[8] Richard Rorty, "A Reply to Dreyfus and Taylor," *The Review of Metaphysics* 34 (1980) 39.

would settle the issue on every point where statements seem to conflict."[9] Among the human sciences, nothing close to commensurability has ever been achieved.

Moreover, when discourses are commensurable their practice constitutes "normal science." The discourses they cannot make sense of they call "abnormal."[10] Epistemology for Rorty is the ideology of commensurable discourses and normal science. It seeks to justify normal science by providing the transcendental conditions of its possibility, to erect permanent foundations for the expansion of normal science, and, at the limit, to construe the rules for commensurable discourses to apply to every statement, no matter how odd, in the interest of reaching consensus:

> The dominating notion of epistemology is that to be rational, to be fully human, to do what we ought to do, we need to be able to find agreement with other human beings. To construct an epistemology is to find the maximum amount of common ground with others. The assumption that an epistemology can be constructed is the assumption that such common grounds exist.[11]

As much as epistemology is "a description of our study of the familiar," hermeneutics for Rorty is "a description of our study of the unfamiliar."[12] Hermeneutics is neither a philosophical discipline, nor a method (as Dilthey maintained), nor a research program. It is an attitude characterized by a willingness to forego the quest for Kantian foundations and ahistorical explanatory frameworks in favor of continuing "the conversation of mankind" (Oakeshott) by submitting oneself to the transformative power of a dialogue with the unfamiliar, "in which we do not remain what we were" (Gadamer).[13]

To summarize, Rorty believes the historical difference between the natural and human sciences is a nonnecessary distinction between normal and abnormal sciences correlative to a distinction between commensurable and incommensurable discourses. Conceivably, in the future natural science could become unfamiliar and warrant the guess-and-validate, dialogical attitude of hermeneutics, while the human sciences could "go normal" and spin out

---

[9] Richard Rorty, *Philosophy and the Mirror of Nature* (Princeton: Princeton University Press, 1979) 316.

[10] See ibid., 320–42; Rorty acknowledges that his use of "normal" and "abnormal" discourse generalizes upon Kuhn's distinction between "normal" and "revolutionary" science. See Thomas S. Kuhn, *The Structure of Scientific Revolutions* (2d ed.; Chicago: University of Chicago Press, 1970).

[11] Rorty, *Philosophy*, 316.

[12] Ibid., 353.

[13] Gadamer, *Truth and Method*, 341.

rigorous epistemological self-justifications. As Rorty claims, "there is no requirement that people should be more difficult to understand than things."[14] As a "response" to Dreyfus's first question, however, Rorty's position must be compared with his explicit endorsement of the "edifying" hermeneutic attitude over "systematizing" philosophies like now-defunct logical empiricism, which take as their task the construction of true transcendental theories. The "personal and political difference" of adopting the hermeneutic attitude for Rorty appears to cash out in a reaffirmation of liberalism and the polity of bourgeois capitalist society.[15] The role of the human sciences in this polity may be to provide occasions for dialogue (owing to their "unfamiliar" subject matter), but this dialogue seems to have no critical function in the analysis of social ills. The very abnormality of the human sciences consigns their discourse to the margins of existing political and social systems. Celebrating these systems, as Rorty advocates, would perpetuate the dividing practices underlying human-scientific discourse, but with no guarantee that more abnormal discourse would result in less oppressive systems.

## Jürgen Habermas

Jürgen Habermas is unwilling to surrender the project of objective human studies to Rorty's deconstruction of post-Cartesian philosophy. Against the trend toward universal hermeneutics, Habermas proposes a distinction among empirical-analytic sciences, the historical-hermeneutical sciences, and critically oriented sciences.[16] On this scheme, the Dilthean split between *Natur-* and *Geisteswissenschaften* is further broken down to reflect real distinctions among instrumental reason (which operates in the empirical-analytic disciplines—Dilthey's "nature-sciences"—according to the hypothetico-deductive model), practical reason (operative in the traditional human sciences and history), and critical reason (rendered through, e.g., psychoanalysis and critique of ideology).[17]

---

[14] Rorty, *Philosophy*, 347.

[15] Rorty states:

> On my view, we should be more willing than we are to celebrate bourgeois capitalist society as the best polity actualized so far, while regretting that it is irrelevant to most of the problems of most of the population of the planet. (Richard Rorty, *Consequences of Pragmatism* [Minneapolis: University of Minnesota Press, 1982] 210 n. 16)

[16] See Habermas, *Knowledge and Human Interests* (Boston: Beacon, 1971) 301–17.

[17] The analysis of reason as cognitive interest is part of Habermas's unmasking of scientism in the early 1960s; cf. ibid., 3–5, 301–17, and passim. My exposition of cognitive interests connects with Habermas's later attempt to reconstruct historical materialism as a history of labor and language; for the latter see the essays in Jürgen Habermas, *Communication and the Evolution of Society* (Boston: Beacon, 1979); see idem, "History and Evolution," *Telos* 39 (1979) 5–48.

Habermas is sensitive, however, to the historicity of all reason and thus prefers to speak of cognitive *interests* based on the actual development of the human species through time. Because nature must be subdued for humans to prosper, the history of labor reveals a technical cognitive interest in forging empirical-analytic tools which contribute to the forces of production. The organization of these forces and their social deployment (the formation and reformation of relations of production) proceeds on a separate logic through the medium of language—not labor—and embodies the practical cognitive interest of reaching an understanding. Here the historical-hermeneutical sciences, from within the arena of culture, interpret the meaning of human expressions and debate the proper ordering of society. Last, because the evolution of communication and labor has in fact worked to skew productive and communicative relations to serve particular interests, while simultaneously repressing from conscious awareness any immediate knowledge of these distortions, there exists a cognitive interest in emancipation. Through the medium of power, immanent in disciplined self-reflection, the critical sciences operate to "release the subject from dependence on hypostatized powers."[18] Habermas believes that the three cognitive interests form vantage points from which any feature of individual or social reality can be understood in its truth and brought to conformity with its ultimately humane nature. The three interests apply "with transcendental necessity" to all experience:

> Orientation toward technical control, toward mutual understanding in the conduct of life, and toward emancipation from seeming "natural" constraint establish the specific viewpoints from which we can apprehend reality as such in any way whatsoever. By becoming aware of the impossibility of getting beyond these transcendental limits, a part of nature acquires, through us, autonomy in nature.[19]

In the past few years, Habermas has attempted the theoretical integration of "reconstructive" sciences like Chomsky's structural linguistics, Piaget's developmental psychology, and Kohlberg's theory of moral development into existing critical theory. Success here would allow the critique of concrete situations of discourse and action to proceed under the guidance and authority of norms derived from strictly empirical analyses of language, consciousness, and moral justification. This project of a universal pragmatics harks back to the three-fold analytic of experience and its distinguishable "interests," but now the transcendental character of these interests will be

---

[18] Habermas, *Knowledge*, 310.
[19] Ibid., 313; see also 311.

demonstrated from *within* experience itself, by the reconstructive sciences, rather than postulated to account for the forms of experience *to date*. Universal pragmatics would therefore have a predictive capability absent from any history of the species and its conditions of possibility. This project of a universal pragmatics now includes a search for a theory of communicative competence, adopting as its reconstructive component a version of speech-act theory, and predicated on an assumption of an ideal speech situation operative in all authentic conversation (dialogue in which claims are intelligible, sincerely offered, justifiably asserted, and true).

It is easy to see that for Rorty, Habermas's attempt to "ground" the natural and the human sciences in either a transcendental theory of human interests or its current version, a universal pragmatics, is at best superfluous to the encouragement of unconstrained dialogue and the appreciation of cultural diversity. Habermas is, like Kant, "scratching where it does not itch," in dividing up reality in order to underwrite claims of knowledge and competence in each domain.[20] Rather than continue the search for foundations (the hallmark of epistemology),

> what we need is a sort of intellectual analogue of civic virtue—tolerance, irony, and a willingness to let spheres of culture flourish without worrying too much about their "common ground," their unification, the "intrinsic ideals" they suggest, or what picture of man they "presuppose."[21]

Where Habermas "goes transcendental and offers principles" to account for a social hope of undistorted communication, "the pragmatist must remain ethnocentric and offer examples." In Rorty's case, these are examples of "truth and justice that lie in the direction marked by the successive stages of European thought."[22]

In summary, Habermas strongly endorses a distinction between the natural and the human sciences. The distinction is not based, he claims, on the nature of an ahistorical subject of transcendental consciousness, but on a critique and reconstruction of the actual interests realized in the history of the species. Three interests emerge which demand distinct clusters of sciences for their intelligibility: empirical-analytic, historical-hermeneutical, and critical sciences. Habermas is currently attempting to ground his assertion of

---

[20] Richard Rorty, "Habermas and Lyotard on Postmodernity," *Praxis International* 4 (1984) 34–36.

[21] Ibid., 38.

[22] Rorty, *Consequences*, 173. Habermas responds to the claims made in Rorty, "Habermas and Lyotard," in Jürgen Habermas, "Habermas: Questions and Counter-Questions," *Praxis International* 4 (1984) 229–49, esp. 231–34.

these interests in a universal pragmatics. If successful, this pragmatics will operate on distortions in economic relations, individual consciousness, and communication, through the power of liberating self-reflection.

The possibility of true reconstructive and critical theories has, as one "personal and practical difference," the potential realization of Kant's great dream of freeing men and women from their "self-incurred tutelage" to the direction of others: what Habermas calls their "dependence on hypostatized powers." [23] Another consequence, however, is the acknowledging of the authority of philosophy in society to determine what counts as rational discourse and what does not. This might give one pause, if Habermas did not hasten to reassure us that his philosophy shares "a fallibilistic consciousness" with science, and operates with "a self-imposed modesty of method":

> Philosophy shares with the sciences a fallibilistic consciousness in that its strong universalistic suppositions require confirmation in an interplay with empirical theories of competence. This revisionary self-understanding of the role of philosophy marks a break with the aspirations of first philosophy ... in any form, even that of the theory of knowledge; *but it does not mean that philosophy abandons its role as the guardian of rationality.*[24]

Could this modest philosophy be a "benign dictator?" As Mary Hesse has observed, concluding a discussion of Habermas's use of the reconstructive sciences, "it is not clear that the theories of reconstructive sciences can be 'pure' and ideology free any more than can empirical theories."[25] Inasmuch as the goal of Habermas's recent work is, in Thomas McCarthy's phrase, the "rational reconstruction of universal competences," I think that the relationships among reconstructive sciences, critical theories, and the social practices from which both kinds of reflection arise deserve far more attention than Habermas has given them to date.[26] For only if the social

---

[23] Immanuel Kant, *On History* (Indianapolis/New York: Bobbs-Merrill, 1963) 3.

[24] Habermas, "Questions," 232 (my emphasis).

[25] Mary Hesse, "Science and Objectivity," in John B. Thompson and David Held, eds., *Habermas: Critical Debates* (Cambridge, MA: MIT Press, 1982) 115; for related discussion, see idem, *Revolutions and Reconstructions in the Philosophy of Science* (Bloomington/London: Indiana University Press, 1980) 167–86.

[26] Thomas McCarthy, *The Critical Theory of Jürgen Habermas* (Cambridge, MA: MIT Press, 1978) 278. Habermas's separation of reconstructive sciences and the social practices underlying them ignores that the human sciences are themselves practices. As Hilary Putnam has argued, the idea of an objective social science only had appeal as long as physics could stand as the paradigm of reflection unencumbered by a cultural matrix, and so could be "objective." But as Putnam observes,

> there is no key to objectivity. Or rather, the idea of a kind of objectivity that does not

practices supporting critical and reconstructive theorizing are ignored can Habermas offer analyses of knowledge formation which are not at the same time analyses of power. The relation between power and knowledge should have a prominent place in Habermas's reflection on the role of the human sciences in contributing to the normalization of social relations.

Such reflection has not been forthcoming. For Habermas, power *constrains* (negatively) or *liberates* (positively), but it does not *produce* either that upon which it operates: the order of words, consciousness, the conscience, communication; nor that through which contemporary knowledge of these anthropological givens is gained: psychology (consciousness), linguistics (the order of words), moral development theory (the conscience), or speech-act theory (communication). Philosophy, the "guardian of rationality," defends reason against power with the power of reason. The question, whence derives philosophy's power and that of the human sciences, is never asked by Habermas because the answer seems evident: from reason itself, whose authority is derived from nature and the order of things.

The following positions can be seen as falling between Rorty's hermeneutic laissez-faire and Habermas's project of a universal pragmatics. They are the views of Charles Taylor and Hubert Dreyfus, both of whom, I believe, take more seriously than Rorty or Habermas the power of social practices for the formation of knowledge.

# The Primacy of Practices

*Charles Taylor*

Charles Taylor claims that the human sciences are very different from the natural sciences because "human beings are self-interpreting animals."[27] This means that how the world is for us is, to the extent that it is a *human* world, determined by the meanings or imports we ascribe both to the world and to ourselves. These ascriptions, or "desirability-characterizations," cannot be ignored or formalized by a study of the human modeled on the

---

spring from and is not corrected by a human practice is absurd. History, philosophy, sociology are human practices. Their standards of objectivity must be created, not found by some transcendental investigation (not even one that calls itself "epistemology naturalized"). (Putnam, "On the Status of the Social Sciences," unpublished paper, 1986)

On the status of "postempirical science," see Hesse, *Revolutions*, esp. 172–73. For Putnam, standards are made in the doing of good work in all disciplines, not by the wholesale imitation of the effective procedures of physics.

[27] Charles Taylor, *Human Agency and Language* (Philosophical Papers, vol. 1; Cambridge: Cambridge University Press, 1985) 45.

example of natural science. Natural science observes the "requirement of absoluteness," which is "to give an account of the world as it is independently of the meanings it might have for human subjects, or of how it figures in their experience."[28]

Taylor's argument is that our use of the language is not merely or primarily to "point" to things "out there," but is actually to *constitute* our very experience as subjects, and to *validate* this experience by reference to a pregiven "field" of intersubjectively determined meanings. To require the human sciences to describe our experience and this field apart from their significance for us as subjects, therefore, would be comparable to requiring an ornithologist to explain avian flight without reference to wings. As Taylor summarizes:

> The requirement of absoluteness can (and indeed, we all agree that is must be made) of natural science, but it is inapplicable to human science. For one thing which is eminently clear is that the properties described by desirability-characterizations are paradigmatic subject-related properties.[29]

The idea that the human world is composed of intersubjective meanings stems from Dilthey. Taylor's importance seems to me to be his insistence on linking the world to a subject's use of language, this same use to specifiable social practices, and these practices to politics. For example (to take one of Taylor's frequent cases), the phenomenon of shame cannot be understood apart from reference to a subject who experiences something shameful; shame is a "subject-related property." But experiencing shame (like other emotions) is intimately connected with learning to use the world "shame" properly, distinguishing it from related terms (like "humiliation" and "embarrassment"); in this way, "language is constitutive of our subject-referring emotions" in that "language articulates our feelings, makes them clearer and more defined; and in this way transforms our sense of the imports involved; and hence transforms the feeling."[30] Yet the validity of subject referring emotions is not idiosyncratic. What counts as shameful (or honorable or amoral ) behavior is determined within a matrix of social practices. Practice determines valid language use, while (to switch to Rorty's jargon) normal discourse validates practices and abnormal discourse challenges them. For Taylor, language and social reality are so close that their distinction is "artificial":

---

[28] Charles Taylor, "Understanding in Human Science," *Review of Metaphysics* 34 (1980) 31.
[29] Ibid., 32.
[30] Taylor, *Human Agency*, 71.

> The situation we have here is one in which the vocabulary of a given social dimension is grounded in the shape of social practice in this dimension; that is, the vocabulary would not make sense, could not be applied sensibly, where this range of practices did not prevail. And yet this range of practices could not exist without the prevalence of this or some related vocabulary. There is no simple one-way dependence here.[31]

Determining social reality and normal discourse, in turn, does not consist in a universal pragmatics but, in part, in the realization of political programs. The "personal and practical difference" of Taylor's strong distinction between the natural and human sciences is a concommitant obligation for the interpreter to take cognizance of the "hierarchical relations of power and command" immanent in all social discriminations, and to resist dehumanizing practices accordingly.[32]

Taylor's work calls into question Habermas's claim that power has only a positive (not to say productive) function when it coincides with critical reflection. Language not merely liberates practices from their ideological distortions; practices in turn determine language. By taking seriously the social context of true utterances, Taylor implicitly assigns a productive role to power. Rorty's "conversation" is similarly brought down to earth: the demise of logical empiricism has not spelled the end of the scientific-technological culture it validated, nor the parameters of language and practices that culture still sustains. Announcing the reign of universal hermeneutics does not substitute for political engagement.

## Hubert Dreyfus

Hubert Dreyfus contends that the reason the human sciences have never been able to achieve the disciplinary coherence and regular success of the natural sciences is not because people are intrinsically inscrutable and physical objects are not, nor because the human scientist is involved in an intersubjective world of meaning with the entities she or he studies. It is not even, as Dreyfus himself once believed, because the human scientist can never thematize the background practices delimiting the realm of his or her professional concern, and so reach agreement with other such scientists as to what counts as a relevant feature of behavior for their given discipline.[33]

---

[31] Charles Taylor, "Interpretation and the Sciences of Man," in Rabinow and Sullivan, *Interpretive Social Science*, 45.

[32] Ibid., 33.

[33] Dreyfus thought that "if the human sciences claim to study human activities, then the human sciences, unlike the natural sciences, must take account of those human activities which

Dreyfus now believes that the human sciences cannot make reliable predictions (and so be truly scientific) about the events they observe because the events themselves, qua relevant data, are determined by those studied to be significant features of their experience of an everyday world, whose varying demands and opportunities allow for changes in practices and changes in regularities of behavior, and reports of this behavior. This varying context of the appearance of relevant data must "recede" for the data to be isolated and manipulated to test thoeries; an unproblematic requirement for natural science, but a fatal one for a reliable human science:

> Insofar as [human] sciences follow the ideal of physical theory, they must predict and explain everyday activities, using *decontextualized* features. But since the context in which human beings pick out everyday objects and events whose regularities theory attempts to predict is left out in the decontextualization necessary for theory, what human beings pick out as objects and events need not coincide with those elements over which the theory ranges. Therefore predictions, though often correct, will not be reliable. Indeed, these predictions will work only as long as the elements picked out and related by theory happen to coincide with what the human beings falling under the theory pick out and relate in their everyday activities.[34]

Significantly, the "picking out" of events and objects is not achieved by testing hypotheses within a general theory of, for example, speech or labor, but relies for its success on the acquisition of skills. Dreyfus points to the example of Pierre Bourdieu's criticism of Lévi-Strauss's structuralist theory of gift exchange.[35] Bourdieu argues that Lévi-Strauss's formal, reversible

---

make possible their own disciplines" (Dreyfus, "Holism and Hermeneutics," *The Review of Metaphysics* 34 [1980] 17). Such a taking account of, however, he believed was impossible since the human scientist's "fore-sight" (early Heidegger's *Vorsicht*) was framed by a totality of cultural practices (*Vorhabe*) available only in particular skills, not to theoretical reflection. His revised analysis has been developed in response to criticisms to "Holism" in Mark B. Orkent, "Hermeneutics, Transcendental Philosophy and Social Science," *Inquiry* 27 (1984) 23–49.

[34] Hubert L. Dreyfus, "Studies of Human Capacities Can Never Achieve Their Goal," in Joseph Margolis, ed., *Rationality, Relativism, and the Human Sciences* (Dordrecht: Nijhoff, 1986); an earlier version of this essay is "Why Current Studies of Human Capacities Can Never Be Scientific," (Cognitive Science Report no. 11; Berkeley: University of California, 1984).

[35] Pierre Bourdieu, *Outline of a Theory of Practice* (Cambridge: Cambridge University Press, 1977). Bourdieu claims:

> To restore to practice its practical truth, we must therefore reintroduce time into the theoretical representation of a practice which, being temporally structured, is intrinsically defined by its tempo. ... To substitute *strategy* for *rule* is to reintroduce time, with its rhythm, its orientation, its irreversibility. Science has a time which is not that of practice

rules for gift exchange cannot accurately predict actual transactions because it omits the context of the exchange—and it is the context which, in each situation, supplies the crucial element of timing. As Dreyfus observes, "the meaningful context does more than provide a necessary cover-up of the formal skeleton of the transaction. The tempo of the event actually *determines what counts as a gift*."[36] Learning the proper tempo, and so being able to give gifts and recognize ("pick out") what counts as a present, is acquiring a skill, or rather, a set of skills drawing on the resources (material and cultural) at hand in a given society. These skills, or "background practices," are what Dreyfus believes the human sciences must ignore in order to work up the data for their theories.

Could there be a theory of the background practices, perhaps like Habermas's theory of communicative competence? Here Dreyfus analyzes the relation of rules to skills, and concludes that "the features and rules used in acquiring skills play no role in the exercise of expertise." If so, attempts to rationalize paradigm cases of skill deployment must fail, since the expert actor's original "features and rules" (what would count as the elements or primitives of the skill) are not available to analysis.[37] The Cartesian method does not apply. I believe Habermas's reconstructive sciences, therefore, cannot claim to supply the conditions of the possibility for all competent communication. At most, they would formalize the patterned features of experience picked out as significant by skilled members of distinct linguistic communities. Pragmatics ignores the interpretive relation of the agent to his or her practices when it confuses the formalization of certain of these patterns with the reconstruction of a general competence.

Dreyfus admits, however, that a human science that did not begin by abstracting features of everyday experience, but approached the background practices in some other way, could conceivably arrive at conclusions which were complete and predicably sound. A science of human capacities is possible.

---

. . . because science is possible only in a relation to time which is opposed to that of practice, it tends to oppose time and, in doing so, to reify practices. (pp. 8 – 9)

[36] Dreyfus, "Why Studies." Dreyfus has explored the importance of context for determining significance of features in *What Computers Can't Do* (rev. ed.; New York: Harper & Row, 1979) esp. 256–71.

[37] Dreyfus, "Why Studies." The relation of rules to performance is analyzed in detail in Hubert L. Dreyfus and Stuart E. Dreyfus, "From Socrates to Expert Systems: The Limits of Calculative Rationality," in Carl Mitcham and Alois Huning, eds., *Philosophy and Technology II: Information Technology and Computers in Theory and Practice* (Boston: D. Reidel, 1986); see also idem, *Mind Over Machines: The Power of Human Intuition and Expertise in the Era of the Computer* (New York: Free Press, 1986) esp. 101–21.

But, one must add that since we have no precedent for such a theory, no reason to believe the abstract features it would require exist, and no way to find them if they did, this abstract philosophical point casts no light on the past, present or future difficulties facing the social sciences.[38]

The "personal and political difference" made by Dreyfus's distinction between the human and natural sciences is a repudiation of all attempts to provide a totalizing theory of human being and behavior, a theory which would claim to formalize the background practices on the basis of isolatable features. Instead, Dreyfus urges us, with the later Heidegger, to hold "always before our eyes the extreme danger" of technology and its transformation of unruly and abnormal thought and action into an orderly, "standing-reserve" of disciplined potential. [39] This cashes out in Dreyfus's recommendation of

> *first*, what Foucault calls genealogy, i.e., amassing and interpreting the historical details of how we got to be where we are, and *second*, the as-yet-unnamed hermeneutic activity devoted to interpreting and preserving the inherited understanding of what it means to be, dispersed in our everyday activities—an understanding which makes possible normal as well as abnormal disciplines and gives meaning and seriousness to our lives.[40]

## Beyond "Objective" Human Science

The foregoing can be read as an indication of the degrees of seriousness with which some current philosophers treat the role of social practices in determining the truth of theoretical statements about human beings. Both the practices of human scientists (for Taylor) and the practices of the people they study (for Dreyfus) have been offered as grounds for distinguishing human from natural science. The ubiquity of the hermeneutic circle, recognized in some measure by all those studied in this chapter, has forced those who would maintain a distinction between the two enterprises to argue for a basis of differentiation apart from the traditional, Dilthean opposition of explanation and understanding, appropriate to the intellectual assimilation of "natural" and "spiritual" realities. A pressing issue in contemporary reflection on the human sciences is not whether there can be an "objective" social science, where "objective" means value free or disinterested, but

[38] Dreyfus, "Why Studies."

[39] Martin Heidegger, *The Question Concerning Technology and Other Essays* (New York: Harper & Row, 1977) 33.

[40] Dreyfus, "Holism," 23.

whether a nonobjective social science may yet make claims which are universally valid.

Habermas and Rorty think there can be, but for very different reasons. For Rorty, normal discourse about the human is always a formal possibility, but only that: a generally true statement about people still tells us nothing about a trans-historical human nature. For Habermas, on the other hand, the formal possibility of a universal pragmatics is realized only when it coincides with depth knowledge of the human in concreto as a laboring, speaking, reflecting being; that is, the formal possibility of universally valid knowledge of the human is always a possibility of material information (hence the "quasi-transcendental" status of the cognitive interests).

Taylor and Dreyfus doubt that human-scientific claims can have general validity, and point to the social context of utterances to support their positions. Taylor holds the anthropological view that we are self-interpreting animals who partially constitute both ourselves and our world from out of linguistic resources, such resources in turn being a function of our sociopolitical environment. Dreyfus argues against a theoretical holism accounting for background practices through the formalization of their isolatable features, by defending the role of the interpretive community or individual in deciding, on the basis of ongoing and variable life interests, what will count as an object or event, and thus, what will count as data for the human sciences.

Whether or not the human sciences can make universally valid, albeit interested, claims may depend on their historical specificity. To what extent is the debate on the human sciences a debate on human nature, and why is this nature questionable in the first place? Has it ever been otherwise for disciplined reflection? These questions will be addressed in Chapter 2 in the context of a discussion of Foucault's archaeology of the human sciences.

Also, the conviction held by all those considered in this chapter that what counts as serious ("normal") talk about the human has a history, is joined in Taylor and Dreyfus by the belief that everyday practices, whose order cannot be formalized, nonetheless play a decisive role in the historical determination of this same serious talk. In Chapter 3, I shall look to Foucault's genealogies of modern Western practices for insight into the elusive connection between background behavior and the agent's perception of relevant events and objects (between what Dreyfus, following Heidegger, terms *Vorsicht* and *Vorhabe*). How, in our day, are some discourses validated and others not? Can we see patterns to our contemporary discriminations, linking observed regularities, which perhaps cannot be formalized by reconstructive sciences or critical theories, but which are nevertheless operative in our society?

Also, in Chapter 3, I shall present Foucault's constructive ideas for assuming responsibility for contemporary life. I will look briefly at their relationship to the values of the Enlightenment, and conclude by attempting to determine some of their consequences for the human sciences and the humanistic philosophy those sciences support.

# 2

# Archaeology of the Sciences of "Man"

In considering the question of a possible valid role for the human sciences in Enlightenment-based theologies, I have chosen, for reasons I shall articulate in this chapter and the next, to focus on the work of the late French philosopher, historian, and activist, Michel Foucault. Foucault's diverse research programs—including, inter alia, studies of madness, clinical medicine and the teaching hospital, the *sciences humaine*, and language, as well as histories of the prison and sexuality—have, since their initial appearance in the early 1960s, been the objects of academic controversy.

## Preliminary Remarks

Foucault has been described as a poststructuralist and "young conservative" (Habermas), a Marxist functionalist, French intellectual leftist, pluralist, and political theoretician of local resistance (Waltzer), a metaphysician and philosopher of history in the grand style of Vico, Hegel, and Spengler (White), a cultural relativist and irrationalist (Putnam), an historicist (Hoy and Ross), an antihistoricist (Megill), a philosopher of immature science (Hacking), a Nietzschean antitheorist (Rorty), and simply as the "mandarin of the hour" for ardent francophiles (Steiner).[1] Clifford Geertz, in a 1978 review of

---

[1] This roster of commentators is meant to be illustrative of the range of published opinion on Foucault. For the following citations when more than one work by a particular author is given, the first text is the text in which the view I attribute to the author is presented; other, selected works by that author which address Foucault follow this citation immediately. See Jürgen Habermas, "Modernity versus Postmodernity," *New German Critique* 22 (1981) 3–14; idem,

*Discipline and Punish*, captures the bewilderment of many of Foucault's readers in this description of Foucault's career:

> Michel Foucault erupted onto the intellectual scene at the beginning of the Sixties with his *Folie et deraison*, an unconventional but still reasonably recognizable history of the Western experience of madness. He has become, in the years since, a kind of impossible object: a nonhistorical historian, an antihumanistic human scientist, and a counter-structural structuralist.[2]

I will not be concerned here with making the "impossible object" possible; that is, with searching for a finally adquate label resolving conflicting interpretations of Foucault. Rather, after recapitulating the relevant features of Foucault's work, in this chapter and the following, I shall pose to Foucault the two questions of Dreyfus which guided the previous chapter; namely, is there a difference between the human sciences and the natural sciences, and, if there is, what personal and political difference would it make?

---

"The Entwinement of Myth and Enlightenment: Re-Reading *Dialectic of Enlightenment*," *New German Critique* 26 (1982) 13–30; idem, "Taking Aim at the Heart of the Present," *University Publishing* 13 (1984) 5–6; Ian Hacking, "Michel Foucault's Immature Science," *Nous* 13 (1979) 39–51; idem, "The Archaeology of Foucault," *The New York Review of Books* 28 (May 14, 1981) 32–37; idem, "Five Parables," in Richard Rorty, ed., *Philosophy in History* (Cambridge: Cambridge University Press, 1984) 103–24, esp. 119–24; idem, "Self-Improvement," *University Publishing* 13 (1984) 4; David Couzens Hoy, "Taking History Seriously: Foucault, Gadamer, Habermas," *USQR* 34 (1979) 85–95; Allan Megill, "Foucault, Structuralism, and the Ends of History," *Journal of Modern History* 51 (1979) 451–503; idem, "Looking Back: Philosophy and Myth," *University Publishing* 13 (1984) 13; Jean Piaget, *Structuralism* (New York: Harper & Row, 1970) 128–35; Hilary Putnam, *Reason, Truth and History* (Cambridge: Cambridge University Press, 1981) 155–62; Richard Rorty, "Comments on Hacking's 'Michel Foucault's Immature Science,'" read at the Western Division Meeting of the American Philosophical Association, April, 1979 (as cited by Thomas E. Wartenberg, "Foucault's Archaeological Method: A Response to Hacking and Rorty," *The Philosophical Forum* 15 [1984] 345–64); Rorty, "Habermas and Lyotard on Postmodernity," *Praxis International* 4 (1984) esp. 40–42; idem, *Consequences*, esp. 203–10; Stephen David Ross, "Foucault's Radical Politics," *Praxis International* 5 (1985) 131–44; George Steiner, "The Mandarin of the Hour—Michel Foucault," *The New York Times Book Review* 8 (February 28, 1971) 8, 28–31; idem, "Steiner Responds to Foucault," *Diacritics* 1 (1971) 59 (Steiner's side of a polemic; Foucault's contributions are, "Monstrosities in Criticism," *Diacritics* 1 [1971] 57–60; and, "Foucault Responds/2," *Diacritics* 1 [1971] 60) ; Michael Waltzer, "The Politics of Michel Foucault," *Dissent* 30 (1983) 481–90; Hayden White, *Tropics of Discourse* (Baltimore: Johns Hopkins University Press, 1978) 230–60; idem, "Michel Foucault," in John Sturrock, ed., *Structuralism and Since* (Oxford: Oxford University Press, 1979) 80–115. (Since the completion of this dissertation, several of the above have become available in a collection. The interested reader is invited to consult *Foucault: A Critical Reader* [David Couzens Hoy, ed.; Oxford: Blackwell, 1986].)

[2] Clifford Geertz, "Stir Crazy," *The New York Review of Books* 24 (January 26, 1978) 3.

Foucault believed strongly that the human and natural sciences are distinct enterprises. In retrospect, one can discern two main ways he argued for their difference: one, through an analysis of the historical forms of serious discourse about the human since the Renaissance (the archaeology of the human sciences); two, by writing genealogies of Western practices which show the human sciences beginning in and still dependent upon particular social institutions. I will begin, in the present chapter, with Foucault's first argument.

*The Order of Things* takes as its point of departure what Foucault claims to be the belief of most French historians of science that mathematics and the natural sciences exhibit in their development "the almost uninterrupted emergence of truth and pure reason," while the disciplines concerned with "living beings, language, or economic facts" are too "empirical," that is, "too exposed to the vagaries of chance or imagery, to age-old traditions and external events" to offer evidence of regularities (*OT*, ix).[3] To this assumption Foucault opposes the hypothesis that past empirical knowledge at a particular time and in a given culture did possess retrievable regularities, that "the history of nonformal knowledge [has] itself a system" (*OT*, x).

Foucault's history, however, is like no other. He is uninterested in writing a history of the human sciences, à la Comte, which would trace their slow but inevitable articulation upon the successes of mathematics, physics, and chemistry. *The Order of Things* is "a comparative, and not a symptomatological, study" (ibid.) that tries to "describe not so much the genesis of our sciences as an epistemological space specific to a particular period" (*OT*, xi). This space allows all serious discourse about living things, languages, and economic realities to proceed in tandem within any given period. The speakers of such discourse observe rules in forming every enunciation. They do so unconsciously; the reconstructive historian, or "archaeologist," brings these rules and the system of possible positive knowledge they order to light. Thus, in the period, or "episteme," which Foucault calls Classical,

> unknown to themselves, the naturalists, economists, and grammarians employed the same rules to define the objects proper to their own study, to form their concepts, to build their theories. It is these rules of formation, which were never formulated in their own right, but are to be found only in widely differing theories, concepts, and objects of study, that I

---

[3] Foucault respects the work of Georges Canguilhem, whose histories of biology and medicine exhibit the same methodological orientation toward the location of discontinuities as Foucault's studies of the clinic and the human sciences. See Michel Foucault, "Georges Canguilhem: Philosopher of Error," *I & C* 7 (1980) 51–62. For Foucault's reflections on the principle of discontinutiy for historical research see *AK*, 3–17.

have tried to reveal, by isolating, as their specific locus, a level that I
have called, somewhat arbitrarily perhaps, archaeological. (Ibid.)

Some of the difficulties raised by the task of archaeology will be
addressed below in the final section of this chapter. For now, it is only
important to see that Foucault in *OT* rejects the criticism which says that the
human sciences have failed to achieve normalcy because, as their history
well indicates, they have consistently been over involved with transient,
"empirical," circumstances and have thus failed to demonstrate the regularities associated with the work of mathematicians, physicists, and cosmolo-
gists. Foucault believes the regularities are there if a method can be found to
disclose them. His goal is to set forth these discursive events (*énoncés*) in
their orderliness, by articulating the rules of formation governing the appearance of statements in the discourses on significant human realities since the
Renaissance.[4]

## The Classical Episteme

### *The Rise of Representation*

The Classical episteme is the immediate prior context of the appearance of
the human sciences. It follows the demise of the Renaissance period; the
latter being an essentially mythical episteme in which thinking and speaking
were organized around the principle of *resemblance*. The order of being was
determined by God, whose providence set forth what there was to be known
while providing the means to know it. These means took the form of "signatures" on entities, which related each thing to every other. "Every resemblance receives a signature" (*OT*, 29) means that first, no two things are radically different (like the Classical *res cogitans* and *res extensa* will be), and
second, each bears upon itself some intrinsic mark or sign that subtle
interpretation can use as a key for unlocking the natural meaning of the thing,

---

[4] Note that Foucault is not saying that the human sciences become normal once we understand their order. The human sciences, as Modern discourses, owe their abnormality precisely to
their order, which is premised on the transcendental-empirical oddity, "man." Neither do the
analysis of wealth, natural history, and general grammar of the Classical period become normal
for us once their conditions of epistemic possibility are grasped (though the study of human
interests within that episteme would likely have appeared normal to its practitioners, since the
human as *res cogitans* was thought capable of clear and distinct knowledge, and thus in principle
able to surmount the empirical obstacles to certain knowledge of living nature, wealth, and
language).

as well as its relationship with the rest of being.[5] In the Renaissance episteme, even language appears as a thing with a nonarbitrary meaning to be revealed:

> In its raw, historical sixteenth-century being, language is not an arbitrary system, it has been set down in the world and forms a part of it, both because things themselves hide and manifest their own enigma like a language and because words offer themselves to men as things to be deciphered. (*OT*, 35)

The resemblance of each thing to every other gave way, according to Foucault, in the early seventeenth century to distinctions between words and things, money and wealth, visible structures and living beings. General grammar, analysis of wealth, and natural history arose within a new epistemological field whose principle of organization was *representation*. This field is the Classical episteme.

The rise of representation was premised on "the dissociation of the sign and resemblance" (*OT*, 63). Epitomized by Descartes's *Rules* (1628), the Classical period substituted the analysis of appearances for the hermeneutics of deep meanings, and the reconstruction of logical interrelationships for Renaissance semiology (*OT*, 29). What Foucault calls the "general science of order" pursued in the Classical episteme moves in two, complementary directions: toward the identification of "simple natures" and their ordering according to a universal method (a mathesis); and, toward the organization of empirical "complex representations" in interlinked taxonomies (a genesis; *OT*, 72). These two projects only appear to be in competition (a sterile "mechanism" versus a protomodern "dynamism") when one ignores "the region of signs" extending between mathesis and genesis creating the space, or "table," for the ordered appearance of representations and the discrimination of identities and differences (*OT*, 73). It is the universal susceptibility of manifest things to virtual representation, and the possibility of their coordination with other signifiers previous to them in time, that inspires the Classical project of a general science of order.

---

[5] For example, because the outside of the walnut "resembles" the human brain its contours are "signatures" of its healing powers for internal head ailments; the seeds of the plant aconite likewise signal their therapeutic potential in their similarity to the eye and eyelid (*OT*, 27). Renaissance astronomy, as Arthur O. Lovejoy (*The Great Chain of Being* [New York: Harper & Row, 1936] 99 – 121) has shown, likewise plays on innate parallels between one aspect of reality and another; hence, Kepler can say God the Father is to the Holy Spirit and the Son as the sun is to the planets and the stars. Lovejoy sees the period more as a composite of "modern" and "medieval" mind-sets than as an episteme with unique conditions of possibility for serious discourse about the cosmos.

Despite their differences, these three domains [of natural history, general grammar, and the analysis of wealth] existed in the Classical age only in so far as the fundamental area of the ordered table was established between the calculation of equalities and the genesis of representations. (Ibid.)

## Classical Sciences

An important assumption about language is implied by the above. No longer is it one thing among others, bearing secrets to be deciphered. In the Classical episteme, "Language has withdrawn from the midst of beings themselves and has entered a period of transparency and neutrality" (*OT*, 56). From the appearance of the Port-Royal Grammar (1660) until the first philological works of Schlegel (1808), Grimm (1818) and Bopp (1816), serious discourse about language assumed "the vertical division between language and that lying beneath it which it is the task of language to designate" (*OT*, 107).

The analysis of wealth is likewise concerned in the Classical age with the ordering of representations. In the Renaissance, the value of metals was plainly visible in their signatures of rarity, utility, and desirability (*OT*, 169). Coins "stood for" wealth through their mintage by participating in the stuff of wealth itself. In the Classical episteme, money represents wealth as its pledge; nothing has an intrinsic value (*OT*, 184). Establishing a monetary system (as a system of signs) raised the question of value: why are some things valuable and others not? Both the Physiocrats and their opponents, who based value, respectively, on production and utility, responded within the same epistemic parameters of Classical thought, rejecting innate values and searching for an answer compatible with the project of an analysis of wealth as representation (*OT*, 189–200).

Last, from Linnaeus until Cuvier, the study of living beings proceeded as natural history. Here again it was necessary for signs to detach themselves from that which they signified, to become transparent and subject to rational organization; in short, it was necessary "for History to become Natural" (*OT*, 128).[6] "Natural history," Foucault claims, "is nothing more than the

---

[6] In the Renaissance, when "signs were part of the things themselves" (*OT*, 128), Aldrovandi's *History of Serpents and Dragons* could include, of necessity, the signatures of an animal's virtues, medicinal and food uses, legends and lore, place in heraldry, and proper method of capture, i.e., "the whole semantic network that connected it to the world" (*OT*, 129). Fifty years later, in 1657, Jonston's *Natural History of Quadrupeds* analyzed the horse under the categories of name, anatomical parts, habitat, ages, generation, voice, movements, sympathy and antipathy, and uses—all treated by Aldrovandi, who included much more information besides.

nomination of the visible" (*OT*, 132). A living thing is represented in the Classical table insofar as it appears, preeminently, to the eye in black and white, revealing to the power of the gaze only "lines, surfaces, forms, relief" (*OT*, 133; see also *BC*, 96 on observation as representation). Like the Physiocrats and utilitarians, "Mechanism from Descartes to d'Alembert and natural history from Tournefort to Daubenton were authorized by the same episteme" (*OT*, 128).

In the Classical period the locus of representation is epitomized by the Cartesian res cogitans and its power of intuition. Intuition makes possible the isolation of simple natures, and their representation in the table of being. In the case of the human, intuition confirms thinking to be that nature. The "thing which thinks" can be assigned a place in the Classical table, insofar as thinking is synonymous with "discovering the truths of nature."[7] What cannot be tabulated in the Classical episteme is the being who orders representations in a table (*OT*, 308–10). The Classical divorce of signs from a signifying world did not imply their reinvestment in a signifying subject: the invisibility of signs from the perspective of Descartes's "pure and attentive mind" authorized the project of a general science of order, but foreclosed in advance the possibility of including in that science the site of signification itself.[8] Once that site could become problematic, after Kant, it has never ceased to occupy the center of disciplined reflection.

## The Modern Episteme

### *Sciences of the Finite*

Between approximately 1795 and 1825, Foucault claims, an epistemic shift occurred in the West ending the possibility of serious discourse about the

---

As Foucault observes, "The essential difference lies in what is *missing* in Jonston. The whole of animal semantics has disappeared, like a dead and useless limb" (ibid.). What has changed so abruptly is the grid of intelligibility (*dispositif*). The normative goal of an interpretation of resemblances has changed to an analysis of representations. Foucault's comparison of the Classically organized clinic and pre-Classical medicine makes a similar contrast:

> The clinic is a field made philosophically 'visible' by the introduction into the pathological domain of grammatical and probabilistic structures. These structures may be dated historically, because they are contemporary with Condillac and his successors. They freed medical perception from the play of essence and symptoms. ... The patient [no longer] both conceals and reveals the specificity of his disease. A domain of clear visibility was opened up to the gaze (*BC*, 105).

[7] René Descartes, *Philosophical Essays* (Indianapolis: Bobbs-Merrill, 1964) 156.
[8] Ibid., 154.

human proceeding on the principle of representation (*OT*, 221). In its place, *analogy* and *succession* appeared as the organizing principles of the newly emerging disciplines of biology, economics, and philology, which eclipsed natural history, the analysis of wealth, and general grammar (*OT*, 218). Cuvier, Ricardo, and Bopp mark the appearance of the Modern episteme and the possibility of human science.

The anthropological basis of the Modern period is my main concern, but to approach this topic, I will look for a moment at the study of living beings as it transformed itself early in the nineteenth century. In the Modern episteme,

> the general area of knowledge is no longer that of identities and differences, that of nonquantitative orders, that of a universal characterization, of a general *taxonomia*, of a nonmeasurable mathesis, but an area made up of organic structures, that is, of internal relations between elements whose totality performs a function. (Ibid.)

In biology, the description of visible structures gave way to the classification of characters, themselves based on the "functions essential to the living being" (Ibid.). Discerning these characters has something in common with the Renaissance project of decipherment of signatures, since for both, a character is "a visible sign directing us toward a buried depth"; however, for Modern interpretation,

> what it [the character] indicates is not a secret text, a muffled word, or a resemblance too precious to be revealed; it is the coherent totality of an organic structure that weaves back into the unique fabric of its sovereignty both the visible and the invisible. (*OT*, 229)

The "sovereignty" of organic structures is their irreducibility to either so many entries in the Book of Nature or to representations of ordered visible surfaces, in a comprehensive table. Organic structures assume their own destinies and origins.

To take the case of Modern medicine, Foucault in his archaeology of medical perception argues that in that episteme, "Deviation in life is of the order of life, but of a life that moves toward death" (*BC*, 156; see also *OT*, 277). Sickness and death are no longer, as in the Classical period, calamities impinging upon the (extended) physical vessel of pure consciousness; like birth, they are intrinsic and necessary moments in the development of the individual: "Disease is a deviation within life" (*BC*, 153). Classical medicine literally saw the being of a disease as the concatenation of its symptoms (pleurisy, e.g., was known by difficulty in breathing, coughing, fever, and side pains; it was their point of intersection [*BC*, 5]). The Modern episteme allowed things to be organized for knowledge differently. Bichat's pathological anatomy could be taken seriously (unlike Morgagni's study of corpses forty years earlier, in 1760) because understanding a disease no longer consisted in relating representations, but rather in tracing symptoms back to their original site within the body; and for this, the dissection of corpses, revealing the past presence of disease in its modification of tissues, was essential.

> Disease is no longer a bundle of characters disseminated here and there over the surface of the body . . . it is a set of forms and deformations, figures, and accidents and of displaced, destroyed, or modified elements bound together in sequence according to a geography that can be followed step by step. It is no longer a pathological species inserting itself into the body wherever possible; it is the body itself that has become ill. (*BC*, 136)

One could say that Modern pathological anatomy was concerned with making original sites visible so that they could be understood, whereas Classical medicine was interested in making symptoms understandable so that they could be cured.[9] The order of things is now deep inside them:

> It was not that [Bichat and his disciples] rediscovered Morgagni beyond Pinel or Cabanis; they rediscovered analysis in the body itself; they revealed, in depth, the order of the surfaces of things. . . . One passed from an analytical perception to the perception of real analyses. (*BC*, 131)

The order of life, studied by biology and pathological medicine, is the order of organic structures, arising within an organism and developing according to internal laws. The arrangement of labor and language in the Modern episteme also attests to the organizing principles of analogy and succession. "Historicity was introduced into the domain of languages in the same way as into that of living beings" (*OT*, 292), so that in studies of

---

[9] The transition in pathological medicine from the Classical to the Modern episteme was not smooth:

> Late-eighteenth-century medicine never knew whether it was concerned with a series of facts whose laws of appearance and convergence were to be determined simply by the study of repetitions, or whether it was concerned with a set of signs, symptoms, and manifestations whose coherence was to be sought in a natural structure. It never ceased to hesitate between a *pathology of phenomena* and a *pathology of cases*. (*BC*, 103; see also 127)

Foucault appears to have in mind the virtually simultaneous appearance of Pinel's Classical texts *Médecine clinique* (1802) and *Les Révolutions de la Médecine* (1804), and Bichat's Modern work, *Anatomie générale* (1801); see *BC*, 146.

language "fraternities" like that of Bopp, "the heterogeneity of the various grammatical systems emerged with its peculiar patternings, the laws prescribing change within each one, and the paths fixing possible lines of development" (*OT*, 293). Like philology, economics turns away from the project of composing a system of equivalences. Ricardo's dissociation of the creation of value from value's representivity (*OT*, 255) was followed by the correlation of value with unmet needs. Political economy in the nineteenth century studied the history of the attempted satisfaction of these needs as the history of production:

> It is no longer in the interplay of representation that economics finds its principle, but near that perilous region where life is in confrontation with death. . . . *Homo oeconomicus* is not the human being who represents his own needs to himself, and the objects capable of satisfying them; he is the human being who spends, wears out, and wastes his life in evading the imminence of death. (*OT*, 257)

It was Kant, according to Foucault, who was responsible for ending the Classical dream of a complete table of being by calling into question the basis of representation itself and asking about its limits; "the Kantian critique . . . marks the threshold of our modernity" (*OT*, 242).[10] Kant does not deny that objective experience is experience of representations;[11] his Modernity consists in the constitutive role he assigns to the transcendental imagination in the production of these representations. Henceforth, all experience will be contingent on forms of perception (space, time) and concepts of the understanding which the transcendental subject brings to bear on a sense manifold. Finitude, the enemy of "clear and distinct" intuition, becomes the sine qua non of objective experience. In the Modern episteme, after Kant, "labor, life, and language appear as so many 'transcendentals' which make possible the objective knowledge of living beings, of the laws of production, and of the forms of languages" (*OT*, 244). The *limits to* Modern experience are at the same time the *forms of* that experience. Foucault doubts that it is possible

---

[10] Cf. the observation on Kant in Michel Foucault, *Language, Counter-Memory, Practice* (Ithaca: Cornell University Press, 1977) 38.

[11] At least in the A-Edition of the first Critique. The Refutation of Idealism takes pains to argue that the permanency we attribute to any object of our experience "is possible only through a *thing* outside me and not through the mere *representation* of a thing outside me" (Immanuel Kant, *Critique of Pure Reason* [New York: St. Martin's, 1929] B 275). Nevertheless, Kant, in the Analogy, clearly designates time as just this permanency: "All appearances are in time; and in it alone, as substratum (as permanent form of inner intuition), can either coexistence or succession be represented" (ibid., A 182; B 224). The phrase, "as permanent form of inner intuition," places the permanent *in us* and not in the thing perceived, even though we may have to *believe* it is in the object in order to understand our experience.

to make a critique of languages, productivity, or life which is not at least implicitly an "anthropology"; that is, a reflection on the being of the entity who speaks, labors, and lives:

> It is probably impossible to give empirical contents transcendental value, or to displace them in the direction of a constituent subjectivity, without giving rise, at least silently, to an anthropology—that is, to a mode of thought in which the rightful limitations of acquired knowledge (and consequently of all empirical knowledge) are at the same time the concrete forms of existence, precisely as they are given in that same empirical knowledge.[12]

In the Renaissance, God's providence was the foundation of speech, living, and working. In the Classical episteme, the idea of God grounded an order of things accessible to the cogito's intuition. Now, in the Modern episteme, reflection by all intelligent, reasonable, and responsible persons (any transcendental subject and moral agent) on the "empirical contents" of their experience, should reveal the foundations, or conditions of the possibility, of those same contents. Reconstructive sciences and critical theories should show the way to a scientific anthropology. Yet, as I demonstrated by examples in the previous chapter, the idea of a critical science of the human is very much contested within the philosophy of science itself. The "forms of existence" (life, labor, and language) may be transcendentally "concrete" (*OT*, 248), but they have resisted to a high degree all attempts at their formalization. Foucault's analysis of "man" offers a reason why.

---

[12] *OT*, 248. The projective capability of Habermas's universal pragmatics sharply distinguishes it from Foucault's archaeology of the human sciences. Both *The Order of Things* and "Toward a Reconstruction of Historical Materialism" (Habermas, *Communication and the Evolution of Society* [Boston: Beacon, 1979] 130–77; see idem, "History and Evolution," *Telos* 39 [1979] 5–48) treat labor and language as radically specific to distinguishable epochs. However, Foucault's epistemes appear to have no intrinsic continuities among them to be reconstructed because Foucault's archaeology is putting into question the validity of developmental thinking itself, as a dogma of anthropology.

This same belief in the possibility of human evolution allows Habermas to take up the categories of cognitive-developmental theorists and reconstruct the effects of a "endogenous learning mechanism" producing surplus technical knowledge, which challenges innate logics of social relations to come up with more adequate arrangements of both this knowledge and its material results. From Neolithic societies to the Modern Age, Habermas's new historical materialism tells the story of Foucault's historico-transcendental subject, "man," without ever questioning the historicity of the human sciences themselves—upon whose results he builds his case—or the anthropological object of their investigation. Cf. Habermas, "Toward a Reconstruction of Historical Materialism."

*Modern "Man"*

"Modern culture can conceive of man because it conceives of the finite on the basis of itself" (*OT*, 318). Foucault believes that the "experience taking form at the beginning of the nineteenth century" and continuing to this day in the West, is an experience that involves the human in "the interminable to and fro of a double system of reference" (*OT*, 316). On the one hand, Modern "man" can know nothing which does not present itself as one of the "positive contents" of life, labor, and language: "If man's knowledge is finite, it is because he is trapped, without possibility of liberation, within the positive contents of language, labour, and life" (ibid.). If this were all "man" is, he would have nothing to fear from the manifestly diverse reports of his activity: the myriad of data which the sciences of "man" have produced since the nineteenth century.

But "man"'s finitude is not imposed on him from without. He experiences his limitations in all areas as intrinsic. Just as sickness and death are the natural conditions of his body as an organism, so are misunderstanding and opacity endemic to communication, and alienating toil an integral part of laboring. "Man" is the condition of his own finite forms of self-experience. So Foucault can say, "Inversely, if life, labour, and language may be posited in their positivity, it is because knowledge has finite forms" (ibid.). "Man" is the source of his own apparent diversity. There are not just many different ways of working, speaking, and living; these ways are only possible objects of knowledge because they are united by transcendental conditions of finite experience, which, by definition, are shared by everyone. For every positivism that would exhaust "man" by formalizing the instances of his language, life, and labor, there is potentially opposed a metaphysics which would understand the ground of these same anthropological functions. The cross-reference of Modern culture back and forth between "man"'s positivities and his foundations is analyzed by Foucault in terms of three sets of tensions, or "doubles."

The first double is the empirico-transcendental (*OT*, 318–22). As indicated above, the project of human studies in the Modern episteme is "revealing the conditions of knowledge on the basis of the empirical contents given to it" (*OT*, 319). One way the human sciences have tried to do this is by looking for the anatomophysiological conditions of knowledge, its place in bodily structures; that is, by positing a nature of human knowledge which human science endeavors to describe. Comte and Mill take this route. The other direction of the sciences of "man" is signaled by Marx. Here, the truth about "man" is to be found not in the nature of knowledge, but in its history. Knowledge is shown to have "had historical, social, or economic conditions" (ibid.) and to exist nowhere apart from these conditions. The two directions these analyses follow—toward nature and history—seem to be unrelated, but, Foucault claims, they are authorized by the same presupposition about truth.

This presupposition is: "there must . . . exist a truth that is of the same order of the object," a truth that the object—either the body or social relations—has in itself and the sciences of "man" seek to bring to language; however, "there must also exist a truth that is of the order of discourse—a truth that makes it possible to employ, when dealing with nature or history of knowledge, a language that will be true" (*OT*, 320). Does truth reside in the object or in discourse? If in the object, be it nature or history, an uncritical positivism results from systematically ignoring the historicity of the discourse of the scientist. If truth is assigned to discourse on the basis of its power to bring about the ultimately real, then an eschatological human science, like Marx's historical materialism, is the consequence. Here, "It is the status of this true discourse that remains ambiguous" (ibid.), inasmuch as the empiricities which would validate its claims are, by definition, not yet in being.[13]

> Comte and Marx both bear out the fact that eschatology (as the objective truth proceeding from man's discourse) and positivism (as the truth of discourse defined on the basis of the truth of the object) are archaeologically indissociable: a discourse attempting to be both empirical and critical cannot but be both positivist and eschatological; man appears within it as a truth both reduced and promised. (Ibid.)

"Man"'s relationship to what is known in his empiricities and what remains to be grasped is the relation between *the cogito and the unthought* (*OT*, 322–28). This second double assumes that "man" is a self-transcending subject capable of comprehending the being of any entity. In this, "man" resembles the cogito of Classical thought. But in the Modern episteme, because the forms of finitude are the limits to all experience, what

---

[13] For instance, one could ask about the status of Habermas's "eschatological" discourse on the function of critical theories:

> The *critique of ideology*, as well . . . as *psychoanalysis*, take into account that information about lawlike connections sets off a process of reflection in the consciousness of those the laws are about. Thus the level of unreflected consciousness . . . can be transformed. . . . [Self-reflection] releases the subject from dependence on hypostasized powers. (Habermas, *Knowledge*, 310)

The truth of the "information" is vouchsafed by its power to "set off" liberating transformation in the reflecting subject. The discourse of the ideology critic and psychoanalyst as information mediators is true, not by reference to empirical states of affairs, but by linking the destinies of those empiricities to ideal situations of labor and consciousness, as the proper (transcendental) conditions of "man"'s experience.

"man" is unclear about is not the order of representations of an external world, a world of extended things distinct from his "pure and attentive mind" (Descartes); rather, "man" is unclear about his own being whenever he finds life, labor, and language opaque—and he always does. Just as "man"'s experience of particular empirical events never coincides with experience of their conditions of possibility (my speech never occurs in the ideal speech situation), so does "man"'s knowledge of himself never exhaust the depths of what he is qua knowable. The unthought is that toward which thinking is directed, be it the unconscious of Freud or the false consciousness of Marx, but which can never be represented in its entirety by and to the conscious mind. In the Modern episteme, the cogito is "the constantly renewed interrogation as to how thought can reside elsewhere than here, and yet so very close to itself; how it can be in the forms of non-thinking" (*OT*, 324).

The alteriority of madness, for example, is an otherness within "man," not his slide into animality or possession by a demon. Because madness has its root in some common ground with reason (a ground that is constantly sought but never articulated, because it has no independent existence apart from the movement of thought toward what eludes it), the Modern cures for madness have focussed on the interior transformation of the insane, rather than their simple confinement and social invisibility (*MC*, 247–78). Likewise, the organization of nineteenth-century penology assumed the old principle of confinement, but added the task of technically transforming the delinquent individual into a model citizen (*DP*, 231–35).

What remains unrecognized in any given instance, in ourselves or another, is the unthought (*OT*, 326–27); what gives one hope for correction or cure is the anthropological premise that Modern "man" can and must bring what has not been thought to consciousness, and from understanding to reform. The Modern institutions of the human sciences—the prison, asylum, and the discourses of critical theories—are devoted to the execution of this goal, and a fortiori to the resolution of the second double in favor of the cogito : "modern thought is advancing towards that region where man's Other must become the Same as himself" (*OT*, 328). The resistance of the Other to cognitive assimilation, however, has been argued by Taylor and Dreyfus, while Rorty allows for the conceivable success of a normal human science, and Habermas awaits the day of its coming (see Chapter 1).

Toward what are critique and clarification directed? The third and final double, *the retreat and return of the origin* (*OT*, 328–35), constrains "man" both to seek his origin in a misty past before labor, language, and human life, and to posit his essential nature in some future state which is always just beyond his reach. Critique and clarification are not subsumed by the third double, but they would be unproblematic if "man," the condition of the possibility of the appearance of things in time, could represent himself in time as one being among others (as the fallen soul in God's time, for the Renaissance, or the "thing which thinks" outside of time, for the Classical episteme).

Instead, every attempt to retrieve a past before his arrival fails because "man" 's reflection must begin with data organized by the forms of finitude. There is no clear perception of a founding act of labor, life, or language, standing out against a background of the nonorganic and prehistoric, because "man" only recognizes himself by appearing within an anthropological "frame":

> Man ... can be revealed only when bound to a previously existing historicity: he is never contemporaneous with that origin which is outlined through the time of things even as it eludes his gaze ... the origin of things is always pushed further back, since it goes back to a calendar upon which man does not figure. (*OT*, 330, 331)

The origin of "man" cannot be assigned a place in the histories of the origin of things, because "man" is, in the first place, the foundation of the appearance of things that have histories.[14]

The origin of "man" lies before him as well. In Hegel, Marx, and Spengler, the movement of nature and history toward totality is the "perfection" of "man" (*OT*, 334); the work of Hülderlin, Nietzsche, and Heidegger posits the return of the origin, on the contrary, only in the origin's "extreme recession—in that region where the gods have turned away, where the desert is increasing, where the techne has established the dominion of its will" (*OT*, 334). For both lines of Modern thought, the culmination of "man" 's destiny is not far off. The return of the origin is imminent. Yet life goes on—and labor and language, too, while "man" continues "waiting for Godot."

With his analysis of the third double, Foucault brings us back again to temporality as the central problem of Modern reflection. "Man" finds himself in the grip of a power that is not foreign to him, but

> disperses him, draws him away from his origin, but promises it to him in an imminence that will perhaps be forever snatched from him. . . . This power is that of his own being. Time—the time that he himself is—cuts him off not only from the dawn from which he sprang but also from that other dawn promised him as still to come. (*OT*, 335) Finitude, which

---

14 That Foucault's analysis of the third double implicitly addresses the early Heidegger's philosophy is the thesis developed in Hubert L. Dreyfus and Paul Rabinow, *Michel Foucault* (2d ed.; Chicago: University of Chicago Press, 1983) 37 – 41.

initially revealed itself as a new-found density in living beings (life), economic relations (labor), and communication (language), can now be assigned a more fundamental level in the archaeology of the human sciences: "it is the insurmountable relation of man's being with time." (Ibid.)

## Human and Counterhuman Sciences

"The human sciences," claims Foucault, "are addressed to man insofar as he lives, speaks, and produces" (*OT*, 351). Psychology, literary criticism, and sociology are the sciences of "man" that have emerged from nineteenth-century biology, philology, and political economy (*OT*, 353 and 366–67). Though at first glance, "they provide the outlines of completely positive configurations" (*OT*, 366), that is, they appear to refer, in a scientific manner, to stable empirical objects, in fact their implicit anthropological orientation undermines their claims to universal validity:

> It is useless, then, to say that the 'human sciences' are false sciences; they are not sciences at all; the configuration that defines their positivity and gives them their roots in the modern episteme  at the same time makes it impossible for them to be sciences. (Ibid.)

Nothing would appear for sociology, psychology, and literary criticism to study if it were not already a positive determination of "man"'s finite existence, and as such, were not even then related to a receding or expected origin, a domain of the unthought, or a transcendental ground synonymous with time itself. There cannot be, Foucault argues, a scientific study of the human as long as "man" remains its object, because the foundations of speaking, laboring, and conscious life—Kant's "common" but "unknown" source of intuitions and concepts—are not available for thematization and formalization, they themselves making possible all reflection and formal redescription whatsoever.[15] To say that the foundations elude the gaze, and

---

[15] My reference to Kant's "common" source of intuition and concepts is not gratuitous: early Heidegger, as Dreyfus and Rabinow have argued, is Foucault's implicit target and prime example of Modern thinking in this century, and Heidegger's own desire, in the 1920s, to renew a search for the grounds of metaphysics which Kant began, is explicit. Heidegger claims Kant is the first philosopher since the Greeks "to raise once again . . . the question of the Being of essents as a question to be unfolded" (Martin Heidegger, *Der Satz vom Grund*, quoted in J. L. Mehta, *The Philosophy of Martin Heidegger* [rev. ed.; New York: Harper & Row, 1971] 163). In 1929, two years after *Being and Time*, Heidegger expressly identified time with Kant's transcendental imagination, which, he argues, constitutes the hidden root of sensibility and understanding. See Martin Heidegger, *Kant and the Problem of Metaphysics* (Bloomington: Indiana University Press, 1969) 140. Richardson has argued that *Kant* was sketched-out between 1925 and 1926; thus,

that the critique of positive configurations can yield no finally scientific conclusions, is only to admit that "man"'s fundamental temporality makes him an impossible object for science. Paradoxically, then, it is not because "man" can and must *transcend* time that he resists scientific explanation, but because he *is* time.

> It is therefore not man's irreducibility, what is designated as his invincible transcendence, nor even his excessively great complexity, that prevents him from becoming an object of science. Western culture has constituted, under the name of man, a being who, by one and the same interplay of reasons, must be a positive domain of *knowledge* and cannot be an object of *science*. (*OT*, 366–67)

Foucault, in *The Order of Things*, holds out hope that "counterhuman sciences" may arise which would overcome the to and fro of the doubles by relativizing anthropological discourse altogether. Psychoanalysis, ethnology, and linguistics appear to be such sciences, replacing psychology, sociology, and literary criticism by questioning "not man himself, as he appears in the human sciences, but the region that makes possible knowledge about man in general" (*OT*, 378).

The particular success of those structuralisms Foucault seems to have in mind—Lacanian psychoanalytic theory and the work of Claude Lévi-Strauss—is less important than, first, the fact that Foucault turns away from the entire task of making a neutral analysis of the conditions of representations, mental and social, after 1971; and, second, the useful contrast the idea of a counterhuman science provides, as the idea of a serious postanthropological discourse, to the ongoing conversations of the sciences of "man." Foucault's move away from structuralist ideals and toward a genealogy of Western practices builds on the conclusion of *The Order of Things*:

> One thing in any case is certain: man is neither the oldest nor the most constant problem that has been posed for human knowledge. . . . As the archaeology of our thought easily shows, man is an invention of recent date. And one perhaps nearing its end. (*OT*, 386–87)

---

*Being and Time*, can be considered the result of Heidegger's reflection on the problematic addressed in the first *Critique*. See William Richardson, *Heidegger: Through Phenomenology to Thought* (The Hague: Nijhoff, 1974) 86. Foucault's analysis indicates that both Kant and the early Heidegger signify attempts to ground "man" in his temporality by analyses of his positivities (for Kant, the objects of experience; and, for Heidegger, *Dasein*'s worldly modes of self-understanding).

## Archaeology Reconsidered

Foucault's archaeology of the human sciences works best when it does not try to explain the causes of the discursive regularities it traces. In his endeavor "to throw off the last anthropological constraints" (*AK*, 15) hindering our thinking about the past, Foucault dedicates archaeology to the project of "a *pure description of discursive events*" (*AK*, 27):

> [Archaeology] is nothing more than a rewriting; that is, in the preserved form of exteriority, a regulated transformation of what has already been written. It is not a return to the innermost secret of the origin; it is the systematic description of a discourse object. (*AK*, 140)

But Foucault, in *The Archaeology of Knowledge*, sometimes speaks as though the description of discursive regularities is really the prescription of their formal conditions of possibility, their "system of formation":

> By system of formation, then, I mean a complex group of relations that functions as a rule ... [i.e.] the system of rules that must be put into operation if such and such an object is to be transformed, such and such a new enumeration appear ... without ever ceasing to belong to this same discourse. (*AK*, 74)

Here Foucault is sensitive to the fact that "one cannot speak of anything at any time" (*AK*, 44), that the organization of serious speech acts is constrained by circumstances. He locates these circumstances, however, not in the social practices and institutional contexts embodying enunciations, but in rules which are indistinct from the enunciations themselves; they "belong to this same discourse" (*AK*, 74). As Dreyfus and Rabinow observe, "The result is the strange notion of regularities that regulate themselves."[16] Discourse does not merely follow rules to organize statements; it establishes relations between social entities as well:

> When one speaks of a system of transformation, one does not mean the juxtaposition, coexistence, or interaction of heterogenous elements (institutions, techniques, social groups, perceptual organizations, relations between various discourses), but also the relation that is established between them—in a well-determined form—by discursive practice. (*AK*, 72; see also 73–74)

Once again, Foucault is attentive to the orderliness of social "institutions"

---

[16] Dreyfus and Rabinow, *Michel Foucault*, 84.

and "techniques": one cannot do anything at any time. But because the archaeologist has bracketed the seriousness of anthropological discourse, the arrangement of social life cannot be construed to follow rules that are in nature, in the human transformation of nature (labor), or in the minds of intending subjects (*AK*, 54–55). Once posited, there is no place to locate these rules except in discourse itself.

I think this is asking an awfully lot of discourse. Not only must we believe that the archaeologist can (1) describe discursive regularities, and (2) "excavate" the rules operating their systems of formation, but now we must accept that (3) these rules establish relationships among social entities when they are deployed in discourse. This implies, for example, that people speaking in the Classical era were thereby following innate rules, of which they could not be aware, and which *caused* and did not just *accompany* the French monarchy, the Port-Royal Grammer, Linnaeus's taxonomies, *Candide*, the debate between the Physiocrats and utilitarians, and any other aspect of Classical life one cares to name. Foucault emphasizes the causative power of these rules when he names their site in the mind, the "positive unconscious" (*OT*, xi).

Foucault's own dissatisfaction with the task of archaeology as *AK* presents it is evident in his exploration of the very different method of genealogy two years after *AK*'s publication. Those who describe Foucault's "turn" as a shift from discourse to practices miss, I believe, the most significant feature of Foucault's later work: the absence of attempts at reconstructing implicit systems of formation of discursive regularities, and the development of the new concept, "power/knowledge." Foucault does not abandon discourse; he lets go a structuralist preoccupation with its rules. Inasmuch as power is always shifting, "capillary," and strategic, so are the conditions of serious speech acts and true discourse. (I will address Foucault's genealogies in the next chapter.) Now, another criticism must be made of archaeology.

Even if one ignores the temptation to read *The Order of Things* retrojectively through the structuralist lens of *The Archaeology of Knowledge*, one must question the possibility of a pure description of discursive regularities. Hilary Putnam strikes at this weakness in Foucault's program when he says, "There is no objective place to stand in ideological matters (except of course, for the mysterious standpoint of Foucault's own allegedly objective 'Archaeology of Knowledge')."[17] Dreyfus and Rabinow take up the criticism in depth, arguing that by proposing to study the past in an utterly

---

[17] Putnam, *Reason*, 156. That the "mystery" of Foucault's standpoint conceals an inconsistent relativism, see Hilary Putnam, *Realism and Reason* (Philosophical Papers, vol. 3; Cambridge: Cambridge University Press, 1983) 235; idem, *Reason*, 162–64; and my discussion below in Chapter 3.

detached manner, beyond the "anthropological" quests for deep truth and meaning, and without their characteristic earnestness, Foucault puts himself outside the realm of reasoned public conversation altogether. There is no reason anyone should take him seriously, if he genuinely has severed all ties to the concerns of contemporary people.[18]

Foucault, in his reflection on the archaeological method, makes statements that support this conclusion. He admits, "my discourse, far from determining the locus in which it speaks, is avoiding the ground on which it could find support . . . it is trying to operate a decentering that leaves no privilege to any centre" (*AK*, 205). Foucault, whose own standpoint thus has no "privilege," nevertheless proposes for archaeology "the intrinsic description of the monument" (*AK*, 7), the pure recording of the structures of historical data. But, as Dreyfus and Rabinow ask,

> Is a pure description possible? Is there no interpretation involved in the choice of descriptive categories? Must we not be able to ask: Are these descriptions accurate or distorted? But doesn't this reintroduce truth?[19]

If archaeology is unsound because (1) it proposes to excavate deep rules of formation in discourse which no one has shown to be even possibly there; and (2) it requires the archaeologist to assume a posture of neutrality toward the data at hand which is impossible; then what significance, one may ask, do *The Order of Things* and other, "pregenealogical," works of Foucault have? I believe they have a limited, but important significance, which I have tried to bring out in the manner of my exposition of their leading points. Rather than offer the archaeology of the human sciences as an articulation of discursive systems of formation, I have presented the chronology of broad areas (epistemes) of human-scientific reflection, each ideally organized around the principles of resemblance, representation, or analogy/succession. An episteme does not "cause" its positivities, even though a synchronic comparison of the structures of these positivities can proceed by reference to a single epistemic principle of organization. In the following definition of "episteme," then, I attribute only a logical function to the "relations" that "unite" discursive practices: "By episteme, we mean . . . the total set of relations that unite, at a given period, the discursive practices that give rise to epistemological figures, sciences, and possibly formalized systems" (*AK*, 191).

---

[18] See Dreyfus and Rabinow, *Michel Foucault*, 79–100, esp. 85–90. Foucault (*The Use of Pleasure*, vol. 2: *The History of Sexuality* [New York: Pantheon, 1985] 8) acknowledges the importance of these critics to the development of his later work.

[19] Dreyfus and Rabinow, *Michel Foucault*, 85.

By distinguishing the logical conditions of actual serious speech about life, labor, and language in diverse historical periods from the conditions of the possible performance of serious discourse, one frees Foucault's archaeology from the impossible burden of explaining why positivities at a given time actually occur, or why their conditions of possibility abruptly change. Archaeology becomes the description of dividing practices that have been presupposed in the utterance of serious statements in the discourses of the human sciences and their Classical predecessors. This removes from discourse the burden of accounting for its regularity by reference to immanent "rules," and creates a methodological space for the genealogical analysis of these same discursive formations. [20]

*The Order of Things* remains a description whose author is naïve with respect to his own structuralist standpoint. However, what Foucault thought his research implied is, in this instance, less important than the research itself. One can distinguish among empirical knowledge, framework assumptions, and philosophical knowledge about these assumptions.[21] In Foucault's case, the analysis of "man" yields empirical knowledge of the order of Modern human sciences. They have set themselves the task of reconciling "man"'s positivities and his foundations. Foucault's background assumptions include the structuralist belief that mental and social reality are the effects of rule-governed systems of transformation. The *Archaeology* is Foucault's philosophical reflection on this assumption. One can disagree with both the project of archaeology as pure phenomenology and the methodological premises of structuralist history, and still find convincing (as I do) Foucault's analysis of Modern "man" and his doubles.

The problem of the formation of true discourses was not abandoned by Foucault after he gave up his search for implicit discursive rules. As long ago as 1967, in an interview with Raymond Bellour, Foucault claimed that archaeology "owes more to the Nietzschean genealogy than to structuralism properly so called."[22] Foucault's development of a genealogical method, complementary to the systematizing operation of archaeology, is the subject of Chapter 3.

---

[20] Foucault's failure to account for epistemic shifts is cited by Piaget (*Structuralism* [New York: Harper & Row, 1970] 128–35) as evidence of the failure of archaeology to become a "dynamic" structuralism.

[21] These three distinctions are made and used to support a related argument in Thomas E. Wartenberg, "Foucault's Archaeological Method: A Response to Hacking and Rorty," *The Philosophical Forum* 15 [1984] 346, 353);

[22] Raymond Bellour, "Deuxième entretien avec Michel Foucault: Sur les façons d'écrire l'historie," *Les Lettres françaises* 1187 (juin 15–21, 1967) 9 (quoted from Megill, "Foucault, Structuralism, and the Ends of History," *Journal of Modern History* 51 [1979] 494).

# 3

# Toward a Genealogy
# of the Human Sciences

After 1971 and *The Discourse on Language*, Foucault's analyses of the human sciences no longer assume that the conditions of serious speech acts are coextensive with implicit, unconsciously operating rules of discursive formation. Although discourse remains highly organized, its systematicity is no longer for Foucault the sufficient cause of its appearance. Foucault retains archaeology as a critical method which aims at showing how particular discourses embody principles of exclusion, rarity, and ordering in the construction and deployment of statements (*AK*, 234); its practitioner's attitude is one of "studied casualness" (ibid.), not the detached seriousness of the pure observer. Criticism reveals the limits of particular discursive formations by indicating what counts, for example, as evidence of pathology for Pinel and Bichat (surface symptoms versus tissular modifications), or the appropriate authority to administer discipline (the Classical sovereign, religious and moral figures, justices of the state, or representatives of the human sciences); in short, criticism tries to elucidate for a given discourse who can speak seriously and who cannot, what makes one statement true and another false, what "morality of knowlege" is in play by serious speakers in any given instance.

## From Archaeology to Genealogy

Foucault conceives of a complementary research tool which will study the formation of discourses as the history of the social practices that engender and support them. This method is genealogy. "Criticism analyzes the processes of rarefaction, consolidation and unification in discourse; genealogy studies their formation, at once scattered, discontinuous and regular" (*AK*, 233). Where criticism looks for the limiting conditions of discourse, genealogy constructs a history of the relations of power in which these conditions have had effect. "The difference between the critical and the genealogical enterprise is not one of object or field," claims Foucault, "but of point of attack, perspective and delimitation" (ibid.);

> Critical and genealogical descriptions are to alternate, support and complete each other. The critical side of the analysis deals with the systems enveloping discourse; attempting to mark out and distinguish the principles of ordering, exclusion and rarity in discourse. . . . The genealogical side, by way of contrast, deals with series of effective formation of discourse: it attempts to grasp it in its power of affirmation, by which [I mean] . . . the power of constituting domains of objects, in relation to which one can affirm or deny true or false propositions. (*AK*, 234)

Genealogy builds upon methodological principles shared with archaeology. Foremost of these is the positive value assigned to the discontinuous in history. In the Introduction to *The Archaeology of Knowledge*, Foucault advocates the examination of discontinuities elided many times over by an historiographical imagination dedicated to, for example, Troeltsche's three principles, or committed to "the progress of consciousness, or the teleology of reason, or the evolution of human thought" (*AK*, 8). What Foucault terms the "new history" calls into question "the themes of convergence and culmination . . . had doubted the possibility of creating totalities" (ibid.). The new history is antianthropological, insofar as it refuses to take as its point of departure the analytic of finitude and its subject/object, "man"; instead, the transcendental subject, the unconscious, and "man"'s quest for his origin are all studied as discursive formations and as the products of an "effective history" (Nietzsche's *wirklische Historie*; see *NGH*, 152–57).

Genealogy shares with conventional historiography an appeal to publically available evidence: "Genealogy is gray, meticulous, and patiently documentary" (*NGH*, 139); it works on well-known sources and others—police blotters, medical reports, memoirs, newspaper accounts—whose obscurity genealogy seeks to overcome by relativizing the *dispositifs*, or grids of intelligibility, that made these sources unimportant in their day. Because genealogy does not treat our contemporary sources with Modern seriousness (because it does not wish to be commentary on "man"), Foucault can say genealogy is practiced in the "mood" of "felicitous positivism" (*AK*, 234). Genealogy is a "gay science" (Nietzsche); it is post anthropological scholarship.

In what sense is genealogy history-writing? Foucault, following Nietzsche, distinguishes three meanings of "origin." The origin as *Ursprung* is "the exact essence of things, their purest possibilities, and their carefully protected identities ... the moment of their greatest perfection" (*NGH*, 142, 143). As *Ursprung*, the origin is that double of anthropology "forever promised in an imminence always nearer yet never accomplished" (*OT*, 332),

> the original foundation that would make rationality the *telos* of mankind, and link the whole history of thought to the preservation of this rationality, to the maintenance of this teleology, and to the ever necessary return to this foundation. (*AK*, 13)

Conventional historiography contributes to this search for "man"'s origin. Consider Dilthey's evaluation of *nacherleben*: "It is the triumph of reexperiencing that it supplements the fragments of a course of events in such a way that we believe ourselves to be confronted by continuity."[1]

Empathy's "triumph" lies in persuading the historian that the strangeness of the past can be overcome when it is seen as the original actors saw and experienced it. Since they presumably experienced their present as a unified, purposeful world, the Modern historian seems fully justified in his or her attempt to "supplement" history's "fragments" with a continuity they ostensively lack. Empathy restores to the past what time itself, paradoxically, has apparently taken away: its orderliness. To do so, howe ver, the historian must oppose to the unruly past "the general model of a consciousness that acquires, progresses, and remembers" (*AK*, 8); in short, an original foundation (here, a transcendental ego) which acts as the substrate for the events that the Modern historian faithfully narrates.

In contrast, Foucaultian genealogy "rejects the metahistorical deployment of ideal significations and indefinite teleologies. It opposes itself to the search for 'origins'" (*NGH*, 140). It proposes instead to trace "man"'s "descent" (*Herkunft*) and "emergence" (*Entstehung*).[2]

---

[1] Wilhelm Dilthey, "The Construction of the Historical World in the Human Studies," *Dilthey: Selected Writings* (Cambridge: Cambridge University Press, 1976) 226. Foucault criticizes the goals and principles of *Verstehen* at *AK*, 139–40.

[2] According to Foucault's reading of the relevant primary texts, Nietzsche stressed "*Ursprung*" when he intended a pejorative commentary on, e.g., metaphysics and religion, and their search for a pristine, atemporal origin of their respective subjects. Thus, the "miraculous origin" (*Wunderursprung*) of metaphysics is stressed, as is the "*Ursprung*" or original basis of morality, sought since Plato, and the divine foundation of religion. Unstressed, *Ursprung* appears alternately with *Enstehung, Herkunft, Abkunft,* and *Geburt*. Foucault readily admits that Nietzsche's own conception of genealogy varied between a search for origins similar to those

Writing the history of "man"'s origin as his descent refers the genealogist to those beginnings overlooked by Dilthean historians, with their love of continuity and faith in the identity of appearances in time:

> If the genealogist refuses to extend his faith in metaphysics, if he listens to history, he finds that there is 'something altogether different' behind things: not a timeless and essential secret, but the secret that they have no essence or that their essence was fabricated in a piecemeal fashion from alien forms. . . . What is found at the historical beginning of things is not the inviolable identity of their origin; it is the dissension of other things. It is disparity. (*NGH*, 142)

Tracing descent is a deconstructive operation, in which the genealogist "disturbs what was previously considered immobile; it fragments what was thought unified; it shows the heterogeneity of what was imagined consistent with itself" (*NGH*, 147). As a hermeneutics of suspicion, genealogy questions a conventional interpretation of a text or an event in order to reveal, on the basis of hitherto ignored or irrelevant evidence, the "lowly" or "shameful origins" (Nietzsche's *pudenda origo*) glossed over or elided by traditional exegesis or historiography.

Unlike Freudian or Marxist hermeneutics of suspicion, however, genealogy does not look for a repressed or disguised significance beneath the first. This would be to restore a continuity to the text or event, though now at a "deep" level. Genealogy would be back to the doubles and the infinite task of seizing "man"'s foundations on the basis of the critique of his positivities. Genealogy would become the next critical theory, instead of what it is, namely, postanthropological history writing.

If genealogy is not the recovery of deep psychic and social structures, it is because it affirms the materiality of discourse, the discontinuity of history, and the role of chance in making the present what it is (*AK*, 231). Can Foucault, however, relativize all structures and still have a history? Isn't Foucault again proposing "a decentering that leaves no privilege to any centre" (*AK*, 205); though now Foucault has not cut *himself* off from his discourse object (as he did in the *Archaeology*), he has dissolved the *object* by repudiating both everyday and "deep" attempts to explicate an apparent or hidden continuity. The genealogy of "man"'s descent seems to deconstruct itself as a history.

This would be a fair complaint if genealogy were only a deconstructive operation involved in tracing "man"'s descent. However, the emergence (*Entstehung*) of historical entities is also genealogy's concern.

---

which Nietzsche denounced, and a "true" conception of a history of power relations (*NGH*, 140–42).

Foucault's archaeology of the human sciences showed that the human has not always been thought of as an evolving entity; "man"'s intrinsic development is a premise of the Modern episteme. Before that, the human was the Classical cogito and the rational soul of the Renaissance. The clarity of archaeology's epistemological disjunctions, however, was offset by that method's inability to explain how epistemic shifts occurred, why thought about the human would change at all and in the directions it has.

Genealogy develops Foucault's idea of discontinuous historical change by introducing power as a constitutive principle for the emergence of entities in any episteme. The unity ascribed to objects, and their continuity through time, is only false when conceived of apart from power relations. When genealogy traces the emergence of "man," it writes the history of successive technologies of the body, the "endlessly repeated play of dominations" which "is fixed, throughout its history, in rituals, in meticulous procedures that impose rights and obligations. It establishes marks of its power and engraves memories on things and even within bodies" (*NGH*, 150). These "meticulous procedures" by which things emerge in their positivity are not metaphysical, only obscure. Foucault's genealogies of the prison and the sexuality of ancient Greek and Modern individuals do indeed relativize structures to social practices (procedures of confession, confinement, diatetics, household economy, and erotics). To this extent, a decentering of sexuality, criminality, and conventional interpretations of Greek life has been achieved. Nevertheless, when power is assigned a productive role in the formation of discursive and nondiscursive practices, the decentering of these practices does not mean their slide into unintelligibility. Rather, they can be understood as the articulation of social conflicts:

> The isolation of different points of emergence does not conform to the successive configurations of an identical meaning; rather, they result from substitutions, displacements, disguised conquests, and systematic reversals. (*NGH*, 151)

Genealogy differs from ideology critique and related critical theories because it withholds "faith in metaphysics" and does "listen to history" (*NGH*, 142), and so refuses to seek a comprehensive, theoretical framework for the explanation of the social conflicts, the relations of power, it describes.

In fact, genealogy specifically opposes "the coercion of a theoretical, unitary, formal and scientific discourse . . . the scientific hierarchisation of knowledges and the effects intrinsic to their power" (*PK*, 85). It opposes not "the contents, methods or concepts of science," but

> the effects of the centralising powers which are linked to the institution and functioning of an organised scientific discourse within a society such as ours . . . it is really against the effects of the power of a discourse that

is considered to be scientific that the genealogy must wage its struggle. (*PK*, 84)

The effects of scientific discourses have included the elision of historical conflicts between the speakers of the discourse and those they address (doctors and patients, teachers and students, parents and children, for example), resulting in "historical contents that have been buried and disguised in a functionalist coherence or formal systemisation" (*PK*, 81); also, the prioritization of scientific discourses has devalued "particular, local, regional knowledge," those "naive knowledges, located low down on the hierarchy, beneath the required level of cognition or scientificity" (*PK*, 82). An erudite retrieval of elided conflicts and the empowerment of disqualified knowledges, these are the goals of genealogical researches: "Let us give the term *genealogy* to the union of erudite knowledge and local memories which allows us to establish a historical knowledge of struggles and to make use of this knowledge tactically today" (*PK*, 83). Because genealogy is methodologically committed to the "insurrection of subjugated knowledges" (*PK*, 81), insead of contributing to the expansion of the effects of scientific discourses, it is imperative that it take as its point of departure those discursive and nondiscursive practices operative today; genealogy must be the "history of the present" not the "history of the past in terms of the present" (*DP*, 31), that is, not the past as it can be assimilated by the "disciplined" reflection of traditional historiography and the human sciences.

Foucault's understanding of power and its relationship with knowledge can be studied in terms of his specific genealogical research. The rise of the human sciences provides one focus for this understanding.

## Genealogy of Modern "Man"

The particular project of Modern human science is, as we have seen, the articulation of "man"'s foundations (the forms of his finite existence) through the critique of the positive manifestations of life, labor, and language. Foucault's genealogy of Modern "man" argues that the appearance of positivities, far from being the spontaneous manifestation of innate drives or the effect of deep anthropological structures, is in fact the result of technologies operating on the body and within the person. Foucault describes two kinds of technologies, or "techniques": those of domination and of the self. The development and deployment of these techniques link the Modern episteme with previous western history, since their genealogical roots lie in the practices of coercion and confession developed by ancient Greek, Stoic, or early Christian societies.

*Techniques of Domination*

"The body becomes a useful force only if it is both a productive body and a subjected body" (*DP*, 26). In the Modern West, reflection on the rise of capitalism insofar as it concerns the body has centered largely on "man" as the bearer of natural forces, which are mediated for labor through the body's organs.[3] Foucault's genealogies of the prison and sexuality invite us to discover the body as a subject of discipline and surveillance, and the history of the Modern West as the history of the deployment of techniques of domination of individual bodies and their collective subjection to the discursive and nondiscursive practices of entities not reducible to the agents of a self-interested capitalism (*PK*, 58–60) Foucault does not deny that capitalism has a history which can be written in terms of the body as a site of productive forces; he insists, however, that these forces, considered genealogically, have only been available for economic exploitation because the bodies of individuals have been subjected to Classical and Modern techniques of domination:

> If economic exploitation separates the force and the product of labour, let us say that disciplinary coercion establishes in the body the constricting link between an increased aptitude and an increased domination. (*DP*, 138)

Disciplinary methods long used in monasteries and workshops became, in the seventeenth and eighteenth centuries, refined and applied to the general population whenever bodies could be made more useful by becoming more obedient, and conversely: primary and secondary schools first, then the hospital, the military, and the prison. Foucault attributes the extension and refinement of these techniques not to an amorphous "will to power," but to (1) specific systems crises unique to western societies of the 1600s and 1700s: industrial innovation, renewed outbreaks of epidemic diseases, the invention of the rifle, the victories of Prussia (ibid.), and most significant, the dramatic increase of the floating population and populations of schools, hospitals, and peace time armies (*DP*, 218); and (2) the response to these crisis-inducing overloads of productive forces and antiquated relations by new

---

[3] This is how Marx conceives the body when, in analysis of the labor process, he writes:

Labour is, first of all, a process between man and nature, a process by which man, through his own actions, mediates, regulates and controls the metabolism between himself and nature. He confronts the materials of nature as a force of nature. He sets in motion the natural forces which belong to his own body, his arms, legs, head and hands, in order to appropriate the materials of nature in a form adapted to his own nature. (Karl Marx, *Capital: A Critique of Political Economy* [3 vols.; New York: Vintage, 1976] 1. 283)

practices aimed at "the administration of bodies and the calculated management of life" (*HS*, 140).

Consider, first, the administration of bodies. Enlightened universities, prisons, armies, hospitals, and related bureaucracies make bodies "docile" (*DP*, 136). A docile body is one which "may be subjugated, used, transformed, and improved" (ibid.). It is not simply the vessel of a will, obedient or in revolt to a higher power such as the authority of the Classical sovereign. It serves purposes by becoming the site of possible knowledge; or rather, the multiple sites of information gleaned by the analysis of physical forms, motions, and the space they occupy into elements; the conceptual recombination of these elements according to a rule (a rule of productivity, prison conduct, classroom demeanor, military "drill," or a rule of pathological appearance—mental or "biological"—and one of therapy); and the concrete application of this rule to individual bodies. The techniques of hierarchical observation, examination, and normalizing judgment all work toward the administration of docile bodies (*DP*, 170–94). Foucault calls the slow elaboration of these techniques and their deployment in institutions of discipline the appearance of "political anatomy" or "mechanics of power," which defines "how one may have a hold over others' bodies, not only so that they may do as one wishes, but so that they may operate as one wishes, with the techniques, the speed and the efficiency that one determines" (*DP*, 138). The "body politic" to which these techniques are applied is not the state as a contractual community of wills, but

> a set of material elements and techniques that serve as weapons, relays, communication routes and supports for the power and knowledge relations that invest human bodies and subjugate them by turning them into objects of knowledge. (*DP*, 28)

At the same time there arose strategies assuring the calculated management of life. Techniques of social organization developed in the Classical period responded to the profound and threatening increase in population not only by administering bodies but by attending to life, or the "species body":

> The body imbued with the mechanics of life and serving as the basis of the biological processes . . . propagation, births and mortality, the level of health, life expectancy and longevity, with all the conditions that can cause these to vary. (*HS*, 139)

Concern for the species body evoked new discourses and new practical arrangements centered on the bodies of children, their sexuality, their relations to other family members, birth control, and public hygiene (*PK*, 172–77); a "biopolitics of the population" (*HS*, 139) was begun.

At the end of the eighteenth century, a "new technology of sex" emerged which made sex "a matter that required the social body as a whole, and virtually all of its individuals, to place themselves under surveillance" (*HS*, 116). The management of children's sex was undertaken through a moral and religious pedagogy aimed at the practice of masturbation; women's bodies were targeted by medical discourse as the site of unique pathologies governed by obscure laws; "population" was constructed and inquiries begun by demographers. Later, medicine and psychology in the nineteenth century would isolate a sexual instinct and create categories of deviancy for the serious discourses of psychology, sexology, psychiatry, and medicine. In summary,

> Four figures emerged from this preoccupation with sex, which mounted throughout the nineteenth century . . . the hysterical woman, the masturbating child, the Malthusian couple, and the perverse adult. Each of them corresponded to one of these strategies which . . . invested and made use of the sex of women, children, and men.[4]

Sequentially, anatamopolitics and biopolitics converged on the discipline of the individual. In prisons, schools, factories, and the home, techniques of domination ensured a healthy, prosperous, well-managed and moral society—necessarily subtended by the ill, mad, poor, delinquent, and perverse. Foucault calls this ensemble of concrete arrangements, which marks "the entry of life into history" (*HS*, 141), "biopower" (*HS*, 140).

The successful investment of biopower into the lives and activities of western people since the eighteenth century has been "an indispensable element in the development of capitalism" (*HS*, 140–41), providing for "the controlled insertion of bodies into the machinery of production" by applying anatamopolitical techniques of docility, and "the adjustment of the phenomena of population to economic processes" (*HS*, 141) through biopolitical strategies of surveillance and intervention (*PK*, 171–72). In contrast to the regulation of productive relations by the great and conspicuous institutions governed by the state, the development and effective management of economic processes relies on bio-power and its "always meticulous, often minute techniques" of discipline (*DP*, 139). Through the "microphysics of power" (ibid.) practiced by diverse social entities (family, schools, hospitals, armies, prisons, asylums), Modern capitalist economies became possible:

---

[4] *HS*, 105. A different view of the "civilization of the family" in nineteenth-century Europe and the United States is Peter Gay's psychohistory, *The Bourgeois Experience: Victoria to Freud*, vol. 1: *Education of the Senses* (New York/Oxford: Oxford University Press, 1984) esp. 421–38, "Social Science as Cultural Symptom," and 468–69 on Foucault's *The History of Sexuality*, vol. 1: *An Introduction*.

> The adjustment of the accumulation of men to that of capital, the joining of the growth of human groups to the expansion of productive forces and the differential allocation of profit, were made possible in part by the exercise of biopower in its many forms and modes of application. The investment in the body, its valorization, and the distributive management of its forces were at the time indispensable. (*HS*, 141)

Finally, it must be emphasized that the emergence of the human sciences in the Modern episteme was similarly made possible by the concrete arrangements of power between analyst and analysand, warder and prisoner, doctor and patient. The knowledge gained by human science relies on the docility of bodies and their susceptibility to surveillance and management, to the techniques of domination practiced by anatamo- and biopolitics. Foucault claims:

> The archaeology of the human sciences has to be established through studying the mechanisms of power which have invested human bodies, acts and forms of behaviour. .... And this investigation enables us to rediscover one of the conditions of the emergence of the human sciences: the great nineteenth-century effort in discipline and normalisation. (*PK*, 61)

Foucault had studied the relation of particular political interests to the designation and confinement of medical "undesirables" in *Madness and Civilization* (see esp. *MC*, 221–40).[5] His specifically archaeological researches thereafter, however, with their shared goal of "a structural analysis of discourses" (*BC*, xvii; see also *OT*, xiv), had the effect of systematically avoiding or occluding the question of the relation of power to truth. This changed with the advent of *Discipline and Punish* and *The History of Sexuality*. The truth of human-scientific discourses is linked genealogically to the growth of normalizing institutions and techniques of domination. The prison is one such institution; though it did not "cause" criminology, nor the spread of carceral techniques (hierarchical observation, examination, normalizing judgment), the human sciences would not have been possible without these techniques and their affiliation with the constraint, analysis, and modification of bodies:

> I am not saying that the human sciences emerged from the prison. But, if they have been able to be formed and to produce so many profound

[5] The relativity of mental illness to the norms of culture was addressed early in his career in Michel Foucault, *Maladie mentale et personnalité* (1954). See the English translation of the 1966 revised edition (*Maladie mentale et psychologie*) entitled, *Mental Illness and Psychology* (Alan Sheridan, trans.; New York: Harper & Row, 1976) esp. 59–88.

changes in the episteme, it is because they have been conveyed by a specific and new modality of power: a certain policy of the body, a certain way of rendering the group of men docile and useful. (*DP*, 305)

The reciprocity of knowledge and power for Foucault is clear: "The exercise of power perpetually creates knowledge and, conversely, knowledge constantly induces effects of power" (*PK*, 52); and again, "Far from preventing knowledge, power produces it" (*PK*, 59).

The genealogy of techniques of domination alone, however, cannot account for our knowledge of Modern "man." The human-scientific search for "man"'s foundations especially relies on strategies equally as old as the coercive technologies. These strategies—which presume in many cases the constraint of the body but employ different methods for the production of different truths—are the techniques of the self. Their historical modes of operation in the West have been self-examination and confession.

## Techniques of the Self

In 1980 Foucault said that through his analyses of sexuality he had become aware that all societies employed

techniques which permit individuals to effect a certain number of operations on their own bodies, on their souls, on their own thoughts, on their conduct, and this in a manner so as to transform themselves, modify themselves, or to act in a certain state of perfection, of happiness, of purity, or supernatural power, and so on.[6]

Foucault argues that the techniques of the self practiced in ancient Greece aimed at achieving complete self-mastery, not the repression of desire and the refusal of pleasurable acts (*aphrodisia*). Through careful attention to the moderate use of *aphrodisia* in all domains of life it was possible for some Greeks "to give their existence the most graceful and accomplished form possible."[7] Some but not all, the techniques of the self were the privilege of free male adults; women and slaves were excluded from these techniques, and boys, as simultaneously elements in adult males' *aphrodisia* and future men in their own right, were never integrated in an unproblematic way.[8]

---

[6] Michel Foucault, "Truth and Subjectivity, Part I," Howison Lecture, University of California, Berkeley, 20 October 1980.

[7] Foucault, *The History of Sexuality*, vol. 2: *The Use of Pleasure* (New York: Pantheon, 1985) 250–51.

[8] Ibid., 187–246, esp. 187–203.

The examination of the self conducted in conjunction with these techniques was, according to Foucault, unlike Stoic and early Christian practices. Whereas the Greeks conceived of self-mastery as the rational integration of pleasures into an optimum style of living, attending to behavior in order to facilitate this integration, the Stoic Seneca advocated a daily examination of one's deeds in order to see how they aligned with universal rules of conduct; he is a "permanent administrator of himself" who examines his life, act by act, to bring about a unity of his will and his knowledge of how one should behave. Seneca can be a master of the disciple Cerenus because he knows these rules. When Cerenus "confesses" his state of inner unrest to Seneca, he is not looking for absolution or judgment, but a diagnosis which effectively changes his will to become one with the rules of conduct. To achieve this unity, he must speak the truth of himself (his attachment to certain worldly things) to Seneca, the master:

> The truth Cerenus needs . . . is a force which is able to transform pure knowledge and simple consciousness in a real way of living. That is what Seneca tries to do. . . . This truth is not something which is hidden behind or under consciousness in the deepest and most obscure part of the soul. It is something which is in front of the individual as a point of attraction, a kind of magnetic pole which pulls him toward a goal.[9]

Foucault's studies of late Hellenistic and Roman technologies of the self is followed by analyses of Christian confessional practices and techniques of self-examination. Calling Christianity "the cradle of Western hermeneutics of the self," Foucault contrasts "the religion of a self which has to be deciphered" with the ethics of a self to be periodically recorrected (in Stoicism) or mastered (in Greek society). Foucault's analysis of confession in the writings of the church Fathers concludes that

> the revelation of the truth about oneself cannot be dissociated from the obligation to renounce the self. We have to sacrifice the self in order to discover the truth about one's self. And we have to understand this sacrifice not only as a radical change in the way of life, but as a consequence of a formula.[10]

By "sacrifice the self" Foucault means that the Christian is under an obligation to detect the presence of evil in the movement of his or her thoughts and in actions, and to publicly renounce the self, and thus its complicity with evil,

---

[9] Foucault, "Truth, I."

[10] Michel Foucault, "Truth and Subjectivity, Part II," Howison Lecture, University of California, Berkeley, 21 October 1980.

in ceremonies of penitence. Only through constant autosurveillance can the Christian begin the hermeneutics of the self which necessarily culminates in the production of truth, either through ceremonies of visible self-mortification (Foucault cites Jerome's description of the penitent Fabiola's *publicacio sui*) or the "permanent, exhaustive, deep, and sacrifical verbalization of the thoughts" before one's confessor or religious community.[11]

If early Christian practices of self-examination and confession introduced the hermeneutics of the self, it was only possible because these practices were part of a new organization of individuals that contributed to the production of truth through those same techniques. Foucault calls this new arrangement "pastoral power." It is characterized by constant, individualized attention by a supervisor or his or her delegate ("pastor") to each person under their care (each one of the "flock"). The exercise of power relations in the pastoral modality distinguishes Christianity in several ways from royal power, the Stoic concern for the self, and the Greek preoccupation with a beautiful life: it aims at assuring the salvation of individuals in the next world; it not merely commands but is prepared to sacrifice the pastor's life for any of the flock's—it is oblative; it attends to the welfare of each individual, in detail; to achieve the latter, it requires a knowledge of the conscience, the inner most self, and the ability to direct it (*SP*, 214).[12]

It was on the basis of the technologies of pastoral power that the secular state took form in the eighteenth century following the decline of ecclesiastical institutions:

> I don't think that we should consider the "modern state" as an entity which was developed above individuals, ignoring what they are and even their very existence, but on the contrary as a very sophisticated structure, in which individuals can be integrated, under one condition: that this individuality would be shaped in a new form, and submitted to a set of very specific patterns.[13]

The new state continued the individualizing function of pastoral power but for the new purpose of securing the well-being of persons in this life, rather than the next. The "worldly" aims of increased wealth, health, security, and protection from accidents replaced the religious aims of the traditional

---

[11] Ibid.

[12] On pastoral power, see Michel Foucault, in Sterling M. McMurrin, ed., *"Omnes et Singulatim*: Towards a Criticism of 'Political Reason,'"* The Tanner Lectures on Human Values* (2 vols.; Salt Lake City: University of Utah Press; Cambridge: Cambridge University Press, 1981) 2. 225–40.

[13] *SP*, 214. On the genealogy of the state, see Foucault, *"Omnes et Singulatim,"* 240–54; and idem, "Governmentality," *I & C* 6 (1979) 5–21.

pastorate. The officials of pastoral power increased at the same time: in addition to the older institution of the family, newer administrators including the police, private philanthropists, and medical personnel worked to achieve the new goals. Finally, the goals and agents of contemporary pastoral power center on producing a distinct knowledge of the human, as at once one of a global population and as an individual. Detached from its former ecclesial forms and invested in the concrete arrangements of the secular state, pastoral power has contributed to our contemporary government of individuals and our knowledge of them (*SP*, 213–15)

This brief account of the development of pastoral power and governmentality returns us to the material conditions of contemporary experience: the techniques of domination (by administration of bodies and management of life) which have flourished in the Modern episteme, and their inadequacy alone to account for the knowledge of "man" which the subjectifying human sciences (psychology, psychiatry, jurisprudence, and clinical medicine) claim to offer. The disciplines of "man" which study him as the bearer of deep truth may employ means that are very old (self-examination, confession) and which are in no way foreign to power:

> The confession is a ritual of discourse in which the speaking subject is also the subject of the statement; it is also a ritual that unfolds within a power relationship, for one does not confess without the presence (or virtual presence) of a partner who is not simply the interlocutor but the authority who requires the confession, prescribes and appreciates it, and intervenes in order to judge, punish, forgive, console, and reconcile. (*HS*, 61–62)

The interpretation of the deep truth of the self—what the self fundamentally is—cannot, if one respects the genealogical method, be considered apart from the concrete techniques governing the production of true statements about the self and the power relations those techniques imply. Together with the technologies of domination, those of the self have in our day given us the human sciences.

## Power and Truth

*Can the Human Sciences Be Exact?*

Returning to the questions posed in Chapter 1, we may ask, first, does Foucault believe that there is a difference between the natural and the human sciences? The answer is ambiguous: because Foucault is a genealogist and therefore avowedly against theoretical generalities, he could only sustain a difference between human-scientific and natural-scientific discourses by writing the archaeology of the natural sciences and the genealogy of their specific techniques for the pr oduction of truth. Since he did not undertake this task (and did not offer speculation on the roots of the natural sciences), we cannot answer the question in a way which would respect Foucault's own criteria of truth.

However, it is clear from his texts that Foucault was not much concerned with the difference as an abstract question of philosophy of science. In his hands, the ongoing conversation regarding the status of the human sciences becomes a struggle among what I regard as three kinds of knowledge: the knowledge of the "exact sciences" which is rigorous, coherent, predictive, and complete; that of the "dubious disciplines" of the human sciences, which aspire to be exact; and the knowledge of genealogical "anti-sciences" (*PK*, 83), which oppose the efforts of the human sciences to emulate the exact sciences in the domain of human being.

For instance, speaking of Marxist critical theory and psychoanalysis in their attempts to establish clear scientificity, Foucault asks:

> What types of knowledge do you want to disqualify in the very instant of your demand: 'Is it a science'? Which speaking, discoursing subjects— which subjects of experience and knowledge—do you want to 'diminish' when you say: 'I who conduct this discourse am conducting a scientific discourse, and I am a scientist'? Which theoretical-political *avant garde* do you want to enthrone in order to isolate it from all the discontinuous forms of knowledge that circulate it. When I see you straining to establish the scientificity of Marxism . . . [for me] you are investing Marxist discourses and those who uphold them with the effects of a power which the West since Medieval times has attributed to science and has reserved for those engaged in scientific discourse. (*PK*, 85)

Because "one cannot speak of anything at any time" (*AK*, 44), the ability to make serious speech acts is not a right of every discourse but must be won in contest with opposing regimes of power-knowledge. Why the exact sciences in the West have been eminently successful may or may not have something to do with the availability of their (natural) objects; why these discourses were institutionally legitimated, however, is a question for genealogy and political history, not epistemology and philosophy of science. Foucault relativizes the latter to the former, and his own investigations of the dubious disciplines reveal their roots to lie not in the solid ground of mathematics, physics, and chemistry's apparent advances, but in historically specific technologies and a transfer of sovereign authority from the Classical monarch to the agents of disciplined normalization:

> What I have wanted to demonstrate in the course of the last few years [as of 1977] is not the manner in which at the advance front of the exact

sciences the uncertain, recalcitrant, confused dominion of human behaviour has little by little been annexed to science: it is not through some advancement in the rationality of the exact sciences that the human sciences are gradually constituted. I believe that the process which has really rendered the discourse of the human sciences possible is the juxtaposition, the encounter between two lines of approach ... on the one hand there is the reorganisation of right that invests sovereignty, and on the other, the mechanics of the coercive forces whose exercise takes a disciplinary form. (*PK*, 107)

Can the human sciences become exact sciences, once the former are analyzed archaeologically and genealogically? Three responses at least are possible:

1) No. The archaeological description of the Modern episteme shows anthropological reflection to be caught in an endless task of reconciling "man" 's positivities and his foundations;
2) Yes. The genealogy of the human sciences shows the production of true discourses about the human to be linked to specific technologies aimed at the normalization of human behavior and self-understanding. If they succeed in extending biopower throughout all social practices, reflection on normalized practices will yield normal sciences;
3) No. The techniques of self-examination and confession practiced by the so-called subjectifying human sciences are intrinsically pleasurable for both analyst and analysand (*HS*, 70ff). Normalization of social practices would obviate the need for serious discourse about a deep truth of the self. Disciplines that employ the techniques of the self do not want to become exact sciences if this implies surrendering these same techniques. "Critique is its own reward."

The last response suggests that the endless to and fro of the doubles is no more mysterious than the pleasure of the confessional conversation itself.[14] The practitioners of disciplined discourse have obviously an economic stake as well in its perpetuation. Nevertheless, the "pleasure of analysis" (*HS*, 71)

---

[14] As Nietzsche said, "In the end one loves one's desire and not what is desired," *Beyond Good and Evil* (New York: Vintage, 1966) 93. Cf. Rorty's view:

Given leisure and libraries ... the conversation which Plato began will not end in self-objectification—not because aspects of the world, or of human beings, escape being objects of scientific inquiry, but simply because free and leisured conversation generates abnormal discourse as the sparks fly upward. (Rorty, *Philosophy*, 389)

The Foucaultian twists on this would include (1) abnormal practices generate abnormal discourses, in the forms of genealogical antisciences; (2) self-objectification, at least through the technologies of the self, generates and does not oppose abnormal discourse.

suggests that a normalization of the population is not in the best interests of the subjectifying human sciences.[15] The reluctance of "man" to fade beneath the gaze of structuralist, counterhuman sciences may be due in part to the continued vitality of technologies of the self (which Foucault had not studied when he suggested "man"'s imminent demise in 1966), and their anthropological postulate of a deep self in need of therapeutic recovery through relentless self-examination and confession.

Ethical implications of Foucault's genealogy of Modern "man" arise from the human sciences' attempts to assimilate their histories to the rational progression of the exact sciences; in effect, denying their constant familiarity with techniques of domination and the self for the production of their true discourses. The "lowly origins" of human sciences raise several questions for ethics.

If power is a constant in any institutionalized discourse about the human, does this thereby undermine the validity of human-scientific claims, so that one may speak with equal respect for, say, medieval hylomorphic theory and the late-Freudian tripartition of id/ego/superego? The Divine Right of Kings and democracy? If an analysis of reason itself cannot answer the question of a possible ground for ethics, where can we turn? Is Foucault obligated to give us such a foundation? In the context of the two questions posed in Chapter 1, we can ask: what personal and political difference does it make that the human sciences aspire to be exact sciences and do so through specific technologies of domination and the self?

## Reason and Power

Several recent critics of Foucault believe that his thought does not contain a coherent answer to the question above; that is, that Foucault does not offer a compelling reason why the "difference" he saw between accepting and opposing the spread of biopower should matter to anyone else, nor why anyone should respond just in the way he did.[16] One form of this objection is the following argument.

---

[15] Foucault remarks on the oppositional effect early psychoanalysis had on the racist and normalizing discourses of nineteenth-century eugenics and biologism (*HS*, 119 and 150). This opposition can be seen as a strategy defending traditional Western techniques of the self against techniques of domination not requiring the subjective testimony of individuals for the production of their essential (racist) truth.

[16] In addition to the objections voiced by Habermas (see the sources at Chapter 2, n. 1), cf. Nancy Fraser, "Foucault on Modern Power: Empirical Insights and Normative Confusions," *Praxis International* 1 (1981) 272 – 87; Rorty, *Consequences*, 203 – 10; and Charles Taylor, *Philosophy and the Human Sciences* (Philosophical Papers, vol. 2; Cambridge: Cambridge University Press, 1985) 152 – 84.

Hilary Putnam thinks that Foucault's analyses of powerknowledge lead to the conclusion that whenever we believe some part of our present stock of knowledge is rational, we are wrong—it is irrational: "Foucault is not arguing that past practices were *more* rational than they look to be, but that all practices are *less* rational, are, in fact, mainly determined by unreason and selfish power."[17]

If Foucault is right, then making a rational argument is an illusion. But then Foucault's own arguments would be illusory in their claims to rational attention. They would be irrational "projections" (as one commentator has implied in claiming that Foucault makes "a problem out of a personal question").[18] Putnam continues, saying that our actual practice of making judgments "shows that we *do* have a regulative idea of a just, attentive, balanced intellect, and we do think that there is a fact of the matter about why and how particular thinkers fall short of that ideal."[19]

If Foucault's arguments qua arguments are wrong, then, it is not because his claims to reasoned discourse are disguised power plays, but because his particular beliefs do not stand up to critical scrutiny. Some arguments can be right for good reasons; that is, for reasons that reflect the "virtues of criticism and impartiality," which

> tend to weed out irrational beliefs, if not at once, then gradually, over time, and to improve the warranted assertibility of our final conclusions. Rationality may not be defined by a 'canon' or set of principles, *but* we do have an evolving conception of the cognitive virtues to guide us.[20]

But because Foucault reduces all rational arguments to mere rationalizations, he is unable to address coherently the very question of ethical conduct which his work seems to raise. His ultimately reductionist background assumptions make his elaborate empirical studies a canard for those sincerely concerned with finding a ground of values or a framework for debating social and political issues.

---

[17] Putnam, *Reason*, 162. Putnam (ibid., 156, 160) reiterates his thesis on Foucault; and Hilary Putnam, *Realism and Reason* (Philosophical Papers, vol. 3; Cambridge: Cambridge University Press, 1983) 192, 198.

[18] The commentator is Fons Elders, mediator of a conversation between Foucault and Noam Chomsky published as "Human Nature: Justice versus Power," in Fons Elders, ed., *Reflexive Water* (London/Ontario: Souvenir Press [Educational & Academic] Ltd., 1974) 161. Foucault's response: "No, I'm not making a problem out of a personal question, I make of a personal question an absence of a problem" (p. 162).

[19] Putnam, *Reason*, 163. See Putnam, *Realism and Reason*, 113, for a reiteration of this point.
[20] Ibid.

Putnam takes Foucault to be saying that all practices, however reasonable in appearance, are "mainly determined" by "selfish power." Putnam assigns Foucaultian power a purely negative function in Foucault's genealogies. Sometimes Foucault *does* speak as if power is something selfish, which must hide its base motives behind a facade of rational discourse, as when he says "it is the court that is external and subordinate to the prison," the prison being one institution in a "carceral city" that sees to "the formation of the insidious leniencies, unavowable petty cruelties, small acts of cunning, calculated methods, techniques, 'sciences,' that permit the fabrication of the disciplinary individual" (*DP*, 308). The moral "charge" such a passage carries is unequivocal: our practices of justice, nondiscursive (detention) and discursive (the reasoned arguments of lawyers and judges), are actually rationalizations, screens for someone's petty but precise cruelties that covertly work to "fabricate" criminals.

More often, and with greater coherence, Foucault's "power" functions as what I have called a constitutive principle for the emergence of entities in any episteme. It is not opposed to rational discourse, but makes it possible by defining the parameters of serious speech acts in any given situation. This understanding of power as that which enables a directed conversation to take place (be it a psychiatric session or getting the right time of day from someone), or an economic transaction or rational ordering of other people's bodies (in a prison or supermarket line), this conception of power is affirmed by Foucault when he says,

> What defines a relationship of power is that it is a mode of action which does not act directly and immediately on others. . . . Instead it acts upon their actions: an action upon an action, on existing actions or on those which may arise in the present or the future. (*SP*, 220)

Power is what makes it possible for the anthropologist to distinguish customary from nonintentional behavior, as well as enabling native subjects to sort relevant from irrelevant speech and actions (as Dreyfus has argued, these two *dispositifs* need not coincide). As that which makes possible what one can say or do, power is not some "thing" at anyone's disposal (*HS*, 94–95); it is not a commodity to be owned or alienated, but is itself the circumstance of any possible ownership or dispossession.

Power is not, however, a denial of human freedom, but instead presupposes it. Power is "always a way of acting upon an acting subject or acting subjects by virtue of their acting or being capable of action" (ibid.). Its opposite "can only be passivity" (ibid.); where there is no possibility of resistance by acting subjects, there is no power, only force and obedience:

> Power is only exercised over free subjects, and only insofar as they are free. . . . By this we mean individual or collective subjects who are

faced with a field of possibilities in which several ways of behaving, several reactions and diverse comportments may be realized. (*SP*, 221)

These two theses, that power conditions discourse and action, and that power relations only exist where resistance is possible, come together in Foucault's examples of successful resistance strategies. In the following, serious speech about women sets up the parameters for organized counter discourses:

> For a long time people tried to pin women down to their sexuality. For centuries women were told, 'you are nothing but your sex.' . . . Feminist movements took up the challenge. Sex by nature, are we? Well, let's be that in its irreducible singularity and specificity. Let's follow the consequences of that and reinvent our own type of existence, politically, economically, culturally.[21]

A similar reversal occurs in "the case of homosexuality," and the moral and medical discourses surrounding it since the 1870s:

> After this date they are *all* perceived in a global relationship with madness, as being ill in terms of the sexual instinct. But taking such discourses literally and by that very fact turning them round, there appear replies couched as challenges: all right, we are what you say we are, by nature, illness or perversion, as you wish. Well, if we are what you say, let's be it, and if you want to know what we are we'll tell you ourselves better than you can. A whole literature of homosexuality— quite different from licentious stories—appears at the end of the nineteenth century. . . . This is the strategic reversal of the 'same' will to truth.[22]

Concerning Putnam's objection, then, I believe that there is a sense in which Foucault would agree that a notion like modern democracy is more rational than the theory of the Divine Right of Kings, but this sense is entirely genealogical : we do not have democracy instead of theocracy because reason succeeded in slowly detaching itself from power, but because power relations changed the parameters of what counts as reasonable government. By taking the genealogically specific forms they did (the truth-producing technologies of contemporary biopower), our present parameters of discourse cannot help but make democracy more rational than theocracy. It is all to the

---

[21] Michel Foucault, "The History of Sexuality: An Interview with Michel Foucault," *The Oxford Literary Review* 4 (1980) 7.

[22] Ibid. On the Modern construction of the sexes at this time in France, see Michel Foucault's "Introduction" to *Herculin Barbin: Being the Recently Discovered Memoirs of a Nineteenth-Century French Hermaphrodite* (New York: Pantheon, 1980) vii–xvii.

good of most people's lives that they are not ordered by theocratic principles. But this is a pragmatic good, consistent with the successful deployment of health- and wealth-producing techniques.

Foucault's important contribution to the discussion is to criticize, from genealogical researches, the kind of liberal, Rortian belief that these same techniques will eventually culminate in the improvement of everyone's lot: given time, liberal democracy will make everyone an equal partner in debating social policy. Foucault says we are more rational than the adherents of theocracy, but always at the cost of certain people's respect in society (the mad, deviate, criminal), those targets of contemporary practices that separate serious speech acts from strange and unintelligible utterances. Because these practices are power relations, however, they contain possibilities, and often realities, of strategic resistance. Through local struggles within and against normalizing technologies, the insurrection of these subjugated knowledges can succeed in changing the context of the production of reasoned discourse about the human. In summary, the specification of reason in terms of power relations does not imply that every coherent, meaningful statement is true. But no statement can disown its genealogical ties with power and claim to be rational.

## Humanism and the Modern Ethos

When truth is accepted as correlative with particular configurations of power, the question for ethics ceases to be, how can the search for a rational ground of moral conduct separate itself from unique historical interests (goals, technologies, political and social values and their systems). In his 1984 essay, "What is Enlightenment?" Foucault responds to Kant's famous article by sketching the basis for a contemporary ethics.

In this essay, Foucault is also writing against the views of some who claim that because he criticizes post-Enlightenment normative frameworks without supplying one of his own, he is implicitly committed to irrationalism.[23] In reply, he distinguishes between the Enlightenment and humanism.

Humanism "is a theme or, rather, a set of themes that have reappeared on several occasions, over time, in European societies" (*WIE*, 44). Since the Renaissance, it has appeared as a theme against Christianity, or within Christianity as a theme against ascetic or theocentric religious forms (Erasmus comes to mind). In the nineteenth century, humanism opposed science and, alternately, supported it. Marxism, existentialism, National Socialism and Stalinism have all, at various times, flown under the humanist banner. Since the 1600s, though, what humanisms have had in common are "certain con-

[23] Note the positions represented in the articles cited at n. 13 above.

ceptions of man borrowed from religion, science, or politics. . . . Humanism serves to color and to justify the conceptions of man to which it is, after all, obliged to take recourse'' (ibid.). Foucault is reminding us that the theme of humanism has historically developed as an element in a polemic; that it is parasitic on the interests of specific regions of society. If it proclaims a universal interest, it is only to facilitate the adoption of a particular program. His conclusion is not ''that everything that has ever been linked with humanism be rejected . . . but that the humanistic thematic is in itself too supple, too diverse, too inconsistent to serve as an axis for reflection'' (ibid.). Although Foucault does not explicitly draw the connection, his description of humanism includes the idea of anthropology, which he has consistently attacked as the unsteady basis of Modern human science. Contemporary humanism is an apologia for the figure of ''man,'' simultaneously the ground and object of positive law and ethical precepts.

Against our contemporary humanism, Foucault wants to oppose

> the principle of a critique and a permanent creation of ourselves in our autonomy: that is, a principle that is at the heart of the historical consciousness that the Enlightenment has of itself. From this standpoint, I am inclined to see Enlightenment and humanism in a state of tension rather than identity. (Ibid.)

The importance of the Enlightenment is not its dubious contribution to the thematics of humanism and its normalizing allies, the human sciences. In Kant's hands, Enlightenment was first a renunciation of the ''heteronomous'' authorities of revealed religion and dogmatic metaphysics, and an endorsement of the principle of self-direction in matters of thought and action.[24] Enlightenment is an ''exit'' (*Ausgang*) from an individual and collective immaturity centered on dependence to unnatural authorities, toward a mature autonomy. To think for oneself: this principle, captured in Kant's motto *aude sapere* (''dare to know''), implies a recognition of historical difference at the moment it is adopted. The past is unreliable; one must find a new direction on one's own.

The value of the Enlightenment for Foucault is not in the Kantian critiques of reason and the critical systems that followed. These, as we have seen, tried to find a new foundation for thought and action in universal anthropo-

---

[24] See Kant, *On History* (Indianapolis/New York: Bobbs-Merrill, 1963) 3–4, 9 and passim. Kant (ibid., 5–6) understood self-direction to imply obedience to authorities in matters pertaining to the achievement of ''public ends.'' He calls this the private use of reason, because each person must contribute their unique skills to the successful operation of society, following procedural-rational programs laid down by designated authorities. Reasoning for reason's sake, however, is obedient only to reason's own limits; it is reason's ''public use.''

logical structures. The importance of the Enlightenment for today is its critical "spirit," its renunciation of traditional authorities at the methodological level and its acceptance of responsibility for the forms of future human life.

Without the "liberal hope" and "comfort" of either universal anthropological foundations or the possibility of true statements apart from particular power relations, the self-formation of human life after the Enlightenment should proceed in the awareness that all reflection, writing, speaking, and acting is a risk that may result in the expansion of biopower and its normalizing practices.[25] Foucault states:

> My point is not that everything is bad, but that everything is dangerous, which is not exactly the same as bad. . . . If everything is dangerous, then we always have something to do. So my position leads not to apathy but to a hyper- and pessimistic activism.[26]

One thing we can do to ameliorate the risks implicit in contemporary activism is to treat all discourse, including our own, with less seriousness. The heroic renunciation of heteronomous authorities must be joined by an ironic appreciation of the historicity of discourse and its affiliation with relations of power. Foucault takes the example of Baudelaire as one who countered the seriousness of his day with an ethos of ironic self-determination.

This ethos is the modern attitude. By "modern" Foucault does *not* mean the episteme with "man" as its object. As an ethos, modernity has been embraced by many in the past, when the failure of social practices to sustain a framework for life orientation has challenged individuals to create something new and more satisfactory. As Dreyfus and Rabinow observe,

> In a modernity crisis, a taken-for-granted understanding of reality ceases to function as a shared background in terms of which people can orient and justify their activity and the modernist response is heroically and lucidly to face up to the collapse of the old order. Such was the attitude of Thucydides and the Sophists in Greece, the Gnostics and Stoics in Alexandria and of course, Kant.[27]

For Baudelaire, modernity means treating the present with respect, neither

---

[25] Cf. David R. Hiley, "Foucault and the Analysis of Power: Political Engagement without Liberal Hope or Comfort," *Praxis International* 4 (1984) 192–207. Hiley's article is in part a response to Fraser, "Foucault on Modern Power: Empirical Insights and Normative Confusions," *Praxis International* 1 (1981) 272–87.

[26] Michel Foucault, "On the Genealogy of Ethics: An Overview of Work in Progress" (1983), "Afterword" to Dreyfus and Rabinow, *Michel Foucault*, 231–32.

[27] Hubert L. Dreyfus and Paul Rabinow, "What Is Maturity? Habermas and Foucault on 'What is Enlightenment?'," in Hoy, *Foucault*, 117.

adopting a nihilistic indifference to "the ephemeral, the fleeting, the contingent";[28] nor, as Foucault remarks, treating "the passing moment as sacred in order to try to maintain or perpetuate it" (*WIE*, 40). One respects the present by attending to its peculiar dangers and opportunities; for Baudelaire, in art and in the artist's self-transformation:

> To be modern is not to accept oneself as one is in the flux of the passing moments; it is to take oneself as object of a complex and difficult elaboration. . . . Modern man, for Baudelaire, is not the man who goes off to discover himself, his secrets and his hidden truth; he is the man who tries to invent himself. (*WIE*, 41, 42)

For Foucault, the modern ethos that Kant approached and Baudelaire embodied is what one must be true to if one wants to be faithful to the Enlightenment. Foucault objects to what he terms, "the 'blackmail' of the Enlightenment" (*WIE*, 42) that presents

> a simplistic and authoritarian alternative . . . you either accept the Enlightenment and remain within the tradition of its rationalism . . . or else you criticize the Enlightenment and then try to escape from its principles of rationality. (*WIE*, 43)

The "blackmail" makes the Enlighenment continuous with the projects of certain critical theorists, just as in an earlier and recent time, Enlightenment blackmail was used by scientific philosophers to disqualify the claims to serious attention of nonformalizable language games. Both scientism and reflection on anthropological "quasi-transcendentals" (Habermas) succeed in mixing "the theme of humanism with the question of Enlightenment" (*WIE*, 45), to the detriment of the modern ethos and the genealogical and archaeological analyses practiced by Foucault.

## Foucault and the Future

Foucault's endorsement of the modern ethos leads him to offer the following recommendations for reflection and action. First, in place of a critique of the necessary and universal structures of human being, Foucault suggests "a historical investigation into the events that have led us to constitute ourselves and to recognize ourselves as subjects of what we are doing, thinking, saying" (*WIE*, 46). Archaeology will study particular discursive formations in

---

[28] Charles Baudelaire, *Baudelaire: Selected Writings on Art and Artists* (Cambridge: Cambridge University Press, 1972) 403.

order to present the history of what we have said about ourselves, as an archive for future self-construction. Genealogy writes the history of the relationship of these discourses to specific technologies of power in the present. Its aim is to set out the parameters within which freedom can work to create new social forms by modifying existing practices. The historico-critical attitude, in brief, locates the limits of determined freedom in concrete arrangements of power and knowledge, while simultaneously exposing possibilities within those arrangements for strategic resistance and change.

Second, for this work to be effective it cannot operate on a large scale or claim an ultimate intuition of the real; it "must turn away from all projects that claim to be global or radical" (ibid.). The historico-critical attitude is always an experiment with going beyond the limitations set by present arrangements. It is transgressive of these boundaries at the very specific points at which we each enounter them. The local character of creative transgression implies that our actions are always self-reflexive: those who act are those who are changed. As Gilles Deleuze has remarked, it is Foucault who has "taught us the indignity of speaking for others."[29] Foucault cites recent changes in "relations to authority, relations between the sexes, the way in which we perceive insanity or illness" (*WIE*, 47) as instances of successful self-transformation in society:

> I prefer even these partial transformations that have been made in the correlation of historical analysis and the practical attitude, to the programs for a new man that the worst political systems have repeated throughout the twentieth century.[30]

Third, Foucault offers four guidelines to assist in the critical analysis of "our historical limits" (ibid.). The first functions as a common reminder of the risks of acting within biopower. Cognizant of the particular arrangements we find ourselves in at any time (the discourses and practices that delimit our present existence), there are stakes involved in resistance. Foucault poses the question, "How can the growth of capabilities be disconnected from the intensification of power relations?" (*WIE*, 48). The point is not to extricate one's discourse from power, but to empower this discourse without strengthening the serious and normalizing discourses within which one's resistance occurs and toward which it is directed. Second, historico-critical

---

[29] Michel Foucault, *Language*, 209.

[30] *WIE*, 47. Foucault reiterates his thesis on the modern ethos and considers contemporary attempts at self-transformation in gay and lesbian communities in Bob Gallagher and Alexander Wilson, "Michel Foucault, An Interview: Sex, Power and the Politics of Identity," *The Advocate* 400 (August 7, 1984) 26–30, 58. See also Gilles Barbadette, "A Conversation with Michel Foucault," *Christopher Street* 6 (1982) 36–41.

analyses share a homogeneity of reference domain. This domain is neither "representations" nor deep structures, but "what [people] do and the way they do it" (ibid.): it is specifically the practices individuals engage in (e.g., the ancient Greek technologies of the self), as well as these practices viewed as strategic games whose genealogies trace the course of shifting power relations. Third, reflection on practical systems shares a systematicity by always addressing three questions: "How are we constituted as subjects of our own knowledge? How are we constituted as subjects who exercise or submit to power relations? How are we constituted as moral subjects of our own actions?" (*WIE*, 49). These questions correspond to three axes: "the axis of knowledge, the axis of power, the axis of ethics" (*WIE*, 48). Fourth and finally, historico-critical investigations assume a generality in contrast to the specificity of the discursive and nondiscursive practices they study. This generality is provided by the recurrence in Western society of certain points of conflict, for example, "the problem of the relationship between sanity and insanity, or sickness and health, or crime and the law; the problem of the role of sexual relations; and so on" (*WIE*, 49). The historico-critical analyses of these general concerns do not study them as (anthropologically) necessary issues. They are problematics for our society which have taken determined historical forms, defining "objects, rules of action, modes of relation to oneself" (ibid.). They are interesting to Foucault because they delimit the parameters of the "present" of which Foucault is writing the "history" (*DP*, 31).

Foucault's ethics begins with the adoption of a specific outlook toward history and oneself which is both ironic and heroic. The modern ethos is the prerequisite, I believe, for undertaking the project which Foucault calls "the critical ontology of ourselves":

> The critical ontology of ourselves has to be considered not, certainly, as a theory, a doctrine, nor even as a permanent body of knowledge that is accumulating; it has to be conceived as an attitude, an ethos, a philosophical life in which the critique of what we are is at one and the same time the historical analysis of the limits that are imposed on us and an experiment with going beyond them. (*WIE*, 50)

Unless one shares the modern ethos, the critique of reason will continue to be the search for transcendental limits *of* human nature, rather than the recovery of historical limits *to* the movements of bodies, the use of pleasures, and the performance of serious speech acts. Transcendental critique, eliding the temporally determined conditions of discourse and social practice, is opposed to modernity, even as it (falsely) claims modernity as its proper ethos.

In conclusion, Foucault's later work contains the elements of a coherent ethics in allowing for the self-transformation of people within determined, but strategically exploitable, relations of power. Self-transformation, Foucault makes clear in his writings and by his life, is not self-absorption: the hard work of creating the self proceeds within communities of individuals in response to varying perceived social dangers. As he states, "The ethico-political choice we have to make every day is to determine which is the main danger" and to focus our efforts there.[31] Dreyfus and Rabinow describe Foucault's method thus:

> Foucault's interpretive approach consists in identifying what he takes to be our current problem, describing with detachment how this situation arose and, at the same time, using his rhetorical skills to reflect and increase shared uneasiness in the face of the ubiquitous danger as he extrapolated it.[32]

Foucault offered what he believed were examples of dangerous practices when he chose to write about madness, the prison, the human sciences, and sexuality. If his genealogical analyses of techniques of domination in these areas are unsettling, causing one to call into question the presumed authority of biopower in our day, even moving one to act in concert with others to change the ways we form ourselves, then the historical ontology of ourselves has had ethical consequences. It has made a "personal and political difference" in our lives. The scope of the "we" cannot be delimited in advance of such a recognition of shared distress. This is what Foucault means when he says,

> But the problem is, precisely, to decide if it is actually suitable to place oneself within a "we" in order to assert the principles one recognizes and the values one accepts; or if it is not, rather, necessary to make the future formation of a "we" possible, by elaborating the question.[33]

Foucault "elaborates" the "question" of community by relentlessly exposing the concrete arrangements of power and truth that determine our lives at the present. His genealogical *dispositifs* render familiar situations foreign—

---

[31] Dreyfus and Rabinow, *Michel Foucault*, 232.

[32] Dreyfus and Rabinow, "What Is Maturity?" in Hoy, *Foucault*, 115. In a draft of this essay composed 8 April 1985, the authors conclude: "Unless theories are based on exemplars which disclose shared distress and shared practices, they will not elicit political commitment no matter how rational and universal they may be."

[33] Michel Foucault, "Polemics, Politics, and Problematizations," in Paul Rabinow, ed., *The Foucault Reader* (New York: Pantheon, 1984) 385.

and sometimes ominous. What "our" response is, thereafter, depends on specific opportunities for resistance, and the free decisions of those concerned to act accordingly.

# 4

# The Situation of Contemporary Theology: David Tracy

In the Introduction, I argued that the history of the problem of theological method has entered a new and decisive phase, in which strictly criteriological disputes have yielded to discussions about the reality of the traditional referents of theological discourse. For the first time, the reality of God, of human religious potential, and of salvation history have become questions within the circles of theology itself.

This chapter will examine the current situation from the perspective of revisionist theologian David Tracy. The concept of the "authentic self" will be introduced in the context of Tracy's discussion of the public character of theological discourse. This will be followed by an analysis of the sources of fundamental theology (Chapter 5) in terms of Tracy's understanding of authenticity as an anthropological category. Finally, the ramifications of authentic self-transcendence for revisionist theology will be explored through an analysis of Tracy's methodological turn from phenomenology and transcendental critique to social criticism and the methods of the human sciences (Chapter 6). In each chapter, Foucault's historical criticism of Modern "man" and the human sciences will be brought to bear on Tracy's theological reflection.

## Pluralism and Privatized Religion

Tracy believes that the contemporary theological scene is marked by both an "ever-increasing pluralism" of positions concerning the nature, method, sources, and media of Christian reflection, and by a "crisis of theological self-understanding" unprecedented in Western history (*BRO*, 3, 4). The problem for Tracy is not that theologians have no idea of what they should be doing, nor simply that they have many different ideas (in itself a plus). The problem is that enough of these different ideas are sufficiently disjunctive to raise fundamental questions about the field per se. In this uncertain position, he believes, the theologian is tempted to withdraw from public discourse completely, and adopt "the fatal social view that religious convictions are purely 'personal preferences' or 'private options'."[1]

Tracy frequently employs William James's description of experience as a "buzzing, blooming confusion" to characterize the theological scene in its activity, attractiveness, and chaos. Pluralism is attractive he claims because it "allows each theologian to learn incomparably more about reality by disclosing really different ways of viewing both our common humanity and Christianity" (*BRO*, 3). Yet comparing it to Rudolf Otto's idea of the holy, Tracy observes that pluralism is both *fascinans et tremendum*: "fascinating" in its sheer multiplicity of forms, but fearful in its lack of apparent unity.[2]

In the absence of an articulated ordering principle, the potential richness of multiple Christian worldviews threatens to be lost. Unless the present "chaotic" pluralism becomes a "genuine" and "responsible" pluralism, the likely result will be a "mere" pluralism of opinions, indistinguishable from the *doxa* of subjective relativism (ibid.).

Hindering the organization of theology is the increasing disintegration of a public forum for the adjudication of religious claims. Tracy is convinced that "the question of an adequate paradigm for theology as a public form of discourse remains the most important item on the contemporary theological agenda."[3]

Tracy argues that in the United States, for example, pluralism is "first and foremost an experience, not a theory"; one which is fundamentally affirmed in a civic rejection of religious intolerance and openness to mutual transformation.[4] In the 1960s, pluralism flowered as groups organized around issues of social distinction (race, sex, religion, etc.), and Vietnam drew attention to the global multiplicity of economic, military, political, and

---

[1] David Tracy, "Defending the Public Character of Theology," *Christian Century* 98 (1981) 351.

[2] David Tracy, "Theological Pluralism and Analogy," *Thought* 54 (1979) 26.

[3] David Tracy, "Theology as Public Discourse," *Christian Century* 92 (1975) 280.

[4] David Tracy, "The Questions of Pluralism: The Context of the United States," *Mid-Stream* 22 (1983) 273.

cultural forms and values. However, Tracy believes that pluralism since the sixties has degenerated into a narcissistic particularism:

> As the seventies and now the eighties drew on, the rising political and pluralistic consciousness of the sixties waned and a 'culture of narcissism' began to prevail . . . [Pluralism became] an excuse for groups and individuals to retreat from their responsibilities to the public realm in favor of a retreat to various group 'reservations of the spirit' (Adorno) or even to purely private and finally narcissist personal pleasures.[5]

When the churches join the general retreat into the "swamp of privateness"[6] they threaten to deprive the public realm of "the moral and theological resources [they] can bring to bear on public moral issues." In the 1980s, he believes, "the major movement of the Christian churches in the United States . . . is . . . a return to the demands and responsibilities of the public realm."[7]

Successfully concluding the "crisis of theological self-understanding" thus has implications far wider than the restoration of a single discipline for the sake of those who practice it. Its resolution is ethically mandated by the public at large. But how "large" is this public? And why has it a legitimate claim on the work of theologians? To answer these questions we must look at Tracy's understanding of the public character of theology.

## Theology as Public Discourse

A public discourse, claims Tracy, is one which "discloses meanings and truths which in principle can transform all human beings in some recognizable personal, social, political, ethical, cultural, or religious manner" (*NI*, 23; see also *AI*, 55). The addressee is universal : "any intelligent, reasonable, responsible human being."[8]

Good theology for Tracy is always public discourse. As such, it discloses religious truth about "our actual existence embedded in the Christian classical texts, events, images, symbols, doctrines, and persons," in a way which satisfies specific cognitive criteria (*NI*, 23).[9] At the same time, theology as

---

[5] Ibid., 275.

[6] Tracy, "Defending the Public Character of Theology," 352; see also *AI*, 6.

[7] Tracy, "Questions of Pluralism," 276.

[8] Tracy, "Defending the Public Character of Theology," 351: "To speak in a public fashion means to speak in a manner that can be disclosive and transformative for any intelligent, reasonable, responsible human being."

[9] These cognitive criteria vary according to the nature of the public addressed and their distinct notions of truth. Tracy holds that "radical pluralism in theology erupts with a vengeance" (*NI*, 29) precisely over what constitutes a public claim to truth in theology.

public discourse satisifies ethical demands of this religious truth by allowing "in principle" for the transformation of self and world.

Although all theology endeavors to be universal, disclosive, and potentially transformative, the sociology of knowledge reveals that the single public focus of theology is realized in relationship to three distinct social realities, or "publics": the wider society, the academy, and the church. One of these publics "will be the principal, yet rarely exclusive, addressee" for the theologian (*AI*, 5). More exactly, the concerns of the institutions making up the theologian's public realm will exert a strong, sometimes determinative, influence on his or her thinking. The self-conception of an institution (what it takes to be its "public" function) will support certain "elective affinities" for discourse, including what will count as "a genuinely theological statement" in that particular social locale (as implicitly representing one of the three publics; ibid.).

Nevertheless, argues Tracy, substantial differences among the publics of society, academy, and church are resolved in the striving of each theologian for "a genuine publicness" (ibid.) in discourse, which discloses potentially transformative meanings and truth to the addressee. Because all good theology is devoted to answering common human questions in a universally acceptable manner (that is, in a way acceptable to any reasonable, responsible person), every theologian implicitly addresses all three publics. This is true, says Tracy, even when two publics (society and church) do not take publicness as their explicit concern:

> It is not, of course, the case that all theologians should accept an explicit concern with "publicness" as their major focus. A thrust to publicness must, however, be present in all theologies. Otherwise, theo-logy no longer exists. . . . To speak and mean God-language is to speak publicly and mean it.[10]

Recalling our earlier questions (Why is theology responsible to the public, and how far does this responsibility extend?), let us look at each of Tracy's "publics" in turn.

*Society*

The public of society embraces three regions: the technoeconomic realm, the realm of polity, and the realm of culture (*AI*, 6–31). The first is concerned with the successful organization and allocation of social goods and services. This requires the determination of the most efficient means of

---

[10] Tracy, "Defending the Public Character of Theology," 351; see also *AI*, 29.

achieving a desired end; action in the technoeconomic realm is therefore instrumental rational (Weber).

The polis is "an exemplary limit concept" (*AI*, 9) of an ideal communication situation in which all citizens meet to resolve matters of public concern. In Western societies, the realm of polity presumes for this purpose that all ethical arguments are "grounded in comprehensive notions of practical reason" which open them in principle to "all intelligent, reasonable and responsible persons" (ibid.). Action in the realm of polity, for Tracy, appears to be generically value rational, respecting the specific value of consensual agreement.

Third, in the realm of culture, the "classical symbolic expressions" of society's "major traditions" of art, religion, philosophy, theology, and literature inform society's "ethos and worldview, affectivity, style and cognitive principles of order" (*AI*, 11). These "classical expressions, " in turn, are critically recovered by the appropriate humanistic disciplines for the general enrichment of society.

The theologian works primarily in the realm of culture, as the domain in which the great religious texts and symbols have appeared and received their classic interpretations. However, the realms of technoeconomics and polity also warrant the theologian's attention.

The goals toward which technological resources should be dedicated, for example, can be determined neither by a broad but naïve intuition of the good, nor by a narrow but scientistic worldview. Humanistic reflection, including theological thinking, on the impact of technology upon society is a genuine public obligation, yet one increasingly renounced as art, politics, philosophy, and religion are confined to "enclaves" of subjective preference within the realm of culture (cf. *AI*, 8−9).

Similarly, in the realm of polity, "the one realm where all the citizens of the polis presumably meet" (*AI*, 9), the privatization of religion has allowed the imperatives of bureaucracy and technology to go unchallenged. Because questions of polity affect all citizens, the theologian has a legitimate stake in the outcome of decision making; conversely, the polis can expect the theologian to elucidate the symbols that give rise to ethical and axiological reflection, by showing how they disclose common human meanings and truth. .

Where humanistic reflection on the classic expressions of culture is trivialized as but a "private option" and suppressed from public conversation, the good of society as a whole is jeopardized. Tracy makes clear his view that theology is entitled to a place in the public discourse of society because it reflects on symbols important to all:

> One need not (indeed, should not) absolutize the claims of any religion in order to realize that any major religious tradition does disclose in its

> symbols and in its reflections upon those symbols (i.e., its theologies)
> some fundamental vision of the meaning of individual and communal
> existence providing disclosive and transformative possibilities for the
> whole society. Both ethos and worldview are disclosed in any religion.
> One need not minimize the need for reasoned public discourse upon all
> claims to truth in order to recognize the indispensable role that cultural
> symbols, including the religious, can play in the wider society. (*AI*, 12)

Tracy is not merely arguing, however, that religious symbols and their
theologies have a responsibility only to their particular social matrix of technoeconomic, polity, and culture concerns. When these expressions are
"classics" they represent something fundamentally human which transcends
any set of social circumstances, disclosing "permanent possibilities" for
individual and social life:

> A major assertion of this book can now be stated as a claim: If any
> human being, if any religious thinker or theologian, produces some clas-
> sical expression of the human spirit on a particular journey in a particular
> tradition, that person discloses permanent possibilities for human
> existence both personal and communal. (*AI*, 14)

I will examine the validity of this claim in Chapter 5, when I analyze the
sources of revisionist fundamental theology. For now the above may be sum-
marized as follows.

Tracy believes that theology has a legitimate place in the public discourse
of society. It is active in all social realms: technoeconomic, polity, and culture, because (1) the theologian, as a responsible and reasonable person and
as a citizen of the state, is entitled to a voice in all matters of common concern, and because (2) religion and theology express and articulate the "fundamental vision" (*AI*, 12) of social and personal meaning and existence.
Tracy also suggests, as a principal thesis, that certain cultural expressions and
their commentary are "classics," and that the classics of any culture have a
universal addressee. Thus even as the classics enrich particular realms of
technoeconomics, polity, and culture, they transcend those realms to address
in principle all societies at all times.

*Academy*

The academy also serves as a forum for theological reflection. Here the
demands for publicness are more consciously and conscientiously imposed
on all would-be participants: the requirements for criteria of adequacy, evidence for assertions, warrants and backings, and a recognizable disciplinary

status are firm.[11] Here, too, the absence of a clear paradigm for theology (what Tracy calls "the most important item on the contemporary theological agenda") is felt most acutely.[12]

On this matter Tracy agrees with Stephen Toulmin that the "hard" sciences are paradigmatic for all disciplined reflection, because they illustrate the features that make any discipline "compact" (*AI*, 17).[13] Tracy believes that theology and religious studies should join psychology, sociology, anthropology, and related social sciences as disciplines diverging from the paradigm of the "hard" sciences in significant ways. The social sciences, theology, and religious studies are "diffuse" or "would-be" disciplines that suffer from "first, a lack of a clear sense of disciplinary direction and thereby a host of unresolved problems; second, a lack of adequate professional organization for the discussion of new results" (*AI*, 18). Yet Tracy indicates that theology once was a "compact" discipline, or "seemed" to be:

> Like social science, modern theology as a discipline clearly does not possess a "compact discipline" in theology in the way it once seemed to. Neither the medieval theologians' notion of theology as a subalternated science . . . nor earlier notions of dogmatics now suffice. (*AI*, 19)

For the present, then, "Theology, like the humanities and the social sciences in the modern university, must and can presently content itself with a 'diffuse' or 'would-be' disciplinary status" (*AI*, 20). In this position, theology remains committed to its traditional "struggle" to be "a normative and self-constituting discipline concerned with that elusive reality 'truth.'" (ibid.). The "drive to speak a truth about religious meaning" (ibid.) remains theology's unique mission, distinguishing it from philosophy (with which it is otherwise closely related) and all other humanistic disciplines. This commitment to truth seeking can only be realized nowadays when theology accepts as its own the "highest standards of the contemporary academy" (*AI*, 21) and enters freely into public discussion, albeit as a temporarily diffuse or would-be discipline.

---

[11] Tracy's analysis of the demand for publicness in the academy is indebted to Van Harvey's work on the structure of rational arguments, in Harvey, *Historian*, 38–67, esp. 49–54. Harvey, in turn, relies on Stephen Toulmin, *The Uses of Argument* (New York: Cambridge University Press, 1958).

[12] Tracy, "Theology as Public Discourse," 280.

[13] See Stephen Toulmin, *Human Understanding*, vol. 1: *The Collective Use and Evolution of Concepts* (Princeton: Princeton University Press, 1972) 379.

## Church

The third social reality addressed by every theologian is the public of the church. By "church" Tracy understands a "community of moral and religious discourse" (ibid.) to which the theologian is "internally related" as "an interpreter of tradition" (*AI*, 25.) Whether or not a theologian makes an explicit commitment to an institutionalized church, he or she voluntarily assumes a loyalty to "an interpersonal community and tradition of shared meanings" called "the Christian church" (*AI*, 22) which becomes, with academy and society, a primary reference group for theological statements.

Although sociologically speaking, the church is one public among three, the church's theological self-understanding places it above society and academy "as participating in the grace of God disclosed in the divine self-manifestation in Jesus Christ" (*AI*, 23). At the same time, however, both the church and the theologian's commitment to it are relativized by ("stand under") what Tracy calls "the eschatological proviso of the judgment of God" (ibid.) which, for inner theological reasons, compels the church to admit its nonidentity with the "kingdom of God" and reject the temptation to triumphalism in every and all theological discourse.

This qualification of the church's self-understanding is important for its relations with society and academy, for it implies the rejection of strictly ecclesial criteria of adequacy in favor of publicly available standards (that is, available to members of societal and academic publics) for the determination of the truth of theological claims. Indeed, it is Tracy's contention that a proper theological understanding of society and academy as the "world" addressed by the church, makes them a genuine *source* for theological reflection, and not merely its *object* (*AI*, 23 and 31, and his discussion of the "emergence of the uncanny" in society and academy, AI 339–70). The unity of the three publics in the "common human experience" of their members, and the intrinsic "thrust to publicness" of church and world alike, imply for Tracy that when the church acts "as prophetic social critic or as a transformative sacrament of the 'world' " (*AI*, 25), it does so on the basis of rational criteria in principle agreeable to all.

It is not surprising, then, that Tracy believes that sociological and theological analyses of "church" are finally compatible:

> The theologian should in principle use a correlation model for relating sociological and theological understandings of the reality of the church in the same way one uses a correlation model for the more familiar relationship between philosophy and theology. (*AI*, 24)

Tracy's use of the correlation model in *Blessed Rage for Order*, does not bring together philosophical questions and theological answers (as Tillich had; see also *BRO*, 45–46, 57–58, nn. 12–15). Instead he attempts to correlate the *meanings* of "common human experience" and "Christian texts" after phenomenological and hermeneutic analyses of these two sources (see, e.g., *BRO*, 43–63). In a similar fashion, he suggests that a correlation model could guide the disclosure of the common ground of sociological and theological interpretations of the single reality, "church," in a way which preserves the integrity of both the Christian symbolic and textual tradition and the legitimate secular demand for fully public criteria.

## Summary

I began this section asking why Tracy believes that the resolution of the current crisis in theology is ethically mandated by the public and how far this public extends. It is now possible to say that "the public" legitimately concerned with theological reflection is in fact three "publics": society, academy, and church. The sociology of knowledge describes the theologian's activity in these publics, but cannot tell us why this behavior satisfies a moral obligation. My reading of Tracy's texts suggests the following.

First, as a loyal member of a community of moral and religious discourse dedicated to the meanings and traditions of the Christian church, the theologian is obligated to transform the world in accordance with the beliefs and values of that community. Because, theologically understood, society and academy together constitute the "world," these publics are in principle the addressees of all theologians. When, as now, theology undergoes a crisis of self-understanding, it is for the good of the world (or, more precisely, for the good of the church's mission to the world) that theologians of all public emphases work to achieve a renewed self-identity.

Second, because the theologian is also a member of society and academy, he or she is charged with contributing to the well-being of these publics in as disciplined a way as possible. In society this means working for the deprivatization of religion and the general reintegration of culture and the realms of polity and technoeconomics. Theology's particular contribution lies in its critical reappropriation of the symbols and texts informing society's overall ethos and worldview, for the good of "a particular cultural, political, social or pastoral need which bears genuine import" (*NI*, 25).

Third, speaking the truth, rather than performing the good, is the goal of academic discourse. This goal demands that the strictest possible standards of reasonable discourse be observed by all, so that every conclusion of the academy is in principle acceptable to any intelligent person. For theology, the obligation to seek and speak the truth in a disciplined manner means engaging in philosophical reflection on the meanings of common human experience and Christian texts. Theology's obligation to the academy is fulfilled by elucidating the transcendental conditions of possibility of *all* experience, including "religious" experience, needed to decide religious and theistic claims (*BRO*, 55). Needless to say, the successful accomplishment of this task presumes the resolution of the crisis of theology's self-understanding.

In summary, Tracy clearly believes that theology's current situation consists in a crisis of self-identity which undermines its effectiveness to fulfill obligations in specifiable social contexts. These contexts, or "publics," include the church (theology's traditionally assumed reference group) plus society and academy. The domain of theological responsibility is, on public grounds, therefore coextensive with the world itself (in the broadest sense, as totality of publics, not in opposition to "church").

In addition to the foregoing, a fuller portrait of the current situation as Tracy understands it must include his analysis of the speaker of this multi-form discourse. With an obligation to publicness imposed on every side, what remains unspoken in any contemporary theological statement?

## Publics, Loyalties, and the "Authentic Self"

### Sociology of Theological Discourse

Tracy's sociological analysis of the publics of theological discourse reveals to him a general "thrust to publicness" or moral obligation on the part of the speaker in the regions of society, academy, and church to make only those claims that are both (a) subject in fact to specifiable criteria of adequacy within any given discourse—ecclesial, social, or academic, and (b) acceptable in principle to "any intelligent, reasonable, responsible human being."[14] In brief, Tracy's thesis is that any genuine theological statement, as an instance of public speech, has a universal addressee. This is true even if, in any particular utterance, two of the three publics are only "implicitly" addressed. The challenge for Tracy is to articulate rules of coherence for truth claims occurring in different publics, so that one can be certain that a true statement in, for example, the church would be recognized as true in the academy and society.[15] Until this is done, the unity of theological discourse

---

[14] Tracy, "Defending the Public Character of Theology," 351.

[15] The problem of rules of coherence among truth claims occurring in different publics has been called a "crucial" one for Tracy's position. The convener of the Seminar on Theological Method at the 1982 meeting of the Catholic Theological Society of America (CTSA) asked him, "Can the public audiences of the theologian be differentiated into academy, church and society without surreptitiously reintroducing a division between public and private languages?" In

must remain an ideal of conversation among society, academy, and church, and not its demonstrated precondition. Tracy's analysis of the speaker of theological discourse influences his understanding of the problem of discursive unity itself.

Tracy describes the contemporary theologian as a Christian intellectual living in a complex society, who personally appropriates to some degree the goals and criteria of all three publics. The theologian "speaks not merely to several publics external to the self but to several internalized publics" (*AI*, 4). Internalization requires each theologian to adopt three "sets" of beliefs correlative with the three publics, regarding, first, the normative reference group of theological statements; second, the proper mode of theological argument; third, the appropriate ethical stance toward sources; fourth, the relevance of the theologian's Christian faith (or lack thereof); and fifth, the proper criteria for meaning and truth in theology (*NI*, 24). So different are the three mind-sets that Tracy can speak of "the actual complexity of different selves related to the distinct social locations and therefore to the distinct plausability structures present in each theologian" (*AI*, 5). Phenomenally, the theologian is not one self but three, each capable of making statements which may be intelligible in one context, but possibly incoherent (not to mention unmeaningful and false) in two others.

The diversity of plausability structures distinguishing the three publics might suggest that in any two of them, the theologian is only an occasional "guest speaker" whose "regular appointment" lies in the third. It would be wrong, however, to assume from this impression that every theological statement is directed to one and just one public. On the contrary, Tracy wants strongly to argue that each statement implicitly addresses two nonostensive reference groups; or, put differently, that elective affinities within any single social reality influence but do not determine genuine theological reflection (*AI*, 5, 28–31). Tracy consistently maintains that although theological statements do differ "fundamentally" among their publics, this difference is one of "emphasis" alone (*NI*, 24). He reiterates his claim:

> The theocentric character of any genuinely theological statement, whether explicitly or implicitly addressed, drives every theologian to claims to truth which demand publicness and, at the limit, universality. (*AI*, 80)

---

response, Tracy reaffirmed his commitment to a "hard consensus" model demanding of any true statement the agreement of all communities of inquiry, such consensus to be based on "abstract or transcendental conditions of the possibility of truth and the concrete disclosure and transformation" of meaning and reality, as criteria of adequacy (T. Howland Sanks and Stephen Happel, "Tracy on the Public and the Aesthetic," *Proceedings of the Catholic Theological Society of America* 37 [1982] 182).

Still, it is difficult for the sociological imagination to see what is common to all assertions when he explicitly states, "Theology, in fact, is a generic name not for a single discipline but for three: fundamental, systematic and practical theologies" (*AI*, 31) which properly address the publics of academy, church, and society, respectively (*AI*, 54 – 79). If the differences among the publics are as profound as Tracy wants us to believe, how can he consistently hold that any theological statement implicitly or explicitly addresses all three realities? What, according to Tracy, creates a unitary theological discourse? The religious and moral situations of the theologian begin to supply an answer.

## Morality of Theological Discourse

Although every theologian is three selves to three publics, he or she embraces the same twofold commitment in each one. This commitment is a dedication to the critical investigation of the religious dimension of both a religious tradition and the contemporary situation.[16] Tradition and situation are the two constants of theological reflection. They themselves are not the immediate objects of this reflection. Rather, they are the permanent contexts within which a given subdiscipline formulates, by its own criteriological lights, an understanding of the "religious dimension" of each suitable for critical correlation. They are media through which the immediate objects of theological reflection are discerned and given conceptual form (much as clay is a medium for the creation of a particular sculpture, itself the object of critical, aesthetic attention). Each theologian defends an interpretation of tradition and situation as the precondition for specifically theological discussion. Consensus on what counts as "tradition" and "contemporary situation," and what methods are appropriate for their investigation, is important for establishing warrants for arguments within and among the publics. When tradition and situation are specified according to the criteria of a subdiscipline, they become the sources for theology in that mode.[17]

Commitment to elucidating the religious dimension of a religious tradition has always given theological discourse a kind of unity, namely, a unity of purpose. To see why Tracy insists that the theologian should include the contemporary situation as an obligatory source requires us to consider the

---

[16] See the following: *AI*, 58 – 61; *NI*, 26 – 29; and David Tracy and John B. Cobb, Jr., *Talking About God* (New York: Seabury, 1983) 5 – 7.

[17] The distinction between "media" and "sources" is my own, but it is supported by Tracy's own identification of "common human experience" as one understanding of the situation we share (*AI*, 60), namely, the interpretation appropriate to fundamental theology (*BRO*, 43 and passim), expressly as "source."

fundamental faith and moral posture of the theologian as a Christian and postmodern intellectual.

The modern theologian was a product of the Enlightenment, and shared that movement's disenchantment with the "mystifications" of revealed religion (*BRO*, 4–10). In place of "a morality of belief in and obedience to the tradition and a fundamental loyalty to the church-community's beliefs" (*BRO*, 6), the modern theologian embraced a morality demanding "that every progress in knowledge must be made by the advancement of critical evidence for or against the present reigning theories, methods, and paradigms" (ibid.) in any given field.

Even after the critical spirit of the Enlightenment turned against that period's epistemological and ethical assumptions, the theologian remained committed to the ideal of "purely secular standards for knowledge and action initiated by the Enlightenment" (*BRO*, 8). The theologian is now so fundamentally dedicated to this ideal that it serves as the focus for her or his "faith" as an "authentic" person in the contemporary world.[18] The postmodern theologian *must* address the contemporary situation because he or she shares in "the faith of secularity ... that fundamental attitude which affirms the ultimate significance and final worth of our lives, our thoughts, and actions, here and now, in nature and in history" (*BRO*, 8). The "thrust" or "drive" to publicness is none other than the desire of the theologian to satisfy a moral obligation imposed by his or her faith as an authentic secular person. Having this faith and obligation, the theologian is compelled to speak in a manner responsible to public criteria of adequacy.

Yet Tracy also wants to claim that this faith is not taken over uncritically (as the moderns did), but critically, by subjecting it to "a proper understanding of the explicitly Christian faith" which perfects secular faith by rendering "intellectually coherent and symbolically powerful that common secular faith we share" (*BRO*, 9). More specifically, the contemporary theologian believes

> that only a coherent articulation of the reality of the Christian God can provide an adequate reflective account of both the unavoidable presuppositions of our inquiry and our moral activity, and of the basic faith in the final meaningfulness of an authentic life. (*BRO*, 10)

In the last analysis, the theologian today faces the task of reconciling a "dual dilemma" of "faiths," in the "modern experiment" and in "the God of Jesus Christ" (*BRO*, 4), within each and among all subdisciplines.

---

[18] Tracy defines "faith" as follows: "a basic orientation or attitude which determines one's cognitive beliefs and one's individual ethical actions" (*BRO*, 8).

At this point it is important to see that a unity of theological discourse, what allows one to speak of "implicit" addressees, presumes a single morality of knowledge applied conscientiously to every statement in every public by each theologian. Commitment to the faith of secularity, as a dedication to "purely secular standards for knowledge and action" (*BRO*, 8), precludes any (perhaps unconscious) appeal to the traditional morality of knowledge in any public. This is so even if such appeal would justify a transcendental theory capable of producing true statements (in fundamental theology), or a rejuvenating interpretation of church texts and symbols (in systematics), or an expedient solution to sociopolitical problems (in practical theology). Loyalty to the Christian tradition and loyalty to the traditional Christian morality of knowledge are conceptually distinct attitudes for the contemporary theologian: the first is an unavoidable dedication to the living Christian past (traditio);[19] the second is an unacceptable adherence to a belief in the self-evidence of that tradition's meaning for the present.

The faith of secularity implies the duty of each theologian as a "postmodern intellectual" to "remain in fundamental fidelity to the critical exigencies of the liberal period" (*BRO*, 12). The modern morality of scientific and historical knowledge, now free of positivism's ideological influence, has become in our day the self-critical, radically "suspicious" morality of secular, "postmodern" knowledge (*BRO*, 8, 10–14). This singular moral conviction should inform every act of theological reflection. This is true, argues Tracy, even though "systematic and practical theologies may be more implicit than explicit on models and criteria for truth in theology" (*AI*, 63), and "honest critical inquiry" is the principal "ethical stance" of fundamental theology alone. The theologian's internalization of a single, postmodern morality of knowledge is not the sufficient condition of a unitary theological discourse, but it is a necessary one for genuine conversation, implicit and explicit, among the three publics.

## Anthropology of Theological Discourse

My reconstruction of Tracy's speaker of theological discourse has found the theologian to be (1) three selves devoted internally and externally to three distinct publics and their plausability structures; (2) loyal to two sources of theological reflection: the contemporary situation and the Christian tradition;

---

[19] On the distinction between *traditio* ("the living reality of the past in the present") and *tradita* ("the handed down conclusions of a once living tradition") apropos the American theological scene, see David Tracy, "An Analogical Vision: Some Reflections on the American Roman Catholic Bicentennial Social Justice Program," *Criterion* 15 (1976) 10–16, esp. 11–12; see also *AI*, 422 and passim on "tradition."

and yet (3) committed in principle to a single, postmodern morality of knowledge for the investigation of both sources in all publics. I have said that this moral commitment is, for Tracy, implied by the theologian's faith as an authentic secular person. The concept "authenticity" as it is applied by the contemporary theologian to actions and states of being will be more closely considered in Chapters 5 and 6. For now, the situation of the post-modern theologian, as Tracy understands it, deserves the following observations.

The faith of secularity draws the theologian in two directions. On the one hand, she or he is committed fundamentally to the affirmation of this world, here and now, as the only proper context for the construction of coherent, meaningful, and true statements about reality. In the present day, "The very meaning and hence reality of the self's full experience is intrinsically and systematically relational, social, and temporal" (*BRO*, 173).

On the other hand, as a postmodern intellectual, the theologian is acutely aware of the potential and real distortions of the self's "full experience" in relationship, society, and history. The contemporary belief that the self and its worldly involvements are not transparent to the rational and reasonable mind, but must be subjected to psychological and social criticism for their truth to emerge, does not imply the denial of the faith of secularity. Rather, Tracy maintains, this belief, characteristic of post-modern consciousness, corresponds to a "deepening" of the Enlightenment's commitment to "secular standards of knowledge and action" (*BRO*, 8).

The faith of secularity, therefore, leads the contemporary individual to "the full affirmation of the ultimate significance of our lives in this world" (*BRO*, 8); yet it also implies the recognition of the disparity between our everyday understanding of this world (which may be ideological) and an authentic apprehension of reality. The final significance of our lives in this world cannot be fully affirmed until we systematically free ourselves and our society from the various distortions of communication and/or productive relations which presently operate freely, beneath consciousness, or in opposition to current attempts at transformation. The response of the authentic person in this situation, for Tracy, is one of

> radical commitment to the struggle to transcend our present individual and societal states in favor of a continuous examination of these illusions which cloud our real and more limited possibilities for knowledge and action. (*BRO*, 11)

Tracy describes the contemporary model of human being as one of "self-transcendence" (*BRO*, 11), and cites with approval Bernard Lonergan's well-known imperatives for personal transformation under this scheme:

"Be attentive, be intelligent, be rational, be responsible, develop and, if necessary, change." To such imperatives and to the possibilities for authentic self-transcendence which a fidelity to these imperatives promise, the post-modern intellectual is irretrievably committed.[20]

The tools of authentic self-transcendence include the human sciences. Its aim is liberation of the subject for enlightened social change.[21]

To summarize, the theologian can affirm the ultimate significance of life in a world of distorted interpersonal relations because he or she accepts the contemporary model of self-transcendence as his or her own. Authentic existence is action according to imperatives (such as Lonergan's) which are consistent with this model. The actor's devotion to the secular morality of knowledge is expressed in his or her willingness to act on one such imperative—"be rational"—in the investigation of evidence in any domain (society, academy, or church). Conforming conduct to this morality is therefore itself an act of authentic existence, consistent with the contemporary model of self-transcendence.

Although the above does not pretend to give an account of all conditions for a unitary theological discourse, this much is certain: that were it not for the subject's fundamental self-understanding as a singular speaker possessing the power to transcend phenomenal descriptions of self and world, there could be no unitary discourse, only the several conversations of sociologically separable selves within their respective "publics."[22] At the same time, however, the contemporary subject recognizes him or herself as in some basic way the proper object of sociological analysis, consistent with the faith of secularity and its morality of knowledge. Where faith in self-

---

[20] *BRO*, 12. See Bernard Lonergan, *Method in Theology* (New York: Herder and Herder, 1972) 53–55, 101–5, 231–32; and idem, *Insight* (New York/San Francisco: Harper & Row, 1958) esp. 472–77 (law of limitation and transcendence), 627–33 (problem of liberation), and 634–41 (nature and source of transcendence).

[21] Tracy believes that both empirical and critical human sciences are valid authorities for theological reflection. The critical theories of psychoanalysis, ideology critique, and perhaps communicative competence (*AI*, 146–47, n. 80) must work together with "genuinely prophetic theological critiques" to offer "proposals and hypotheses" explaining the precise, if hidden, causes of a situation's "empirical base," as determined by empirical social science (*AI*, 77). See also *AI*, 69–79, 92–98; and *BRO*, 237–58, esp. 246–48.

[22] Tracy appeals to Kierkegaard's idea of "the single one" to describe the subject of theological discourse in its oneness and resistance to social-scientific reduction/dispersion:

> Theology has always been, as Kierkegaard observed, a question of "the single one" to the single one . . . at its best . . . existential thinking speaks indirectly to an ideal reader, a limit concept of the authentic reader. The concept of the "single one" is the ultimate yet not the penultimate ground for the complex reality of the contemporary self of the theologian. (*AI*, 4)

transcendence frees the subject from the potentially refractive analyses of the human sciences, the faith of secularity binds the contemporary religious speaker to the standards, methods, and conclusions of postmodern critique. The concept "authentic self-transcendence" is the interesting attempt to capture reflectively the dual orientation of the subject of contemporary theological discourse, by postulating the liberation of consciousness (self-transcendence), not *against* but only *by* adherence to secular norms of coherence, meaningfulness, and truth.

## Authenticity and the Modern Ethos

Tracy's "faith of secularity" bears certain resemblances to Foucault's "modern ethos." Both reject religious *tradita* and precritical philosophies as morally unacceptable authorities for contemporary living. Foucault would agree on the need for "purely secular standards for knowledge and action" as well as "the full affirmation of our lives in this world" (*BRO*, 8). Both Tracy and Foucault are advocating, as a premise for ethical conduct, the heroic renunciation of heteronomous authorities in all areas of life.

But while Foucault's modern ethos gives up traditional seriousness for irony, Tracy's secular faith approaches the manifest diversity of publics and discourses with renewed determination to identify their common ground in a transcendental figure. This figure is the "authentic self," whom we meet in this chapter in the role of "any intelligent, reasonable, responsible human being."[23] Under this description, Tracy's transcendental subject functions as the locus of intelligibility for competing discourses.

Not surprisingly, however, the authentic self is related to specific, empirical structures. Like an archaeologist, Tracy recognizes "the actual complexity of different selves related to distinct social locations and therefore to the distinct plausability structures present in each theologian" (*AI*, 5). We might expect Tracy to offer an archaeology of these plausability structures, showing how the regularities he detects within social, academic, and ecclesial discourse, which each theologian assumes in speaking and which set each "public" apart from the rest, are linked to historically specific systems of exclusion (producing true statements, excluding false; sorting rational speech from madness; allowing certain things to be spoken of, prohibiting others; *AK*, 219), to systems of discursive rarefaction (organizing possible speech acts according to disciplines; establishing the ideal object of disciplined "commentary," and the relation of relevant texts to their authors; *AK*, 220–24), and to systems of the rarefaction of speakers (stating who can and

---

[23] Tracy, "Defending the Public Character of Theology," 351.

cannot make a competent claim in any discourse; who can participate in the Western "fellowships of discourse": the highly "serious" formations of religion, medicine, law, politics, and natural science; showing how speakers are rarified by educational institutions and career "tracks"; cf. *AK*, 224–27).

Tracy's five axes for theological discourse, differentiated according to publics of society, academy, and church, go a ways toward recognizing that "one cannot speak of anything at any time" (*AK*, 44). These axes, or "rubrics," again are:

> (1) different primary reference groups; (2) distinct modes of arguments; (3) distinct emphases in ethical stance; (4) distinct self-understandings of the theologian's personal faith or beliefs; (5) distinct formulations of what counts as meaning and truth in theology. (*NI*, 24)

These distinctions point toward an archaeology of theological discourse by allowing us to place statements within some system of discursive rarefaction (all theological statements address a reference group; argue in a certain manner), a system of exclusion (religious knowledge based on intuition is immoral, because irrational; statements are distinguished according to criteria of meaning and truth), and a system of the rarefaction of speakers (Christians can speak qua believers some places and not others; nonbelievers aren't taken seriously everywhere).

Tracy's rubrics point toward an archaeology but are not one. The five axes cannot be subsumed by broader principles of differentiation (Foucault's three "systems") because they privilege the enunciation of serious statements. The rubrics are derived from examples of disciplined reflection, for the sake of guiding the theologian in producing coherent, meaningful, and true claims in any of three ideal discourse situations (society, academy, church). Since his intent is to make *serious* claims, the smallest unit with which Tracy is concerned is the *disciplined* statement. That is why Tracy begins with the sociology of knowledge, not the archaeology of statements. Had he begun without traditional seriousness (with the archaeologist's "studied casualness"), and looked at the production of statements in terms of the application of principles of exclusion, discursive rarity, and speaker rarity, it would have been possible to analyze theological discourse in a comparative way, showing how its dividing practices operate like those of other Western discourses (legal, medical, etc.) to establish what counts as a disciplined statement in the first place.

One could then begin by seeing how the principle of speaker rarefaction determines the public of the church, for example, not only as a place where Christians speak intelligibly, but as a site where the discourse of women is marginalized and the conversation of those not trained in a university is subordinated to the discourse of the educated. Adopting the principle of discourse rarefaction, the "ironic" theologian would start with the Bible as a text at the center of related commentaries (not, taking it with traditional seriousness, as the bearer of deep meanings), organized in disciplines, with distinct attitudes in each toward the significance of the authorial function, attitudes shared by nonbiblical discourses and nontheological disciplines. Finally, an archaeological point of departure would imply, via the principle of exclusion, that discourses peripheral to liberal theology would not be invalidated a priori because they were not well disciplined: certain mystic, fundamentalist, and liberationist theological discourses would be related to post-Enlightenment theological discourse as its exclusions. These same knowledges, "subjugated" to varying degrees in contemporary society, could also be compared, at the archaeological level, with statements occurring in nontheological discourse situations (cf. the order of statements in Latin American liberation theologies and Marxian economic statements).

The archaeology of theological discourse would cut across the "publics" of society, academy, and church (lines determined by the sociology of knowledge) comparing dividing practices and their systematic effects. Tracy's method, which takes the well-formed statements of each general domain (public) as the source of normative "rubrics" for fundamental, systematic, and practical theological discourse, cannot question the authority of the dividing practices operative in each domain for the construction of theological statements of equal seriousness. Revisionist theology is committed in principle to the conservation of whatever discursive practices are in effect in each of its three target audiences. It cannot criticize these practices because it never reaches the level of the formation of statements itself; the point where the principles of exclusion and rarity are initially applied, and where they link theological discourse with other discursive "fellowships."[24]

---

[24] When a group of statements is theologically justified on the basis of their sociological unity and a purported universal addressee, rather than analyzed first in terms of the statements' participation in specific dividing practices, protests arise:

> If systematic theology is primarily concerned with retrieving the tradition—not with subjecting it to the most trenchant criticism modern thought and experience can bring to it and then reconstructing it, perhaps fundamentally—the arrows directed by radical critics can all be safely contained and traditional piety largely reaffirmed. (Gordon D. Kaufman, "Conceptualizing Diversity Theologically," *JR* 62 [1982] 397)

Political theologian Matthew Lamb makes a similar point when he asks:

> To what extent are Tracy's distinctions unintentional ways of immunizing the disciplines of foundations and systematics against the claims of liberation and political theologies? (Matthew Lamb, *Solidarity with Victims* [New York: Crossroad, 1982] 81)

Even if a critical correlation of the subdisciplines can assign a theoretical complementarity to their publics and orientations, actual theological positions, Lamb points out, *within*

Tracy does not aspire to archaeology, however, because his anthropological postulate of the authentic self allows for the ideal unification of sociologically disparate statements. "Authentic self" and "genuinely public discourse" are mutually referring concepts that function in Tracy's statements to elide the relationship of conversation to real constraints. Even though Tracy presents theological discourse as specific to three broad domains (society, academy, church), it is only in order to transcend these separate regions by the "limit concept of the authentic reader" (*AI*, 4), and its corollary, the disclosive, transformative, and universally applicable discourse. Rather than "a historical investigation into the events that have made us to constitute and to recognize ourselves as subjects of what we are doing, thinking, saying" (*WIE*, 46), Tracy proposes a transcendental investigation of sociologically separate discursive formations. Instead of analyzing the practices of serious speakers genealogically, in terms of the formation of different "selves" by techniques operating within, for example, technoeconomic, religious, and human scientific discourses, Tracy posits, then analyzes, an authentic self as addressee of *any* "public" discourse, regardless of the power relations that enable it.

A pragmatic treatment of these important concepts is to be preferred: "authentic self" is a purely regulative idea which makes sense of my experiences of internal diversity by referring them to an individual which I call myself. "Genuinely public discourse," the self's corollary, tries to account for the fact that I can learn to give reasons for what I say (can learn to observe "criteria of adequacy" in making statements), and can sort true claims from false in several language games (can address "several internalized selves"). Had Tracy worked from some version of these simple definitions, his program would not have set itself implicitly against the historico-critical attitude of Foucault's modern ethos and its methods. As Foucault has argued, concepts like "self" and "discourse" can be genealogically and archaeologically specified, and still be useful and used ethically.

---

a subdiscipline may be riven with "alienations and distortions . . . running throughout the academic, ecclesial, and social publics" (ibid., 80).

Transforming these positions "calls for [seeing] dialectical differences rather than complementarity" (ibid., 81). Lamb doubts, however, that Tracy's fundamental theology is adequate to this task, since it relies on phenomenological and disclosive-hermeneutic methods that affirm, not challenge, apparent similarities in difference. Lamb argues that practical theology can be fundamental, too, and when armed with social theories in the tradition of the Frankfurt School, can keep the "arrows" of Kaufman's "radical critics" sharp for targets in all publics. Foucault, though subordinating critical-social theory to an historico-critical anlysis of its effects, likewise agrees that phenomenological and hermeneutic methods conserve epistemological figures rather than challenge their accepted unity (*OT*, 321–22, 325–26).

As it stands, the stage is set for an anthropological drama, in which the self's experiences of adversity, oppression, ecstasy and the sublime are all referred to a depth subjectivity, as its modifications. Neither the dividing practices of social, academic, and ecclesial discourse, nor the techniques of domination and the self, can be the objects of relevant criticism for thinking guided by the anthropologically serious faith of secularity, which takes as its twin points of departure the idea of the authentic self (as specified by appropriately disciplined reflection) and the idea of the genuinely public discourse (as determined by the canons of serious speech acts in each public). How this discourse works to "liberate" the Modern soul from its "profound subjection" (*DP*, 30) is the concern of my next chapter.

# 5

# Revisionist Fundamental Theology and Philosophical Anthropology

Tracy locates most contemporary theological reflection within the last of five models for theology which have been influential in the previous two centuries (*BRO*, 22–42). Each model he describes "discloses" how theologians operating within that model see themselves (the model's "self-referent") and the task before them (its "object-referent"). The order of presentation corresponds roughly to the chronology of the models' respective theologies' appearances in the church and/or academy: orthodox, liberal, neoorthodox, radical, and revisionist.

## Five Models for Theology

For the orthodox theologian, the claims of secular authorities (critical historians and scientists) and non-Christian religions have no inner theological relevance. The self-referent is a believer in a particular community of faith. The object of reflection is the believer's creed and related textual matter of the tradition, which the theologian elucidates in systematic fashion. Tracy cites the reasoning of Roman Catholic theologians at Vatican I as an instance of the wholly "in-house" work that characterizes orthodox thinking.

Liberal theology begins with devotion to both the values of modernity and the claims and values of the Christian tradition. Under this model, which Tracy associates preeminently with Schleiermacher and the Catholic Modernists, the self-conception of the theologian reflects the values of "free and open inquiry, autonomous judgment, critical investigation of all claims to scientific, historical, and religious truth'' (*BRO*, 26). The object of theologizing is the reform of one's church or religious tradition, in accordance with the modern morality of historical and scientific knowledge.

Neoorthodoxy breaks sharply with the liberals' subordination of theological truths to the principles of historical and scientific inquiry (such as Troeltsch's three principles) while nevertheless continuing the criticism of society and religion which distinguishes the liberal tradition. Like the critiques of culture and mind performed by Marx, Nietzsche, and Freud, neoorthodox theologies take aim at the liberals' faith in human nature, their confidence in the inevitability of progress in society and its institutions, including religious ones, and the largely exemplary function in liberal theologies assigned to the historical Jesus.

The principles of neoorthodox criticism, however, are suprarational: the aseity and sovereignty of the biblical God of Jesus Christ, and its corresponding term, the poverty and incompleteness of the human condition, are taken from religious tradition and its picture of the cosmos. The self-referent of the neoorthodox theologian is a human being of authentic Christian faith, who believes ''that justification comes only from grace through faith in God's manifestation of self in the event of Jesus Christ'' (*BRO*, 28). The object of theological thought is reflection on this transcendent God of Christ.[1]

The fourth model described by Tracy is the radical model, with which the Death of God theologians (Altizer, Hamilton, van Buren, et al.) are most often associated. Radical theologians begin with a commitment to the value of critical thinking but reject the God of the neoorthodox as a critical principle. With the ''masters of suspicion'' of postclassical liberalism, radicals reject the existence of God as a conception of the alienated mind. As their object-referent they take, instead of God, Jesus as a ''paradigmatic figure of a life lived for others'' or as ''the decisive incarnational manifestation of a liberated humanity'' (*BRO*, 31).

Tracy's description of the radical model supports my contention that contemporary theology has moved away from purely criteriological debates to question fundamentally the reality of the referents of its own discourse. The strength of the radical model, according to Tracy, is that it raises this question, the question of the reality of God, as one ''which any thinking human

---

[1] Prominent neoorthodox theologians for Tracy include Barth, Brunner, Bultmann, Tillich, and Reinhold and H. Richard Niebuhr. Karl Rahner is also named, as are certain of the ''eschatological'' theologians, Moltmann, Braaten, Gutierrez, and Alves (*BRO*, 27, 30), and, in a later analysis, theologians of liberation including Soelle, Metz, Schaull, and Segundo (*BRO*, 242–46). As Matthew Lamb (*Solidarity with Victims*, 112, n. 7) notes, Tracy amended his classification of eschatological and liberation theologians in *AI*, to recognize their rejection of neoorthodoxy's appeal to supernatural paradox. Tracy now terms them ''theologies of praxis'' operating within a ''transformational model of truth'' (*AI*, 71; see also 69–82, 390–98).

being" must now address, if he or she is to remain both "authentically" Christian and secular (*BRO*, 32; see also 147). Its weakness lies in its own answer to the same question. For, as Tracy asks, "Can one really continue the enterprise of Christian theology if there is no meaningful way to affirm the reality of God" (*BRO*, 32).

Revisionist theologians answer no: a doctrine of God must be the logical centerpiece of any future theological program. Indeed, thanks to the radicals of the 1960s, Tracy states, we are now able to see clearly that "the central cognitive claim of Christianity" is "its understanding of God" (*BRO*, 147). To establish this doctrine, the revisionist theologian draws upon the symbolic and textual resources of the Christian tradition. At the same time, she or he "is committed to continuing the critical task of the classical liberals and modernists in a genuinely postliberal situation" (*BRO*, 32). This means that the revisionist must "try to rectify earlier theological limitations" by adopting the results of "historical, philosophical, and social scientific research" (ibid.), thus pursuing "a radical continuation of critical theory, symbolic reinterpretation, and responsible social and personal *praxis*" (*BRO*, 33).

The revisionist model has been operative historically in the work of certain process theologians, Tracy believes, and others, viz., Baum, Dewart, Gilkey, Harvey, and Novak. Tracy also includes Gordon Kaufman among those practicing revisionist theology (*BRO*, 32 and 41, n. 64).

These thinkers share a self-reference to "a subject committed at once to a contemporary revisionist notion of the beliefs, values, and faith of an authentic secularity and to a revisionist understanding of the beliefs, values, and faith of an authentic Christianity" (*BRO*, 33). The task of theology for those so committed is twofold.

On the one hand, revisionist theology systematically elucidates the "meanings present in common human experience and the meanings present in the Christian tradition" through "philosophical reflection" (*BRO*, 34). Yet because these meanings are not self-evident, the object of revisionist theology can be stated in more dialectical, indeed, therapeutic terms:

> In short, the revisionist theologian is committed to what seems clearly to be the central task of contemporary theology: the dramatic confrontation, the mutual illuminations and corrections, and possible basic reconciliations between principal values, cognitive claims, and existential faiths of both a reinterpreted postmodern consciousness and a reinterpreted Christianity. (*BRO*, 32)

The aim of revisionist theology, then, is nothing less than the integration of contemporary secular and Christian claims, values, and faiths, when each of these are "authentically" understood and "critically correlated." Fundamental revisionist theology, as Tracy conceives of it, is "philosophical reflection upon the meanings present in common human experience and language, and upon the meanings present in the Christian fact'' (*BRO*, 43).

# Analysis of the Source
# "Common Human Experience and Language"

*Fundamental Theology as Philosophical Reflection*

The modern view of fundamental theology, upon which Tracy builds, was first framed by Schleiermacher:

> The part of Christian theology we call philosophical theology utilizes the framework developed in philosophy of religion, in order to present (a) that perspective on the essence of Christianity whereby it can be recognized as a distinct mode of faith, and at the same time (b) the form which Christian community takes, and (c) the manner in which each of these factors is further subdivided and differentiated. Everything that belongs to these three tasks, taken together, forms the work of philosophical theology.[2]

Although it is not possible here to rehearse the modern history of fundamental theology, it is worth noting that Schleiermacher's description of the subdiscipline sets out the terms of the problematic adopted by succeeding theologians in the liberal tradition.[3] Steering a course between a largely discredited "natural" or "rational" theology and the potential fideism of orthodox and neoorthodox Protestantism, modern fundamental theologians have attempted to locate Christian beliefs within a genus of describable religious attitudes, forms, and responses (through the comparative study of religion and philosophy of religion) while arguing for the uniqueness or "absoluteness" (Troeltsch) of traditional Christian claims.

Even when, as in the present, the apologetic task of fundamental theology has assumed the more moderate aim of establishing the nonexclusive validity of Christian beliefs, the exact relationship between what Tillich calls "the 'borrowed' philosophical truth" which theology takes from philosophy of culture, and "theological truth" per se, has not been clearly and unequivo-

---

[2] Friedrich Schleiermacher, *Brief Outline on the Study of Theology* (Atlanta: John Knox, 1966) 25.

[3] On the relationship between premodern natural theology and contemporary philosophical theology as practiced from an existentialist perspective, see John Macquarrie, *Principles of Christian Theology* (2d ed.; New York: Scribner's Sons, 1977) 43–58.

cally agreed upon.[4] Indeed, it is the task of Tracy's fundamental theology to establish just this relationship by a method of correlation, building upon (and, he hopes, improving upon) the earlier work of Tillich.

The modern heritage of Tracy's reflections is evident in his description of the characteristic features of fundamental, as distinct from systematic and practical theology. Fundamental theologies are primarily related to the public of the academy; their arguments are public discourse in "the most usual meaning" of that phrase, that is, "available to all persons *in principle*"; such discourse is conducted from "the ethical stance of honest critical inquiry"; the speakers of the discourse are usually Christian believers, but must "abstract themselves from all religious 'faith commitments' " in the interest of genuinely public conversation; and, finally, fundamental theologies attempt to show the adequacy or the inadequacy of the truth-claims of some given religious tradition "to some articulated paradigm of what constitutes 'objective argumentation' in some acknowledged discipline" (*NI*, 24–25). This discipline is normally philosophy (though he claims it could be "the philosophical dimension of one of the social sciences"), hence the frequent identification of "philosophical" with "fundamental" theology (*NI*, 26).

The thoroughly modern orientation of Tracy's fundamental theology, expressed in the above analysis, is reflected in his choice of methods and sources for the subdiscipline. The first source investigated by fundamental theology is "common human experience and language."

## Semantic Autonomy of the Authentic Self

Tracy's justification of this source brings us immediately into dialogue with this anthropology. He distinguishes, first, between "experience" as a subject's encounter with an object, and "experience" as a subject's encounter with itself. The former notion is a proper description of our mundane sensory contacts with reality, as well as our reports of our own subjective states (feelings, moods, attitudes, etc.) The subject's experience, in the first instance, is strictly and simply experience of the objects in the "phenomenal world" (to employ Kant's understanding of the phrase), the things of "outer" and "inner" sense.[5]

Second, however, Tracy claims for the subject an "experience of the self-as-self" (*BRO*, 65). He also calls this "the self's nonsensuous experience of self" and the self's experience of "an authentic self" (*BRO*, 66). The idea of the "authentic self," analyzed in Chapter IV as the corollary of

---

[4] Paul Tillich, *Systematic Theology* (3 vols.; Chicago: University of Chicago Press, 1951–63) 1. 30.

[5] See Kant, *Critique*, B 67–71.

"genuine public discourse," returns now to assist the revisionist fundamental theologian.

In his oddly brief exposition of this important concept (*BRO*, 64 – 66), Tracy states that the authentic self exists in a relation with reality which is both preconscious and immediate (*BRO*, 66). On the face of it, this assertion is highly problematic to those like Gordon Kaufman, who argue from Kantian epistemological premises that experience cannot be prelinguistic, but must always be experience of something distinct from the subject (*RKF*, 48 – 52, 59 – 63). The idea that experience is separable from reflection and communication (language), and can serve as a valid source for theology, that is, that it has some content apart from language, has been consistently and systematically rejected by Kaufman as incoherent (*ETM*, 4 – 8).

Understanding how the authentic self is related to language is made more difficult by Tracy's vague and inconsistent description of that to which the self is preconsciously and immediately related. Close inspection of Tracy's position shows that he believes the self is related in some sense to a larger context of concerns, a "lived world" (*BRO*, 66). Yet in other accounts, the self is in tune with some essential aspect of its own being, which links it generically with other selves. The "experience of the self-as-a-self" is here taken to be the self's depth encounter with its own humanity.

When Tracy specifies the authentic self in terms of its life-world, he emulates Heidegger's analysis of the human in Division I of *Being and Time*.[6] Here, "authentic" means "phenomenal": the authentic self is the self which "shows itself in itself" as Being in a world of ordered relations (relations with tools, objects, the "they," other selves) for which it has "care." It is the task of phenomenology to make this everyday order explicit, by allowing the authentic self to manifest itself, in its manifold ways of appearing.

Here, the "immediate experience of the self" can be understood as simply the subject's unreflective involvement with entities and people. It does not imply that this engagement proceeds outside language. [7]

---

[6] *BT*, 49 – 63, 67 – 273. George Steiner (*Martin Heidegger* [New York: Viking, 1978] 90) calls Division I "an ontological approach to social theory"; but Hubert Dreyfus ("Beyond Hermeneutics: Interpretation in Late Heidegger and Recent Foucault," in Gary Shapiro and Alan Sica, eds., *Hermeneutics: Questions and Prospects* [Amherst: University of Massachusetts Press, 1984] 66 – 83) argues that for Heidegger, the practices observed by Division I's hermeneutic phenomenology "are simply skills picked up by imitation," not the effects of deep structure.

[7] Though in *Being and Time* he claims discourse as "a primordial *existentiale* of disclosedness" of "Being-in-the-world," one "constitutive for Dasein's existence," early Heidegger subordinated language to being (*BT*, 204; see also 56 – 57, 203 – 10). See also the brief history of Heidegger's reflections on language in Paul Ricoeur, "The Task of Hermeneutics," in Michael Murray, ed., *Heidegger and Modern Philosophy* (New Haven/London: Yale University Press, 1978) 151 – 56, esp. 154 – 55.

If we use Heidegger's analysis of "Being-in-the-world" (Division I) as an interpretive tool for understanding only Tracy's descriptions of the authentic self in terms of its "lived world," we can almost rescue Tracy from Kaufman's objections. The following statement then takes on a more commonsense tone:

> When we state that an appeal to experience is meaningful, we often mean no more and no less than the fact that the appeal "resonates" to our own immediate experience as a self. We also ordinarily attempt to understand, judge, and evaluate that immediacy by such modes of critical mediation as cultural and historical analysis, human scientific analysis, philosophical and theological analysis. In the broadest sense of the term "phenomenological," all these modes of reflective analysis are phenomenological analyses insofar as they mediate the meaning of my experience as a self-in-a-world. (*BRO*, 66)

The above says nothing about the absence of language from experience. It only claims that specialized human sciences can provide lenses for ("mediate") the task of interpreting the meaning of any particular experience. But he goes on to say:

> More exactly, such analyses mediate the immediacy of our lived experience through some particular image, symbol, metaphor, myth, or concept. Throughout, we shall employ the word "meaningful" to refer to that intrinsic relationship between a mediating symbol, image, metaphor, myth, or concept and the immediate lived experience of the self. (Ibid.)

Here it is not the human sciences that mediate our understanding of our experiences, it is the linguistic elements themselves ("symbol, image, metaphor, myth, or concept") of any discourse which "mediate" the self's "immediate lived experience" and the self's understanding of that experience. Experience thus precedes two languages: everyday language, and the specialized discourses of the sciences. It is important to see that Tracy's anthropology does not consistently describe "Being-in-the-world," that is, Heidegger's Dasein (Division I). The authentic self is not, finally, coextensive with its symbolic world: it is beneath it (and, as we shall see, beyond it as well).

It is little wonder that when we turn to consider the second of Tracy's two notions of the authentic self, "experience of the self-as-self," as exponent of humanity, we see that the authentic self is intrinsically remote from its own acts of self-reflection: "Most of us would agree that this experience of the

self as a self is more difficult to attend to than the reports of our five senses"
(*BRO*, 65).[8] He continues:

> Yet, somehow that experience—technically, our "nonsensuous experi-
> ence of the self"—is both prior to our interpretation of our sense-know-
> ledge and more important as source for the more fundamental questions of
> the meaning of our human experience as human selves. (Ibid.)

The authentic self is not only the silent substratum of discourse, a formal
principle of unity joining subject and predicate (as a subject), or implicit in
an address by other speakers, including the human sciences (as an object).
The real self is in constant, "nonsensuous," communication with the inauthentic, phenomenal self. The nature of the communication brings the fact of
the authentic self into the discourses of metaphysics and theology, since the
self inquires into the meaning of its existence, its ultimate end, its orgin and
limits: "Lurking beneath the surface of our everyday lives, exploding into
explicitness in the limit situations inevitable in any life, are questions which
logically must be and historically are called religious questions" (*AI*, 4).

Attending to the "lurking" questions of the authentic self is no longer the
proper business of religious professionals alone: "Most of us would also
agree that this experience of the self-as-a-self demands the most sophisticated
reflective analyses available" (*BRO*, 65). To get at the elusive deep meanings and structures of our immediate experience, we rely on the

> powers of intelligent and critical introspection. . . . When wise we may
> also turn to such trustworthy modes of mediation as friends, or psychol-
> oanalysts, artists, trusted cultural analysts, finely attuned historians,
> social and natural scientists, philosophers and theologians. (*BRO*, 66)

To these authorities the recalcitrant self reveals its secrets; in return, the
"trustworthy modes of mediation" allow the subject to participate in rituals

---

[8] It is remarkable that Tracy views the problem simply as one of paying attention to an
elusive experience, given the powerful and far-reaching objection of Kant to *any* experience of
the self in se: "Consciousness is, indeed, that which alone makes all representations to be
thoughts, and in it, therefore, as the transcendental subject, all our perceptions must be found; but
beyond this logical meaning of the 'I,' we have no knowledge of the subject in itself, which as
substratum underlies this 'I,' as it does all thoughts" (Kant, *Critique*, A 350). Tracy's "authentic self" amounts to an end run around Kant's deconstruction of rational psychology. His
phenomenology of the experiences of this self presupposes that the "I" is available for our
description; it is based, Kant would say, on a "subreption of the hypostatised consciousness"
(ibid., A 402). A good contemporary reconstruction of Kant's position on the unity of experiences and the experience of unity is P. F. Strawson, *The Bounds of Sense* (London: Methuen,
1966) esp. 162–74.

of power (discourse situations) which culminate in the production of true statements about the authentic self.

In summary, the concept of "common human experience" proposed by Tracy as one of two sources for fundamental theology includes the idea of an authentic self related both immediately to itself (sometimes identified with its "lived world") and mediately to its own inauthentic, "everyday" persona. More than a formal principle of the unity of discourse, the authentic self lies beneath words (its own and others) "questioning," as it were, the fact and meaning of its existence. The inarticulate longing of the self for insight into its foundations is brought to language by authoritative disciplines like fundamental theology. Guided by the secular morality of knowledge, however, the foundations described by these disciplines cannot lie outside the human (as they were for orthodoxy and neoorthodoxy), but must be laid bare within the very nature of the authentic self.

## Phenomenology and the Critique of Deep Meaning

Accordingly, Tracy urges the fundamental theologian to adopt a version of the phenomenological method in attempting "to explicate how and why the existential meanings proper to Christian self-understanding are present in common human experience" (*BRO*, 47). The phrase "existential meanings" refers to intrinsic significations of the authentic self, to essential meanings not determined in the play of words in discourse and related social practices, but given in a prelinguistic orientation of the self toward its own nature.[9] The revisionist theologian uses phenomenology to show that any hidden meaning of Christian self-understanding is a meaning shared by everyone, insofar as everyone is also an authentic self.

Yet the more successful phenomenology is in bringing to light the deep meaning of the authentic self's experience—the more the immediate experience of the "self-as-a-self" is brought to language and consciousness—the more problematic does the adequacy of the phenomenological method become. Once the self-evident meaning of an experience is no longer regarded as its true meaning, but rather a symptom or sign of a deeper, more

---

[9] In the everyday world of the self, its meaning is determined in the conventions of the several communities of interpretation in which it lives. Its significance is a function of many discourse situations. Existential phenomenology of the kind advocated by Tracy claims to uncover meanings of the self which are not only prelinguistic (which the existential discourses "bring to language") but foundational for the everyday life of the self. The foundations, in Heidegger's terminology, are the *existentialia* (existentials) associated with "Being-in-the-world." Their realization in the everyday world of the self constitutes *Dasein*'s "existentiell" self-understanding (*BT*, 33, 70–71). The objects of discursively formed self-understanding (human events, artifacts, the constructs of the human sciences) are Foucault's "positivities."

profound meaning, *any* meaning which becomes available to reflection (that is, becomes a phenomenon) cannot safely be trusted to be the final meaning of the experience. At this point, the philosopher-fundamental theologian may conclude that human being is interpretation "all the way down" (Dreyfus) and give up the search for foundations altogether as Heidegger, Wittgenstein, Gadamer, and Foucault eventually did. Or, one may give up only the idea that the authentic self can ever become transparent to phenomenology, that the foundations can be coextensive with their positive appearances, and that therefore a critique is needed to ground our experiences of authenticity. In this case, one may, as Tracy claims to do, construct an explicitly transcendental theory which has as its goal the articulation of the conditions of the possibility for the appearance of the authentic self's deep meaning. Thus, the final significance of an experience is the meaning attributed to it by the transcendental theory. Since the deep meaning is understood to be a universal character of particular everyday experiences, the transcendental analytic can claim to account for the ultimate significance of everyone's experience, not just the experience of the reflecting philosopher/theologian.

One should note, moreover, that Tracy's transcendental moment, as the occasion of theological discourse, seeks to be an ultimate account of the *deepest* meaning of any experience, relativizing the everyday meaning assigned by the reflecting subject to its objective, discrete experiences, and the "serious" meanings determined by the human sciences. Nevertheless, Tracy admits that the results of transcendental reflection are always open to revision, and are in this sense "problematic." Tracy follows the lead of the existentialists in "radicalizing" Kant's critique of reason:

> The task [of postcritical philosophy] can be executed only when the Kantian exclusive attention to the centrality of "understanding" or "reason" is replaced [by] an insistence upon the centrality and comprehensiveness of the originating lived "experience" itself over its clear, distinct—and derivative—expressions in human "understanding." (*BRO*, 68)

The shift from Kant's anthropology of transcendental consciousness to Heidegger's *Existenz* means for Tracy that the structures of existence (the existentials) cannot be as neatly delimited as the structures of mind (the categories), since existence is capable of "revealing" multiple dimensions of experience, dimensions other than that of subject-object, which are as varied in form as human nature will allow. (Indeed, as we shall see, Tracy's concept of the authentic self allows him to project a "religious dimension," in which existence reveals itself in a very peculiar way, and which serves as the raison d'être of all revisionist theology.)

Phenomenology, then, is inadequate alone because it can never grasp the foundations of the authentic self, only the deep, "existential" meaning of its positivities. Transcendental reflection accounts for this meaning, but suffers an essential incompleteness: the authentic self is always potentially more than an inventory of its foundations by any given theologian.[10]

Nevertheless, philosophical-theological reflection must attempt to provide the final meaning of any experience: its judgments seek not only to be valid (coherent and meaningful) but true (adequate to the experience), and "true" not only to a single theologian, but to any reasonable, responsible human being. Tracy makes clear his belief that the fundamental theologian is committed to the joint methodology of phenomenology and transcendental critique:

> Unless one is content with phenomenological investigation alone, he is led by the logic of inquiry itself to ask the question of the basic ground or presuppositions of every and all phenomena or any and all phenomenological reflection. In that sense, both philosophical "moments" (the phenomenological and the transcendental) are two intrinsically linked moments in a single methodological task for any philosopher who wishes to determine the basic and grounding presuppositions of any given phenomenon. (Ibid.)

The foregoing has attempted to elucidate the anthropological assumptions underlying the first source of fundamental theology for Tracy, "common human experience and language," and the twofold method of investigation appropriate to this source: phenomenology and transcendental critique. These assumptions are carried over into his discussion of "the Christian fact."

## Analysis of the Source "The Christian Fact"

*Semantic Autonomy of the Text*

Tracy designates the texts of the Christian tradition as the second source of revisionist fundamental theology because "it seems obvious that any enterprise called Christian theology will attempt to show the appropriateness of its

---

[10] The basic indeterminacy of the foundations of the authentic self—a consequence of the historicization of the subject—allows Tracy to postulate a dimension of experience Kaufman does not. I am arguing that it is consistent with the model of the authentic self (developed by the existentialists and adopted by Tracy) to permit multiple dimensions of experience claiming distinct foundations, so long as every meaningful experience is accounted for in a coherent way, i.e., in a manner respecting the rules of coherence for statements about experience in that dimension.

chosen categories to the meanings of the major expressions and texts of the Christian tradition'' (*BRO*, 43). What is "obvious" to Tracy is (1) that contemporary Christian theology must *show* not *presume* that its discourse is adequate to the meanings of Christian classics, and (2) that the Christian classics are deserving of this attention. The former assumption reflects the revisionist theologian's loyalty to the secular morality of knowledge, the second his or her devotion to the Christian tradition. One content of this tradition is the belief that the Christian anthropology, correctly understood, pertains to all people. Thus, Tracy states, the logic of Christian beliefs and the logic of contemporary, secular inquiry both lead to universalistic claims:

> This commitment to determine methods and criteria which can show the adequacy of Christian self-understanding for all human experiences is a task demanded by the very logic of the Christian affirmations; more precisely, by the Christian claim to provide the authentic way to understand our common human existence. (*BRO*, 44)

Tracy holds that the authentic self is the proper addressee of the Christian scriptures. He is assisted in doing so by the concept "distanciation" developed in the work of Paul Ricoeur, and the idea of a sense-referent relation between the text and reality.[11] First, Ricoeur's theory allows Tracy to claim that the writing of a text fixes its meaning in such a way that the text takes on a life of its own, independent from the significance it had for its original author and addressees. He states:

> What we write is the meaning, the *noema* of our speech events, not the event itself. Once I write, it is my text alone which bears the meaning, not my intention in writing it, not my original audience's reaction to it. (*BRO*, 75)

At this point the meaning of the text (as opposed to its "meaningfulness": potential for disclosing the reader's lived experience) is the same as its "sense," or specifiable structure: "The sense or the meaning of the text is

---

[11] Ricoeur (*Interpretation Theory* [Fort Worth: Texas Christian University Press, 1976] 30) places his work between two fallacies which he calls the "intentional fallacy" and the "fallacy of the text as an authorless entity." The first understands the meaning of the text to be its meaning for its original audience or author; a romanticist hermeneutic follows. The second treats the text like a natural object, ignoring that it was a discourse by someone to someone else, about something. The concept of "distanciation" admits the semantic autonomy of the text, against the claims of the intentional fallacy. Yet it also allows the ideal sense of the text to open up a world "in front of" the text, to which the meaning refers. The text makes a claim on reality a natural object (or the text's ideal meaning alone) cannot. See also ibid., 1–44, esp. 12–22; and idem, *Essays on Biblical Interpretation* (Philadelphia: Fortress, 1980) 15–17, 67–70, 72.

the ideal object which is intended. As ideal, this meaning is purely immanent. The words do not refer to an extralinguistic reality but rather to other words."[12] Determining the meaning of a text is the task of history and the human sciences involved in the study of language ("nonpsychological methods;" *BRO*, 76). The reconstruction of the text—an obligation for the interpreter since Schleiermacher's distinction of the "grammatical" from the "psychological" moment—follows a strict order for Tracy, "the historical method, semantics, [and] literary-critical methods" (*BRO*, 51).

A certain symmetry between the investigation of the text and the phenomenology of common human experience and language here begins to appear.[13] The task of textual reconstruction is to constitute an object for reflection, in a way similar to the preparatory role the human sciences play in clarifying the proper starting point for phenomenological reflection. For the fundamental theologian, the human sciences act as a kind of "divining rod," indicating the presence of "deep meaning." For example, in the next chapter we shall see that the work of psychologists including Abraham Maslow focuses the attention of the fundamental theologian on the particular phenomenon of "peak experiences" (*BRO*, 105–6), beneath which the theologian as existential phenomenologist uncovers the deep meaning of " 'being-in-love-without-qualification' familiar to the authentically religious person" (*BRO*, 106).

Though the history of psychology contains a tradition in support of theological interpretation of its findings (the Jungian), more often the human sciences have understood things to be the other way around: *they* are the depth phenomenologists, whose critical theories of the authentic self (or society) comprehend the discourse of *theology*. For Tracy, however, the human sciences perform a preparatory task which is no less valuable because incomplete: the bringing to language of the penultimate meaning of common human experiences. Revisionist theology works with, not against, the human sciences because they share the same object of investigation: the authentic self. That is why Tracy can claim that fundamental theology and the human sciences are generically phenomenological in method, while upholding the right of theology to have the final say in any anthropology. The model of the dialogue employed below obscures this final right:

---

[12] *BRO*, 76. Ricoeur states: "Without such a conception of meaning, of its objectivity, and even its ideality, no textual criticism is possible . . . the semantic moment, the moment of objective meaning, must precede the existential moment, the moment of personal decision" (*Essays on Biblical Interpretation*, 68).

[13] The analogy between self/text and existential hermeneutics/textual hermeneutics has been developed explicitly by Paul Ricoeur in his essay, "The Model of the Text: Meaningful Action Considered as a Text," in Rabnow and Sullivan, *Interpretive Social Science*, 73–101.

> Only a phenomenology in continued conversation with those of the
> human sciences which investigate the religious dimension in human
> existence, and in conversation with other philosophical methods can
> really hope to succeed.[14]

Returning to the preparatory task performed by history and the sciences of
language, we see that they, too, are inadequate understandings of their object.
Reconstructing a text and establishing its ideal meaning is analogous to the
psychological reconstruction of an experience and seeing in it a generic
significance.[15] Both set up the surface of language as a potential object of
("genuine," "authentic") excavation of the self's/text's foundations: by
existential phenomenology (the self's) and textual hermeneutics (the text's).
With Foucault, we may refer to these complete discursive preparations as
"positivities."[16]

## Hermeneutics and the Critique of Deep Meaning

The idea that the text has foundations which can be distinguished from its
positivities is implicit in Tracy's distinction of the text's meaningfulness
from its meaning, and the assignment of methods from the human sciences to
establish the latter, while reserving "the explicitly hermeneutical" method

---

[14] *BRO*, 48. Tracy admits the authority to interpret "lived experience" only to those who
adhere to his notion of the authentic self, excluding those intellectual trains of the Modern West
(and certain of the East) which do not share his anthropological presuppositions: the
"trustworthy modes of mediation" of the authentic self's experience do not include "the reports
of our five senses" or "controlled experiments," but rather, "that community of interpretation
where the value of the self as a self is reverenced and where modes of raising that experience to
conscious awareness are developed" (*BRO*, 66).

[15] The analogy is not limited to psychology, of course. The reconstruction of a scuffle on a
loading dock can bear the meaning, for a Marxist theorist, of an instance of the class struggle.
Because Tracy's theology is committed to discerning dimensions of experiences, not intruding
theological answers into existential questions, it starts with the understanding of the experience
proffered by secular social science (or similar authorities), and then begins the task of
phenomenological or hermeneutic excavation (cf. Tracy's criticism of Tillich's method, whose
existentialist anthropology he otherwise adopts, *BRO*, 45–46, 57–58, nn. 12–15). Thus class
struggles can be "limit situations."

[16] As noted above, the human sciences do not ordinarily see themselves as providers of grist
for the theological mill. Foucault's analysis shows that they consider themselves to be reconciling foundations and positivities, getting at the nature of "man" (*OT*, 344–48), not making
preparatory analyses for theology. In considering the relationship between existential
phenomenology and these disciplines, one does well to remember that phenomenology arose on
the Continent as philosophy's self-defense to the claims of the newly prestigious human sciences.
Cf. Edmund Husserl, *Husserl: Shorter Works* (Notre Dame: University of Notre Dame Press;
Sussex: Harvester, 1981) 166–97. Tracy's phenomenology of existence continues that defense
on behalf of fundamental theology.

for bringing to light the text's deep meaning, that is, the significance of the text for the authentic self. In Tracy's hermeneutics, the authentic self tries to grasp its foundations once and for all by using the text as a window, through which it perceives itself in a different world, an authentic world, in which foundations and positivities are finally reconciled. Even after the human sciences have done their work, he states:

> Still the meaning of major import *to the theologian* remains a concern that can be formulated by a question like the following: what is the mode-of-being-in-the-world *referred to* by the text? That question is not really answered until an explicitly hermeneutic enterprise is advanced. On this understanding, hermeneutics is the discipline capable of explicating *the referent* as distinct from either the sense of the text or the historical reconstruction of the text. (*BRO*, 51–52)

In the case of literary classics, the text refers to permanent possibilities for authentic human life. The disclosure of these prospects to the reader, as Ricoeur has emphasized, calls for existential decision on the question, "Do I recognize my authentic self in the world this text is presenting or do I not?" which, when "answered" in the affirmative results in the reader's experience of deep meaning.

A meaningful encounter with a sensible text, however, is not enough to guarantee that the reader's experience has anything to do with reality. As I argued above, the more successful phenomenology is in bringing to light deep meaning, the more problematic does the adequacy of the phenomenological (here hermeneutic) method become, for the reason that appearances are inherently symbolic of something more profound about the self, and so cannot be safely trusted to be the last, "true" meaning of any experience. Tracy states: "The further question of the truth-status of the referent explicated by hermeneutics remains" (*BRO*, 52). How can one be sure that the foundations one thinks one apprehends phenomenologically, are really the fundaments of the authentic self?

The transcendental mode of analysis, which Tracy previously described in reference to phenomenology's essential incompleteness, is again introduced as the means by which the truth of a meaningful interpretation of classic texts may be ascertained. That is, the truth of claims about the meanings present in common human experience and language, and in Christian texts, is to be decided by an explicitly theoretical construct—a metaphysics—accounting for the conditions of the possibility of the self's deep meanings. When achieved, the self will be complete: it will understand the final meaning (the truth) of its most meaningful experiences—it will grasp in a fully cognitive way the foundations of its positivities—and it will do so only on the basis of the testimony of the experiences themselves, not by reference to "tradition" or some other heteronomous authority. In short, transcendental critique of the deep meanings supplied by phenomenology and hermeneutics completes the liberation of the subject's consciousness and its entry into authentic self-knowledge.

## Critical Correlation of Sources

As a Christian fundamental theology, however, the transcendental analysis must mediate the results of the investigations of both sources. It must show (1) that the revised understanding of common human experience and language is not only adequate to that experience and language, but adequate to the revisionist interpretation of Christian texts, and (2) that the revised interpretation of scripture is appropriate not only to the Christian classics, but to common human experience and language as well (*BRO*, 79–81). The "critical correlation" of the meanings of both sources must be effected for any transcendental system to claim that its constructs are true.

Note that Tracy attempts to improve on Tillich's method of correlation by requiring that the secular morality of knowledge be followed in the preparation of the meaning of each source; in each source, existential questions are raised and addressed according to fully public methods (phenomenology and hermeneutics). Thus, what is correlated is not a "question" from common human experience and language, and an "answer" from scripture, but two *answered questions*, each acceptable in principle to any reasonable, responsible, intelligent inquirer (i.e., to any authentic self).

What, then, is gained by correlation? We recall that Tracy claimed from the start of his fundamental reflections that the faith of secularity, "our fundamental faith in the ultimate worthwhileness of our present action," is brought to language by "the central beliefs" of Christian faith:

> The Christian theologian holds that a proper understanding of the explicitly Christian faith can render intellectually coherent and symbolically powerful that common secular faith which we share. (*BRO*, 9)

In principle, a revisionist metaphysics accounting for the meaning of common human experience and language, *and* the meaning of the Christian classics, could be constructed without the vocabulary ("the central beliefs") of Christianity. Tracy's revisionist theologian is not obligated to show that only a proper understanding of Christian doctrines can give meaning and meaningfulness to the faith of secularity (make it "intellectually coherent" and "symbolically powerful") but merely that a proper understanding of these doctrines, one which is adequate and appropriate to its sources, can succeed in bringing secular faith to full cognitive awareness.

Because the Christian fact has been "preprocessed" by the interpretive methods appropriate to the second source, rendered intelligible in terms of the anthropology of the authentic self, the propositions of faith can be treated entirely as symbols of deep meaning by the theological metaphysician. They may therefore be kept, discarded, or changed as the revisionist theologian endeavors to construct a system which is adequate to experience, that is, "true." A cognitive claim is true, Tracy states,

> when transcendental or metaphysical analysis shows its "adequacy to experience" by explicating how a particular concept (e.g., time, space, self, God) functions as a fundamental "belief" or "condition of possibility" of all our experiences. (*BRO*, 71)

Returning to our previous question, "What, then, is gained by correlation?" we may answer—much and little. "Little" is gained in the way of insight into the self's foundations which could not in principle be provided by some other, non-Christian discourse. Yet "much" is gained because without some discourse the truth of the meaning of the authentic self's experience of its foundations would remain unknown to it; moreover, without a Christian conceptual framework, the theologian's loyalty to the religious tradition would be betrayed.

## Discursive Formation of Authentic Self-Knowledge

The culmination of theological revision in a transcendental portrait marks the end of a long journey of self-discovery for the subject of theological discourse. Tracy's anthropology assumes an authentic self beneath the subject's phenomenal manifestations. This self slips in and out of discourses, moving through language in its progressive attempt to attain true knowledge of its own foundations and the ultimate meaning of its positivities.

Beginning with the "mixed discourse" conducted by the subject about itself, its experiences of people and things, and the books it regards as familiar and interesting, the authentic self moves into the discursive formations of the human sciences. Here the self isolates its positivities: everyday experiences, unrelated and ephemeral, such as anxiety, boredom, joy, depression, and well-being, become *signs*: of personality types, inner conflicts, social struggles, cultural tendencies. Books become *texts*: autonomous bearers of meaning signifying a potential "mode-of-being-in-the-world" for the authentic self. At the same time, however, the phenomena constituted by the discursive formations of the human sciences estrange the self from its comfortable world of the everyday. The proliferation of texts presents in infinite number of worlds in which the authentic self could dwell, while the human sciences splinter the self into a series of "profiles" (psychological, sociological, ethnographic, linguistic, et al.) whose principle of unity becomes occult; the authentic self recedes from its own gaze.

In pursuit, the reflecting self moves from the discourses of the human sciences to that of existential anthropology. Here the self tries to describe, as accurately as possible, the deepest meaning of common human experience and language, and the deepest meaning of the Christian fact. The task remains phenomenological/hermeneutic: "to disclose or mediate . . . the immediate experience of the self-as-a-self" (ibid.), but now treating the positivities as described by the human sciences *as signs themselves* of the fundamental orientation of the self toward reality.[17] Existential anthropology, as practiced by Tracy, seeks the meaning *of the meaning* of the disparate objects of the human sciences, and retains the observational model of the latter. When the authentic self successfully perceives the "limit character" of Christian texts and the self's immediate experience, including the "limit-of" the world of the text and the self's experience, the penultimate meaning of the positivities becomes clear to it.[18] The alienated, or "distanciated," formations of the discourses of the human sciences are "appropriated" as adequate and suitable representations of the authentic self, as are the Christian classics.

It remains for the authentic self to account for this meaning, which includes an intuition of the self's foundations (an "experienced necessary existent [God]," (ibid.). Until the authentic self attains true knowledge of its foundations, its meaningful appropriation of its positivities exists only "on credit."

Thus moving for a final time, the authentic self leaves the discourse of existential anthropology to take up residence in the explicitly foundational discourses of Christian fundamental theology. Chief among these discourses is the Christian doctrine of God (the religion's "central cognitive claim," [*BRO*, 14] which is adjusted by Tracy to accommodate the self's meaningful

---

[17] An example of the point I am making is Tillich's reflections on neurotic anxiety (as a formation of Modern psychology), which he explicitly takes as a sign of deeper, existential meaning. For that matter, psychology's conception of *healthy* anxiety is, for Tillich, equally disclosive. See Paul Tillich, *The Courage to Be* (New Haven/London: Yale University Press, 1952) 64–85 and passim.

[18] Discussion of "limit situations" will take place in the next chapter. It is worth nothing here that the human sciences are the proper disciplines for determining the "limits-to" the self's powers. Tracy brings along the idea in moving from the phenomenology proper to these sciences to that performed by existential anthropology, which purports to uncover a correlative "limit-of" the self's transcendence.

appropriation of its positivities (its experience of the necessary existent). The result is a "neoclassical theism" (ibid.).

Once the self is established in knowledge as well as in experience, the subject of theological discourse (the revisionist theologian) begins to reconstruct other areas of the Christian symbol system. Now, however, the criteria for reflection can be "experiential" (in Kaufman's sense of "pragmatic," *ETM*, 75–76) rather than ideal:

> As the concerns of fundamental theology move out of their orbit of primarily logical and metaphysical concerns to the orbit of dogmatics (i.e., to a greater concern with the explicit particularity of the Christian symbol system), the concerns of fundamental theology itself may shift from criteria of metaphysical adequacy to criteria of relative experiential adequacy. (*BRO*, 80)

In theory, the resolution of the foundations and the positivities, discovered in the deep meaning of the authentic self and secured cognitively in a doctrine of God, enables the subject of theological discourse to reconstruct the formations of christology, ecclesiology, eschatology, etc., secure in the knowledge that the subject's claims are not only coherent and meaningful, but true as well, and not only for an intelligent inquirer in the academy, but in principle for anyone at all. The resemblance of Tracy's philosophical anthropology to the serious discourse of the Modern episteme is more than casual.

Tracy's "authentic self," like Foucault's "man," is simultaneously the subject and object of an analytic of finitude. As analytical subject, the self bases its phenomenology and critique of deep meaning on a reflective capability proper to the self as a rational being. "One lives authentically," Tracy tells us, "insofar as one continues to allow oneself an expanding horizon," where "expansion" means "going beyond one's present state in accordance with the transcendental imperatives" of Lonergan (*BRO*, 96). As analytical object, the self inquires into the conditions of the possibility of this same rational nature (as the imperatives' anthropological justification), by the disciplined description of the self's positivities and the transcendental critique of their significance.

> What one is reflecting upon is never merely "given" for human consciousness. . . . Rather every object—every phenomenon—has *a priori* conditions. Certain of these conditions are basic and universal for all human knowing and experience insofar as those conditions are conditions of possibility, i.e., they are so constitutive of any performance of cognition or experience that they can be reductively exhibited from it. (*BRO*, 67–68)

The figure of the authentic self is the subject of a virtually unlimited knowledge, an "expanding horizon" of foregrounded reality, and the object of the rational recovery of this same subjective capacity. The authentic self's knowledge can be distinguished from the God's Eye view only because the self must apprehend reality piecemeal, through time. Though potentially unlimited, the self's knowledge of everything, including itself, is finite and must be gained by the critique of positive, temporally determined experiences and cognitive states. Therein lies the difficulty: how to be sure that what critique "reductively exhibits" is really "so constitutive" of the self's positive experience that it counts as a "basic and universal" condition "for all human knowing and experience" (ibid.). How can the revisionist theologian ascertain that self-knowledge is *authentic*?

Posed as a question of becoming clear about the self's epistemic foundations through the analytic of its positivities, the phenomenology and critique of the theological source, "common human experience and language," spirals down the track of the cogito and the unthought. We recall that the unthought is not foreign to the self, but "has an ineradicable and fundamental relation" to it (*OT*, 325). Modern phenomenology is the anthropological method par excellence, specifically dedicated, says Foucault, "to interrogation concerning man's mode of being and his relation to the unthought" (ibid.). As Foucault and Tracy believe, contemporary phenomenology does not specify things in order to relate them to Kantian categories of technical reason. Since Heidegger, its aim is more radical: experiences are specified in order to refer them to "man," the ground of science's particular rationality and that which lies beneath it, in the ontological structures of the unthought itself (*BRO*, 67 – 68; *OT*, 323 – 26).

While Foucault observes phenomenology's Modern turn with "studied casualness," however, Tracy treats it with full seriousness, by linking theology's project of a depth ontology with the logically "shallower" but still authentic and authenticating disciplines of the human sciences:

> Only a phenomenology in continued conversation with those of the human sciences which investigate the religious dimension in human existence, and in conversation with other philosophical methods can really hope to succeed. (*BRO*, 48)

"Succeed," that is, in "ending man's alienation by reconciling him with his own essence, of making explicit the horizon that provides experience with its background of immediate and disarmed proof, of lifting the veil of the Unconscious" (*OT*, 327); in short, succeed in bringing the unthought to thought by making it empirically apparent. Tracy's methodological assimilation of the results of the human sciences follows a pattern of Modern phenomenologies identified by Foucault, according to which the human-scientific obligation to empiricity is matched by an ontological component which relativizes the thinking subject and its knowledge claims about the empirical world:

> The phenomenological project continually resolves itself, before our eyes, into a description—empirical despite itself—of actual experience, and into an ontology of the unthought that automatically short-circuits the primacy of the 'I think.' (*OT*, 326)

The discursive formation of authentic self-knowledge is, therefore, an always unfinished task, but not a cumulative one: the raising of the unthought to consciousness in the empirical description of experiences and psychological states is a matter which varies with the interpretive categories of the human-scientists, the *dispositifs* of their "confessing" subjects, and the social practices of the subjects themselves. The result is the present profusion of competing human-scientific programs. Their corollary is the pluralism of fundamental-theological discourses taking some version of "man" as their object, thereby supplying the ontological component of the phenomenological project. Tracy's postulate of authentic self-transcendence allows for the theoretical integration, in the discourse of ontology, of phenomenologically diverse data about the self. But this same postulate prevents, rather than facilitates, the resolution of theology's present crisis by systematically ignoring the discursive and nondiscursive practices which enable the formation of authentic self-knowledge in the first place.

The cogito proceeds in the manner of a sovereign, exercising its right to self-clarification. Language and practices mediate the transformation of the unthought into the contents of consciousness; specifically, the "powers of intelligent and critical introspection" organized in the discourses of psychoanalysts, culture critics, historians, social and natural scientists, et al. (*BRO*, 66). But because the discourse and practices of these "trustworthy modes of mediation" (ibid.) can only facilitate or impede the liberation of authentic self-consciousness, without affecting the nature of the reflecting individual (compromising the authority of the cogito), their responsibility for creating and sustaining the historico-critical conditions of anthropological discourse goes unnoticed by the revisionist theologian. Perhaps genealogy and archaeology are modes of thinking which do not "reverence" the "value of the self as a self" (ibid.). But the *dispositif* of revisionist fundamental theology, by which it takes "common human experience and language" as one "source," places theology in the double of the cogito and the unthought, maintains it in this useless repetition by systematically eliding the genealogically specific power relations supporting the double, and prevents the construction of postanthropological forms of human being by perpetuating traditional seriousness and the quest for foundations.

Tracy's anthropological assumptions are carried over to his treatment of theology's second source. The interpretation and critique of "the Christian fact" move along the path of the origin's retreat and return.[19]

First, the text must be prepared to function as the site of an origin. This is achieved by distinguishing a text sense, which reflects the specification of writing in retrievable styles and literary genera, and a number of text references (world behind and world before the text), which owe their unity to the inquirer's imagination. Now, if the historian works with traditional seriousness, we have seen that the role of the imagination in reconstructing the past (world behind the text) is to transcend the historian's own circumstances and, taking the sense of the text as a point of departure, to restore a unity to previous events which time has paradoxically obscured (see Chapter 3). Tracy's concern is with a world in front of the text, but like the romanticist historian, he belies that the role of the imagination is to transport the inquirer into an anthropological story, an adventure of "man."

In his essay, "What Is an Author?" (*Language*, 113–38) Foucault discusses a consequence of the demise of the author's sovereignty for interpretation. One contemporary idea of writing (*écriture*) dispenses with the Modern correlative notion of the necessity of deciphering an author's meaning. Literary-critical techniques now define the text's structure without reference to its underlying significance for an originating consciousness. So far, Foucault and Tracy are in agreement: the sense of a text has its own autonomy. But Tracy, like Ricoeur, treats the ideal meaning of a text as the springboard for the recovery of depth significance. Foucault's criticism, directed implicitly at Derrida, applies equally well to the programs of Ricoeur and Tracy:

> It appears, however, that his concept [*écriture*], as currently employed, has merely transposed the empirical characteristics of an author to a transcendental anonymity. The extremely visible signs of the author's empirical activity are effaced to allow the play, in parallel or opposition, of religious and critical modes of characterization. In granting a primordial status to writing, do we not, in effect, simply reinscribe in transcendental terms the theological affirmation of its sacred origin or a critical belief in its creative nature? . . . is this not to reintroduce in transcendental terms the religious principle of hidden meanings (which require

[19] Because revisionist fundamental theology is devoted to the analytic of finitude, any part of it could be analyzed in terms of any of Foucault's three doubles. My choice to see the first source in terms of the cogito and the unthought is motivated by phenomenology's historical association with clarifying thought concerning the structures of *Existenz*. Hermeneutics' involvement with the search for "man"'s origin in liberal theology is the reason I have selected the origin double as my grid for understanding "the Christian fact."

interpretation) and the critical assumption of implicit significations, silent purposes, and obscure contents (which give rise to commentary)?[20]

What the author thought about his or her work is irrelevant not only to its ideal sense, but to its ideal meaningfulness, which the text bears within itself as the reader's origin. When Foucault derisively remarks that we have waited twenty centuries for the Word, he is implicity criticizing the revisionist model of the text-dialogue and truth as disclosure, with the "Modern soul" (the attentive reader) and the classic (the Word) earnestly engaged in the transmission of truth (the genuinely public discourse).[21]

The Word that the classic speaks, however, is not the *totaliter aliter*. As discourse in the Modern episteme, it speaks to "man" about his own deepest potentials, his ontological destiny, that is, his origin as an authentic self.

> Certain expressions of the human spirit so disclose a compelling truth about our lives that we cannot deny them some kind of normative status. Thus do we recognize, whether we name it so or not, a normative element in our cultural experience, experienced as a realized truth. (*AI*, 108)

"The Christian fact," purposefully broad to include any "classic" of the Christian tradition (*traditio*), is amenable to critical, "public" inspection insofar as it refers to the same anthropological construct as the discourses of the academy.

---

[20] Foucault, *Language*, 119–20.

[21] Tracy claims the following:

> The experience of the classic remains a permanent feature of any human being's cultural experience. Indeed, even radical thinkers like Michel Foucault who would eliminate the usual classics (Kant, Hegel, Aristotle) will uncover new candidates (De Tracy, Cuvier) to fill the vacuum left by their genealogical suspicions. (*AK*, 108)

It is very hard to see how the texts of Cuvier and De Tracy function as "classics" for Foucault in the way those of Kant, Hegel, and Aristotle obviously function for Tracy, i.e., as "expression of the human spirit" disclosing "a compelling truth about our lives" (*AK*, 108). The reason is, Foucault's archaeology violates the integrity of the text in order to place it among structurally similar discourses, and to specify these related discourses' epistemic conditions: "I had no intention of describing Buffon or Marx. . . . I wanted to determine . . . the functional conditions of specific discursive practices" (Foucault, *Language*, 114). Whether as functions of rules or practices, Cuvier's texts have their importance for Foucault only in relation to the specifiable conditions of their appearance as occasions for serious discourse. To treat them as "classics" would require the archaeologist to adopt traditional seriousness toward the history of "man," rather than to question the circumstances of validated talk, like Tracy's, about "expressions of the human spirit."

Finally, if the *retreat* of the origin is the bane of Modern Christian biblical scholars (because the Word always eludes the words in which its historical foundations are specified), then the *return* of the origin, as the imminent identity of the authentic reader's sociocultural reality and the world in front of classic texts, is the hope of the revisionist theologian. The critical correlation of the results of the hermeneutics of the Christian fact and the results of the phenomenology of common human experience and language, is the composition of an anthropological story, weaving the authentic commentary on ''man'''s returning origin with the authentic representation of ''man'''s unthought significance. It remains to be shown in Chapter 6 how, according to Tracy, experience in ''man'''s religious dimension works to abruptly clarify the unthought and return the origin, only to be followed by ''man'''s fall back into experiences of unclarity and promise, as ''the negative'' in every situation (*AI*, 355−64) reminds the authentic self of its temporality, and the difference it is.

# 6

# Revisionist Fundamental Theology
## and Self-Transcendence

In the previous chapter I argued that Tracy's construct, "the authentic self," can be usefully described as engaged in a process of intellectual self-liberation which coincides with insight into the ultimate significance of the self's most meaningful experiences. This final significance or "truth" is determined wholly by a transcendental critique of the experiences' conditions of possibility. The meaning and penultimate significance ("meaningfulness") of these experiences are unearthed ("disclosed") by the "generally phenomenological," preparatory work of the human sciences, operating in dialogue with existential-phenomenological and textual-hermeneutic investigations (*BRO*, 68–71).

## Phenomenology of the Religious Dimension

Tracy's fundamental theology aims at providing just such a critique of knowledge and experience. It culminates in a revisionist doctrine of God adequate to the authentic self's drive to know (preeminently evident in scientific inquiry); the human's experience of the world as ultimately trustworthy (assumed in moral argument); and the authentic self's occasional encounters with the "ground" or "foundation" of its intrinsic limitations (in everyday life).[1]

---

[1] In addition to scientific, moral, and "limit" experiences, Tracy includes "the scriptural meaning of God" (*BRO*, 179) as a fact to be criticized by transcendental theological reflection in

Before fundamental theology can construct its doctrine of God, however, its phenomenological/hermeneutic moment must "tag" for reflection those aspects of the self's experience which render them significant for theological critique. Theology must discursively form the "significant implicitly religious characteristics of our common experience" (*BRO*, 93).

The "religious dimension" of human life is, analytically speaking, the experiences of the self viewed from a "religious" perspective. The phenomenology of insight, of moral conduct, and of finitude is the investigation of the religious dimension of the self's experiences whenever these three ways of "being-in-the-world" are considered in terms of their penultimate meaningfulness and meaning for the knowing, acting, finite human.

How does one recognize an "implicitly religious" characteristic of experience? What considerations guide the discursive formation of the religious dimension of the authentic self by the fundamental theologian? Tracy's analysis of "limitation" into "limits-to" and the "limit-of" experience and knowledge provides him a conceptual framework for formulating the disclosure of the deep meaning of human existence effected by phenomenological and hermeneutic reflection.

## Self-Transcendence and Limit Questions

Authentic self-transcendence is a primary category of Tracy's anthropology. It refers to "going beyond one's present state in accordance with the transcendental imperatives" (*BRO*, 96) of Lonergan. The movement "from sensitivity through intelligent and critical reflection to deliberate action" (*BRO*, 97) represents the self's attempt to push beyond the "experienced world of sensitive immediacy" (*BRO*, 96) to an understanding of the actual and logical conditions of possibility of that world; and, having gained insight in this regard, to reform the self's world responsibly.

Because the reflection leading to insight must be performed on the ever-changing patterns of events and experiences of the lived world, the authentic self is constantly challenged to rethink its conclusions, including its understanding of the logical contexts within which these conclusions receive their validity. As Tracy observes, "One lives authentically insofar as one continues to allow oneself an expanding horizon" (ibid.) of intelligibility.

---

constructing its doctrine of God. This dissertation, however, will confine its study to the religious dimension of common human experience and language, as disclosed by phenomenology. It will not take up in any extended fashion the religious dimension of Christian texts (i.e., the limit character of "authentic explicitly religious language"; *BRO*, 119). Tracy's own analysis of the religious dimension of Christian texts is found at *AI*, 163–92 and *BRO*, 119–45. Like the limit situations described in *BRO*, 105–9, the "religious classic" is "an event of disclosure, expressive of the 'limit-of,' 'horizon-to,' 'ground-to' side of 'religion' " (*AI*, 163).

Authentic self-transcendence is a constant challenge, but Tracy believes its achievements are progressive nevertheless. Each insight into the preconditions of a scientific, moral, or existential fact or event deepens the self's understanding of that fact or event, by allowing the self to see reality more clearly as "an intelligently mediated and deliberately constituted world of meaning" (ibid.).

Here Tracy's thinking resembles that of Kaufman regarding the intrinsically perspectival nature of knowledge: the authentic self, like Kaufman's internal relativist, does not claim to have escaped the conditions of historical thinking. One reflects within a "horizon" or frame which is relative to the circumstances of the knower. Yet this horizon is not merely constantly *shifting*. If one abides by the canons of responsible reflection (respects the secular morality of knowledge), this horizon is constantly *expanding* to allow an increasingly comprehensive view of the nature of reality.[2]

Authentic self-transcendence aims at achieving a complete view of the grounds of intellectual, moral, and existential limitation (*BRO*, 97). The "limits-to" scientific inquiry (which serves as a paradigm of self-transcendence for Tracy; *BRO*, 96–100) are coextensive with the intelligible world. The "limit-of" scientific questioning is the ground of questioning itself, thinking's ultimate conditions of possibility. Reflection on the limits to inquiry, Tracy claims, leads logically to reflection on thinking's ground:

> On the level of questions for intelligence the authentic scientific inquirer can inquire into the very possibility of fruitful inquiry. In his scientific research a scientist can and does reach intellectually satisfying answers. Yet he can also ask such limit questions as the following throughout his inquiry: Can these answers work if the world is not intelligible? Can the world be intelligible if it does not have an intelligent ground? (*BRO*, 98)

The logic of inquiry begins in reflection on an experience of limitation (here the scientist's experienced limits to knowledge), and ends in the "disclosure" of that limited experience's necessary preconditions, which ultimately coincide with the "limit-of" intelligent reflection itself:

> [The scientist's limit question] is initially formulated as the question of both a limit-to his inquiry and possibly disclosive of a limit-of that drive

---

2 Cf. Kaufman's remarks on progress in *Relativism, Knowledge, and Faith*:

The only line of progress we can see in thought is a line moving gradually toward our own position in the present, which attempts to take up all other positions of which we are aware within itself. What progress we can discern is progress made possible by taking up what appear to us to be the key threads of the past into our own position, through performing our historical thinking with more comprehensiveness and adequacy. (*RKF*, 123)

(viz., an intelligent ground for intelligibility). In that logical sense, the question can be described as a religious-as-limit question. (Ibid.)

Following the logic of inquiry into the religious dimension is no optional decision on the part of the scientist, but occurs in response to the inquirer's fundamental obligation to act on the imperatives of authentic self-transcendence:

> Unless he wishes to abandon the search for authentic self-transcendence the scientist cannot silence the question of the final horizon of scientific inquiry. ... No inquirer can commit himself to the task of authentic self-transcendence (i.e., intelligent, rational, and responsible thought and action) and then deny his own need to seek the ultimate intelligent, rational, and responsible grounds for such inquiry and action. (*BRO*, 98–99)

Significantly, the necessity of an intelligent ground for reflection (God) remains a postulate of the scientist's experience of objects in an intelligible world. Never does God (the limit of experience) become available to the inquirer's experience. The scientist "may attempt to mediate that final or ultimate limit dimension . . . through symbol, or myth, or philosophy" (*BRO*, 99), but it is not an experience by the scientist which is being "mediated" through language. It is the scientist's conclusion, as an authentic inquirer, that the order of the world as experienced requires the postulation of an intelligent ordering principle, which the scientist is articulating in metascientific terms.

Likewise, Tracy affirms Schubert Ogden's claim that moral discourse presumes a basic confidence in the ultimate trustworthiness of life, a confidence which is "re-presented" in the linguistic forms of explicitly religious language.[3] Theological reflection does not operate upon the inquirer's experience of the source of the world's trustworthiness, an ultimate ground of ethical engagement, but upon an experience of certain features of the world as trustworthy:

> The kind of experience which religious language discloses is thereby clarified: an already present basic confidence has been threatened (e.g., in some "boundary situation" or by reflection upon the limit questions of morality) and needs the reassurance which religious re-presentative language may bring. (*BRO*, 103)

---

[3] Ogden's argument is presented in Schubert Ogden, "The Reality of God," in idem, *The Reality of God and Other Essays* (New York/San Francisco: Harper & Row, 1977) 27–43.

To this point in my analysis, Tracy has argued simply that certain questions arise in one kind of discourse (scientific or moral) whose answers presently lie in another—that of traditional religious language—insofar as the logic of inquiry is followed consistently. As he observes, "neither scientific nor moral uses of argument are entirely self-contained" (*BRO*, 102). In attempting to account for her or his experiences of order and morality, the authentic inquirer moves from a description of the *limits to* scientific and ethical knowledge, to the critical investigation of the conditions of the possibility of these experiences. The ultimate *limit of* trust and true knowledge is not experienced in determining these conditions. The limit of experience is these conditions. The limit of knowledge and experience is postulated in propositions framed in religious or philosophical linguistic forms.

Tracy's phenomenology of limit situations in everyday life departs significantly from the epistemological relationship between inquirer and inquiry's ground described above. In certain uncommon moments, he claims, the limit of experience is itself encounterd by the authentic self.

## Phenomenology of "Positive" Situations

The concept "limit situation" arises in the discourses of existential philosophy and theology.[4] As adopted by Tracy, "the concept refers to those human situations wherein a human being ineluctably finds manifest a certain ultimate limit or horizon to his or her existence" (*BRO*, 105). Tracy distinguishes two main kinds of existential situations in which the horizon of the self's act of being comes into view: "Either those 'boundary' situations of guilt, anxiety, sickness, and the recognition of death as one's own destiny, or those situations called 'ecstatic experiences'—intense joy, love, reassurance, creation" (ibid.). A "genuine limit situation," positive or negative, is a situation "wherein we both experience our own human limits (limit-to) as our own as well as recognize, however haltingly, some disclosure of a limit-of our experience" (ibid.).

Unlike the posing and answering of limit questions in the philosophy of science and ethics, in which separate acts of reflection are required to raise the question of the limits to inquiry (in scientific and moral discourses) and to address that question critically (in religious or philosophical linguistic forms), in a limit situation the self's experience of a "limit to" its powers is joined by an experience of the "limit-of" those capabilities. Speaking specifically of "positive" limit situations, he claims: "That limit-to the everyday also seems to disclose—in the same *ec-stasis*—a limit-of whose graciousness

---

4 Tracy refers the reader to Karl Jaspers, *The Perennial Scope of Philosophy* (New York: Philosophical Library, 1949) 85 – 87, 168 – 80.

bears a religious characteristic'' (*BRO*, 106). Or again, ''Authentic love, both erotic and agapic, puts us in touch with a reality whose power we cannot deny'' (*BRO*, 105 – 6). Explicitly religious language is the occasion of the same affect on the self. Religion

> continues to operate in our common lives as an authentic disclosure which both bespeaks certain inevitable limits-to our lives and manifests some final reality which functions as a trustworthy limit-of life itself. (*BRO*, 109)

Why not simply claim that limit situations show the subject the extent of its powers at any given time (its ''limits-to'')? Why include, as common human experiences, manifestations of the ''limit-of'' these powers? Tracy's own employment of horizon metaphors would suggest the appropriateness of such a tack, since a horizon in everyday experience is merely the furthest visible set of points from any given location, the *limit-to* the observer's sight. The ''ultimate horizon'' would then be just the temporally last periphery of one's knowledge and experiences, not a single, grand horizon which would count as the boundary of all one's possible experiences and knowledge.

Tracy's anthropology contains the seeds of an answer. Recall that the drive to transcend one's present intellectual and moral limits in a reasonable and responsible way is a prime category of authentic selfhood. ''One lives authentically insofar as one continues to allow oneself an expanding horizon'' (*BRO*, 96). The impulse to intellectual self-liberation (insight) demands that each horizon be more comprehensive than the one preceding it.

Once the idea of a progression of horizons is (implicitly) introduced as a corollary of authentic self-transcendence, the concept of an ultimate context for reflection (in science), ethical action (in morality), pain and pleasure (in everyday life) becomes the telos of every transgression of the limits to knowledge and experience. Boundaries are not merely broken; they are surpassed in the subject's endeavor to see clearly and distinctly, once and for all, the destiny of authentic self-transcendence.

This destiny may be ''disclosed'' to the self in rare moments of ecstasy, when the individual is ''put in touch with . . . a final, a 'trustworthy,' meaning to [its life]'' (*BRO*, 106). Tracy claims that in addition, the

> ''world of meaning'' beyond the everyday . . . may also disclose to us, however haltingly, the character of that ultimate horizon of meaning which religious persons call ''gracious,'' ''eventful,'' ''faith-ful,'' ''revelatory.'' (Ibid.)

Ecstatic transgression of limitation brings the authentic self into this extraordinary world of meaning, in which the self experiences the meaning of its life as finally trustworthy. This world, in turn, "may also disclose" the ultimate precondition of this meaningfulness. This precondition or "ultimate horizon," which I have called the destiny of the authentic self, is not disclosed merely by reflection on experience (as the limit of inquiry and morality is disclosed), but is itself experienced as a reality which is religious (*BRO*, 108 – 9). As Tracy concludes:

> The principal cognitive claim involved in religious language, I shall argue, is the explicitly theistic claim: that the objective referent of all such language *and experience* is that reality which religious human beings mean when they say "God." (*BRO*, 109; my emphasis; see also 71)

The model of authentic self-transcendence allows Tracy to interpret ecstatic experiences as personal transits or passages into a world of profound meaning, which in turn sometimes reveals the source of this meaning (God). However, I believe it is less successful in supplying an interpretation of "negative" or "boundary" situations which is equally religious (i.e., equally amenable to theistic critique).

## *"Negative" Situations and the Limits of Phenomenology*

While positive limit situations claim to put the self in touch with life's ultimate trustworthiness, boundary situations confront the self with its own fundamental attitude toward life's significance. The self's initial encounter is a self-encounter, in which negative limit situations act as a mirror of the self's "faith or unfaith":

> That "limit" world of final closure to our lives [revealed through the experience of grave illness] now faces us with a starkness we cannot shirk and manages to disclose to us our basic existential faith or unfaith in life's very meaningfulness. (*BRO*, 105)

The explicit entry of personal responsibility for the meaningful or meaningless appearance of life distinguishes negative from positive limit situations. Ecstatic experiences presume an existential faith which is satisfied or rewarded by the disclosure of a "world of meaning" with God as its foundation. Faith is confirmed in ecstasy, but challenged in tragedy, when adverse circumstances call into question the ultimate trustworthiness of life.

Granted that negative limit situations reveal to the self its basic attitude toward life's meaningfulness, is there yet another disclosure of a "limit-of" existence analogous to the manifestation of God in moments of genuine ecstasy? If there is not, in what sense are negative limit situations disclosive of a *religious* dimension of common human experience?

At this point recall that Tracy is attempting to improve on Tillich's method of correlation by uncovering from within experience both the "questions" and the "answers" to authentic selfhood (*BRO*, 45–46). Tracy's phenomenology of positive limit situations coherently correlated the question of the ground of life's trustworthiness with the answer of God as the ultimate horizon of meaning: once beyond the everyday in an extraordinary world of meaning, the self occasionally encounters the ground or telos of its transcendence.

Phenomenology of negative limit situations, however, does not so clearly reveal the presence of God. Indeed, the "question" of anxiety (to take Tracy's paradigmatic boundary situation) is "answered" not by the disclosure of a ground of existence, but by an experience of the self's own fundamental contingency, according to Tracy's reading of Heidegger:

> Anxiety is a fear of *no-object*-in-the-world-alongside-other-objects. Anxiety is literally, as Heidegger reminds us, a fear of No-thing. More positively stated, anxiety is a fear disclosive of our often forgotten but never totally absent consciousness of our own radical contingency. In anxiety, we do not merely consider, we know that we neither create ourselves nor can we assume the continuance of existence. (*BRO*, 107)

Jolted by circumstances out of our comfortable everyday world into an awareness of our radical contingency, "we find ourselves—as the metaphors of the existentialists and the mystics alike remind us—poised over an abyss, a chasm, whose exact nature we do not know but whose experiential reality we cannot deny" (ibid.).

The juxtaposition of the self and an "abyss" or "chasm," a "No-thing" distinct from the self, possessing its own reality and nature (albeit known inexactly), and attested to by mystics, obscures the anthropological grounding of this reality proposed by Heidegger (discussed below), and harks back to Tillich's concept of the "negative side of the mystery" of finite reason.[5]

---

[5] Tillich's notion of "the mystery" mediates both negative and positive "sides" of the self's experience of its essential finitude. See Tillich, *Systematic Theology*, 1. 108–11. The inability of reason to account for itself is sometimes experienced (negatively) as an "abyss." In "actual revelation" the same "mystery" makes itself known (positively) as reason's "ground." Here mystery "appears as the power of being, conquering nonbeing" (ibid., 110). Tracy's avowed intention to answer existential questions without appeal to revelation leaves him only the "abyss" as a phenomenological datum—not the "ground."

Indeed, Tracy's own analysis appears frustrated in its attempt to uncover, by phenomenology alone, a religious significance of boundary situations:

> What, really, does this analysis of anxiety and similar existentialist analyses manifest?  At the very least, the analysis discloses that the final dimension or horizon of our situation is neither one of our own making nor one under our control.  (Ibid.)

Tracy suggests that "No-thing" answers the question of anxiety by functioning as a kind of ground or horizon of existence (no doubt in a fashion analogous to the ultimate horizon of meaning disclosed in ecstatic experiences ). He says, "In analyzing anxiety we may also see that our situation is, in fact, correctly described as a limit situation.  We are grounded or horizoned by no other thing in the universe, but rather by No-thing" (ibid.).

Are boundary situations really limit situations?  Do they reveal in experience a "limit-of" as well as the "limits-to" human being?  Depending on whether one relies on Division I or II of *Being and Time*, the answers will be "no" and "yes," respectively, but in neither case will the answer be theologically useful to Tracy.

Tracy draws exclusively from Division I in making his analysis of anxiety and refers the reader to sections in that Division to support his argument (*BRO*, 118, nn. 86–88).  The point of Heidegger's discussion, however, is not to illuminate the nature of the "No-thing" which *Dasein* fears, but simply to show how anxiety reveals to *Dasein* that the world and others can offer no final self-understanding of *Dasein*'s "true self."  He says:

> Anxiety thus takes away from Dasein the possibility of understanding itself, as it falls, in terms of the "world" and the way things have been publicly interpreted.  Anxiety throws Dasein back upon that which it is anxious about—its authentic potentiality-for-Being-in-the-world.[6]

---

[6] *BT*, 232. Heidegger's analysis of anxiety in Division I contains no mention of any reality apart from the self (a "chasm" or "abyss") which sets the horizon for or grounds its existence. Everything learned about anxiety tells us something about Dasein's resistance to authentic Being-in-the-world.

> The entire stock of what lies therein [in "the Being of the totality of Dasein's structural whole"] may be counted up formally and recorded: anxiousness as a state-of-mind is a way of Being-in-the-world; that in the face of which we have anxiety is thrown Being-in-the-world; that which we have anxiety about is our potentiality-for-Being-in-the-world. Thus the entire phenomenon of anxiety shows Dasein as factically existing Being-in-the-world. (*BT*, 235)

Put differently, Division I merely attempts to set forth the *limits to* authentic and inauthentic Being-in-the-world. It is a "preparatory fundamental analysis of Dasein" which tries to disclose phenomenologically "those structural items" comprising the "totality" of *Dasein*'s "Being" (*BT*, 274–78). From this point Heidegger moves "to the question of the primordial unity of this structural whole" (*BT*, 275), that is, the question of the conditions of the possibility of these items. The *limit of* the structure of anxiety is only taken up explicitly in Division II.

In short, when anxiety is interpreted solely on the basis of Heidegger's existential phenomenology of Division I, the boundary situation described by Tracy is no limit situation. The "answer" to boundary situations is not in Division I, and Tracy's effort to find one (by hypostatising *Dasein*'s fear of Being-in-the-world into the vaguely sinister "No-thing") is unsupported by Heidegger's text.[7]

Division II of *Being and Time* does offer an analytic of the preconditions, or horizon, of anxiety. Yet the analytic's conclusion is not theologically palatable to Tracy's revisionist program: the "limit-of" the phenomenon of anxiety is *Dasein*'s "Being-towards-death." Already in Division I we are told: "Anxiety makes manifest in Dasein its Being towards its ownmost potentiality-for-Being—that is, its *Being-free* for the freedom of choosing itself and taking hold of itself" (*BT*, 232). This "ownmost potentiality-for-Being" in Division II's analytic of *Dasein*'s temporal structure is clearly identified with death:

> Death, as the end of Dasein, is Dasein's ownmost potentiality—non-relational, certain and as such indefinite, not to be outstripped. Death is, as Dasein's end, in the Being of this entity towards its end (*BT*, 303; emphasis deleted; see also 279–311).

The condition of the possibility of *Dasein*'s experience of anxiety is its Being-towards-death, a potentiality "not to be outstripped" as the ultimate horizon of the self's existence.

---

[7] Tracy rightly regards the experience of the "uncanny" (*Unheimlich*) as a sense of contingency, of the possibility of not being, but he wrongly regards the uncanny as a "characteristic" of an "experiential reality" apart from the authentic self ("wrongly," i.e., as attributable to the phenomenology of Dasein). Rather, the experience of uncanniness, Heidegger makes plain, is a sense of being "not-at-home" (*BT*, 233) among other entities in the world, not the encroachment of "No-thing." Elsewhere Tracy interprets the uncanny as the signal of the explosion of difference out of apparent identity, the disorienting effect of something new emerging from something common-place (*AI*, 339–70). Tracy's move toward dialectical philosophy can be seen as a partial repudiation of the adequacy of existential phenomenology to account for bad experiences. See his remarks in Tracy, "Defending the Public Character of Theology," 355.

In summary, Tracy's analysis in *Blessed Rage for Order*, is unable to exhibit, from a phenomenology of experience itself, a "limit-of" guilt, anxiety, oppression and so on, which encompasses and grounds Heidegger's final horizon of death. Without such a disclosure, however, it cannot be said that Tracy has achieved his purpose of demonstrating *from within experience* a religious dimension of everyday suffering (*BRO*, 71).

# From Phenomenology to Social Criticism

*The Turn to Negative Dialectics*

Tracy admits his own dissatisfaction with his fundamental-theological interpretation of suffering—and his phenomenology of basic trust—in an article published in 1981. Writing in a series entitled, "How My Mind Has Changed," he rejects the idea that on the subjects "of religion, God or Christ" any major changes in his thinking had occurred over the preceding ten years. Yet he continues:

> On one substantive issue, however, I do think that I have experienced something like a sea-change in both sensibility and theological understanding. In my earlier work, I tended to emphasize an approach to religion by means of reflection upon what can be called the positive limit experiences of life ... I do not doubt that fundamental trust remains a crucial ... phenomenon for approaching the issues of religion and God. Yet I have come to doubt that the route from fundamental trust to religions and God can prove as direct or as unencumbered as I once thought. More exactly, *I no longer believe that the "route" of the negative realities (anxiety, responsible guilt, death, illness, bereavement, alienation and oppression) is correctly described as an alternative route to the questions of religion and God.* ... The experience of fundamental trust remains as central to me as it ever was. Yet even that trust has now become subtly transformed by being arrived at only through a route highlighting the negative at every moment of the theological journey.[8]

Tracy's qualification of the "routes" to theological reflection bears implications for the phenomenology of both limit questions and limit situations.

First, by disavowing "the 'route' of the negative realities," Tracy implicitly acknowledges that the "limit-of" suffering is either not disclosed phenomenologically, or that which is disclosed cannot be accounted for by revisionist theology's transcendental "moment." If the "limit-of" the negative realities is by definition God (a ground of the world's trustworthiness),

---

[8] Tracy, "Defending the Public Character of Theology," 355; my emphasis.

then Tracy is conceding that phenomenology of suffering does not reveal or disclose a "limit-of." This brings him back to Tillich. If, alternatively, the "limit-of" suffering is understood as any ultimate horizon of suffering's appearance, a "limit-of" is disclosed, but the limit is death: the intrinsic possibility of nonbeing in which all suffering has its apparent end. This returns him to Division II Heidegger. If the "limit-of" the negative realities is death, then phenomenology of these realities is no "route" to "the questions of religion and God," that is, the discourse of explicitly religious language performed in the transcendental "correlation" of revisionist theology's two sources.[9]

Second, rather than beginning theological reflection by making a phenomenology of fundamental trust (implicitly disclosed in reflection on the limit questions of morality; explicitly manifested in ecstatic experiences), Tracy sets basic trust as a *goal* for a theological "journey" incorporating "the negative at every moment." Tracy continues to qualify his earlier criteriological framework by saying:

> The classic theological language of analogy . . . remains my real theological home. Yet now the analogies emerge more tentatively through (not in spite of) the various languages of negative dialectics. This recognition of the need for both the negative and the positive as always already together in every religious journey has forced me onto a more unsteady route for every question of theology.[10]

Tracy's move toward "the various languages of negative dialectics" should not, I believe, be understood as a retreat to the old "dialectics" of neoorthodox theologies. The problem of the authentic self's foundations will not be addressed by offering neoorthodoxy's revealed "solutions" to existential "problems." (Indeed, Tracy explicitly criticizes liberation thinkers for their unquestioning reliance on the neoorthodox model for their critiques of injustice [*BRO*, 240–50] .)

Nor does Tracy recommend that fundamental theology adopt the truth-as-disclosure model employed in revisionist systematics. Although the latter model is described in terms emphasizing the importance of the negative for

---

[9] Note that the disclosure of nonbeing as the "limit-of" existence is a particular problem for revisionist theology. For neoorthodox theologies like Tillich's, whose method consists in a correlation of an existential "situation" and a Christian "message," Tracy's phenomenology of negative limit situations leads nowhere *except* "the questions of religion and God." See Tillich, *Systematic Theology* 1. 3–11, 59–66; 2. 13–16. Tillich could be addressing Tracy when he claims, "one cannot derive the divine self-manifestation from an analysis of the human predicament" (p. 2. 13).

[10] Tracy, "Defending the Public Character of Theology," 355.

truth's manifestation, and for that reason might be called "dialectical," it, too, suffers from an assumption of the possibility of the self's experience of the ground of the world's trustworthiness (God) that Tracy in his 1981 essay was willing to call into question as a starting point for theological thinking.[11]

Tracy's response to his own criticism of his earlier work is not to seek alternatives to either the phenomenological-hermeneutic method or the truth-as-adequacy-to-experience model. Rather, it is to develop more systematically the link between fundamental theology and a practical theology devoted to "transformative praxis."

## Sublating Theoretical Constructs

Tracy's notion of praxis is indebted to the interpretations of the concept developed in the work of liberation and political theologians. These practical theologians understand praxis as

> not simply practice but as "authentic" praxis (actions in situation) informed by (sometimes informing) theory in accord with perceived personal, societal, political, cultural, or religious needs (for example, the need to overcome the perceived inability of even good theological theory to overcome actual alienation).[12]

"Good theological theory" includes fundamental and systematic reflection

---

[11] Notice in the following passage how the transgression of the "limits-to" experience and knowledge is much more than the mere occasion of truth's disclosure. The denial or "negation" of limitations is the condition of the posssibility of this manifestation, apparently performed by that which is manifested itself, i.e., God:

> Through the negation of the "limit-to" in the limit situations and limit questions of critical philosophies and theologies through the radical negations demanded in all the classic ascents and descents of speculative theologies, to the negations of the ordinariness of the ordinary as ordinary in the concrete disclosure of the ordinary's genuine extraordinariness, to the initial negations of the ordinary itself as "profane" in the journeys of the paradigmatic, *the same kind of negation assumes some central role in the emergence of the event as graced gift of manifestation.* (*AI*, 385; my emphasis)

Tracy elsewhere calls this "event" of manifestation, "a disclosure concealment of the whole of reality *by the power of the whole*" (*AI*, 163). That the systematic theologian speaks one of "the various languages of negative dialectics" is obvious; yet his or her truth claims, Tracy acknowledges, must be "sublated" by the conclusions of the practical theologian (*AI*, 73). The latter speaks another "language" which, in Tracy's work, is also one of negative dialectics, but conducted more "obviously," Tracy would say, according to the secular morality of knowledge and "the imperatives of critical rationality" (*AI*, 69).

[12] Tracy and Cobb, *Talking About God* (New York: Seabury, 1983) 14. See also *AI*, 69–79; *BRO*, 240–50.

conducted according to the criteria appropriate to each subdiscipline. The inability at times of these theologies to "overcome actual alienation" is due to the relative inadequacy of their respective models of truth, compared with the transformation model used in practical theology:

> Insofar as praxis sublates theory, insofar as the speaking of the truth demands doing the truth, insofar, therefore, as truth is always best understood as basically transformative in character rather than metaphysical or disclosive, praxis theology sublates the claims to truth of all alternative formulations articulated by nonpraxis-oriented fundamental and systematic theologies. It may still prove helpful for purely methodological reasons to continue to distinguish fundamental, systematic and practical theologies. *Substantively, however, all claims to truth in all forms of theology are determined by alienated or emancipated praxis and should be judged on those transformative praxis criteria.* (*AI*, 73; my emphasis)

So far Tracy has been summarizing the views of others which he takes to be representative of the practical-theological subdiscipline. Tracy's own practical theology has yet to appear, but from what he has written to date, he is in essential agreement with the tenets of praxis theology outlined above:

> Fundamental theology cannot live on its own. It finds its own inner drive to truth and concreteness necessitates its move to systematics . . . The same drive to the truth of concreteness impels both systematic and fundamental theology to recognize the grounding of their own theories and methods in a praxis deeper than all theory, and their drive to concreteness implies their sublation by practical theory. (*NI*, 36)

By "sublating" the conclusions of nonpraxis, theoretical subdisciplines (foundations and systematics) by the conclusions of practical theology, Tracy means first of all that any statement in the academy or church must be relativized by an analysis of the statement's sociocultural, "concrete," conditions. About his own work, and in reponse to "some Latin American critics," Tracy acknowledges:

> My analysis, like similar analyses by Euro-American theologians, was [in *Blessed Rage for Order*] largely confined to an analysis of those limit situations (either positive or negative) or those reflective limit questions that are likely to become the focus of the reflection of a twentieth-century, educated, middle-class Euro-American.[13]

In the same response, Tracy goes on to "sublate" the particular work of

---

[13] David Tracy, "Christian Faith and Radical Equality," *TToday* 34 (1978) 373.

nonoppressed theologians (like himself) by the reports of oppressed theologians, since the latter have suffered more intensely the negative realities in the course of their daily lives:

> The analysis of serious candidates for "religious dimension" language does and should naturally turn to those persons whose experience of that distortion is clearest and deepest. . . . The various forms of liberation theologies can be viewed as intensified negative disclosures of the limit situation of systematic oppression and as positive disclosures of the limit-demand for justice.[14]

Yet intensity of suffering, or any experience, does not make the experience an authentic disclosure of the "limit-of" (a genuine limit situation). This was Tracy's "precritical" error in *Blessed Rage for Order*: "The intensity of the experience of either love, joy, anxiety, or death cannot ignore the reality of the systematic distortion of our experience which sexism, racism, and classism in fact involve."[15]

Because of the possibly distorted nature of the subject's understanding of its own experiences, the phenomenology of common human experience and language—the keystone of revisionist fundamental theology—can no longer be assumed to provide an adequate description of that experience and language. The subject's sincerity toward the truth of its reports can no longer be taken as the sufficient condition of its authenticity: the subject may be deluded in its belief that is has encountered God. Or conversely, it may be deluded in thinking that it has not encountered the "limit-of," or that the logic of inquiry does not lead to the positing of an intelligent and moral ground.

The real nature of the subject's experiences is no longer determinable merely by phenomenology of the subject's reports of its experiences of "positive" or "negative" realities (pleasurable or painful disclosures of the "limit-of"). Rather, an adequate description of what the self is undergoing requires, for Tracy, the application of critical theories to specific economic and discursive situations. These theories order experience as "authentic" or "systematically distorted" (*AI*, 75–77).

The religious dimension of life remains a central anthropological assumption for Tracy, as does his belief that only authentic experiences diclose that dimension. Yet the measure of authenticity is no longer a function of the experience's *intensity* (its ability to put the self in touch with a "limit-of" through transgressing a "limit-to"), but is a function of its *normalcy*, as understood by critical theories of personality and society:

---

14 Ibid.
15 Ibid.

In the earlier analyses one must distinguish between authentic "anxiety" over our existence and an anxiety on the individual level which is either neurotic or psychotic (and thus systematically distorted). *Thereby one learns to allow the first and disallow the second as serious candidates for a disclosure of a religious dimension to our lives.*[16]

Everyday language has the first word in revisionist theology; human-scientific analyses have the second; and normalization of systematically distorted situations through transformative praxis has the third.[17]

### Empirical and Critical Human Sciences: Methods of Modern Liberation

A closer look at Tracy's understanding of the role of critical theories in revisionist theology underscores its importance for authentic reflection. Below, Tracy links the aspirations of revisionist theology with the goals of the Frankfurt School, and urges the incorporation of critical social theory into theological method for the authentic construction of explicitly religious discourse and images:

> The central demand for the continuing refinement of genuinely critical theory and for its universal applicability to all experience and all symbol systems is the chief distinguishing characteristic of both the contemporary revisionist model for fundamental theology and the "revisionist" model for critical social theory exemplified in the work of the Frankfurt School. ... As the brief reference to the Frankfurt School suggests, a revisionist theology of *praxis* would need at least one further mode of theoretical analysis to supplement and complete the earlier modes of analysis proper to constructive theology. That other necessary mode of analysis can perhaps best be described as a critical social theory. (*BRO*, 276)

Both the Frankfurt School and revisionist theology are marked by a commit-

---

[16] Ibid. My emphasis. One wonders if the discourse and behavior of a Joan of Arc or Margery Kempe would pass muster as "serious candidates" for authentic disclosure of the religious dimension, or would instead be judged "neurotic or psychotic (and thus systematically distorted)." The answer turns on the authority given by revisionist theology to critical theories; as shown below, if the theories criticize situations which have been accurately specified by empirical social science, their authority in theology cannot be contested. See *AI*, 75 and 77.

[17] "Everyday language" is any language people use to say theologically relevant things. It reports experiences which can be classified as limit situations. Among everyday language speakers, Tracy gives priority to the oppressed. Yet even (or especially) the oppressed may be deluded as to the causes of their pain; so enter critical theories. Authentic (i.e., rational) action follows by any intelligent, reasonable and responsible person.

ment to "genuinely critical theory," illuminating the systematic distortions of all socioeconomic and sociocultural relations ("all experience and all symbol systems") now and in the future.[18]

Tracy emphasizes, however, that to ensure that these theories adequately represent reality, they must have "grounding" in analyses of particular situations by empirical social-scientific investigation. Accurate description and normative critique are complementary operations:

> Both strictly empirical *and* theoretical positions (including theories of praxis such as ideology-critique or theories of communicative competence) are necessary. Without that empirical base, the theories are literally groundless as social-scientific evidence and should be treated, and respected, as proposals and hypotheses awaiting empirical testing. Without critical theory and transformative praxis, empirical social-scientific studies are always in proximate danger of simply affirming the present, possibly alienated and oppressive, status quo and in remote but real danger of disallowing any real critique of society. (*AI*, 77)

Only if theory is "confirmed" by the evidence of rigorous empirical studies can it act authoritatively within theology:

---

[18] The following selected sources are useful points of departure for studying the Frankfurt School: on the history of the School from 1923 to 1950, see Martin Jay, *The Dialectical Imagination* (Boston/Toronto: Little, Brown, 1973); primary material written in this period is represented in Andrew Arato and Eike Gebhardt, eds., *The Essential Frankfurt School Reader* (New York: Continuum, 1982); linking the School with the thought of Habermas is David Held, *Introduction to Critical Theory* (Berkeley/Los Angeles: University of California Press, 1980); Thomas McCarthy, *The Critical Theory of Jürgen Habermas* (Cambridge, MA: MIT Press, 1978) is an excellent thematic exposition and analysis of Habermas's work. The 1981 paperback ed. of McCarthy, *Critical Theory* contains an extensive bibliography of Habermas's works, arranged chronologically.

Tracy says that the reason "revisionary theorists like [Richard] Bernstein and Habermas" appeal to him is that their work supports the "recovery (of) practical reason with an emancipatory thrust" (*AI*, 38, n. 36).

> To uncover . . . [systematic] distortions we do need, as Habermas correctly insists, critical theory (i.e., theory which is reflexive and possesses an emancipatory thrust like Freudian psychoanalysis and ideology critique). Whether we also need a "theory of communicative competence" (as Habermas's later work insists) to provide de jure rules for our de facto ability to dialogue and find consensus seems to me far more debatable. (*AI*, 146–47, n. 80)

Yet cf. his inclusion of "theories of communicative competence" (*AI*, 77) together with ideology critique as at least potentially necessary "theoretical positions." Tracy does not discuss why he finds the need for de jure rules for competent communication "debatable." This is, on the face of it, peculiar since adherence to the postmodern morality of knowledge implies an obligation to set forth the conditions of the possibility of any and every phenomenon. This would include communication.

> The empirical evidence for our present situation as systematically dis-
> torted . . . should not be allowed to assume a descriptive and implicitly
> prescriptive force in theology *without rigorously empirical social-
> scientific support.* (*AI*, 75; my emphasis)

Tracy does "agree with the need to employ some form of ideology-critique
in social science, philosophy and theology" founded "not on personal
preference but on a common methodology" (ibid.). This methodology will
respect the findings of authentic empirical social science as the final authority
over critical-theoretical judgments: "Thus all claims for the primacy of
praxis over theory, if they are to prove consistent, must allow for empirical
social-scientific analysis to check all theories against our societal situation"
(*AI*, 75). The critique of oppression begins with empirical descriptions by
social scientists, including analyses of "our actual economic, political, cultural, and social situations," (*BRO*, 246); it includes "rigorous ethical analyses of the possibilities and limitations of the various infrastructural and
superstructural components of our social reality" as well as

> critical retrievals, if possible, or critical interventions, if necessary, of
> various symbol-systems in accordance with their ability both to negate
> the oppressive forces actually operative in the situation, and to project
> those images of social humanity to which the authentic human being can
> commit himself or herself. . . . In brief, the critical-*theoretical* aspect of
> the constructive model would need the expansion of scientifically
> authenticated empirical data, explicitly critical social analyses, and ethi-
> cal analyses. (*BRO*, 247)

In summary, critical theory in revisionist theology is a therapy operating
on situations of systematically distorted communication and productive relations, as diagnosed by empirical social science. It begins where phenomenology and hermeneutics leave off: with the description of the meaning and
meaningfulness of common human language and experience. Achieving
authentic insight into the religious dimension, however, now requires the
(practical) theologian to suspect, methodically, that the phenomenological-
hermeneutic report of this experience and language may be a rationalization
of the reporting subject's vested interests, and therefore a piece of distorted
communication. The testimony of the fundamental theologian and the sys-
tematician is relativized by the results of the critical investigation of the
economic and cultural situation in which the discourse of the academic and
church theologian originates. The result is not merely a transformation of
that discourse, it is an improvement in communciation—a "development"
in the journey of the authentic self toward enlightenment and enlightened
social change:

A practical theology in interdisciplinary conversation with empirical sociologists and economists, and informed by critical social theory would find its *praxis* grounded in, yet authentically be a major and new stage of development upon, the *theoria* of a newly constructed revisionist fundamental and systematic theology and an ever-freshly retrieved historical theology.[19]

By bringing the hermeneutics of suspicion to bear on the hermeneutic phenomenology of trust itself, practical theology overcomes any secret distortions of communication in its original fundamental reflections, and emerges renewed in an emancipated understanding of common human language and experience. That is, until the spiral turns again from construction to deconstruction, from trust to suspicion, as revisionist theology continues its ongoing quest for an adequate transcendental theory; for profound insight into the meaning and meaningfulness of the subject's drive to know and the agent's will to transgress limits; and for certain knowledge of the religious destiny of authentic self-transcendence.

## Theology as Critique of Discursive Formations

Phenomenology of the religious dimension and the theological critique of discursive formations have distinct but related archaeological conditions. The double of empirical knowledge and its transcendental foundations calls for "arbitrary" but "clearly elucidated" divisions (*OT*, 319) for the production of serious discourse, the most important being the division of truth itself. Modern truth, we recall from Chapter 2, strives to be both empirical and critical, and so must be both in the object of discourse and in discourse per se (*OT*, 320). Failing this, anthropology vacillates between truth's two sites.

Put simply, Tracy's fundamental theology situates the truth of its discourse in the object. This object is the manifestation of the "limit-of," God, in experience and reflection. Theological discourse tries to be adequate to its object; when it is, it is true. After 1981 and Tracy's turn to negative dialectics, the truth of his discourse is gradually established in the course of a "theological journey" toward its object. Here, "man"'s truth is in discourse, moving toward liberation through disciplined reflection on systematically distorted empiricities.

---

[19] *BRO*, 248. The idea that revisionist theology is not only an alternative to but an improvement upon all previous models is expressed in the following: "In the favored Hegelian language of the theologians of *praxis*, perhaps the revisionist model can provide an *Aufhebung* and not mere negation of the other dominant models for theology" (*BRO*, 247).

Keeping with Foucault's terminology, we may say that the phenomenology of the religious dimension and its correlative transcendental "adequation" form a theological *positivism*, where "the truth of the object [the self-validating appearance of the "limit-of"] determines the truth of the discourse that describes its formation [revisionist fundamental theology and other 'trustworthy modes of mediation'] (ibid.). Later, the critique of all discursive formations by the privileged discourse of practical theology (privileged because responsive to authentic, critical reflection) is a discourse of theological *eschatology*, in which "the truth of the philosophical [here theological] discourse constitutes the truth in formation" (ibid.).

Tracy himself acknowledges fundamental and practical theology's distinct relations to truth in terms of two "models": "truth-as-adequacy-to-experience," and "truth-as-transformative-praxis" (*AI*, 62–64 and 69–79). He views these models, and their true claims, as "complementary" (*AI*, 79):

> Practical theology . . . should, by its own criteria, be open to the necessary correctives provided by the authentic praxis informing the arguments and theories of fundamental theology. . . . Practical theology can, I believe, sublate the other two disciplines as long as the sublation also includes the truth claims operative in fundamental and systematic theologies. (*AI*, 96, n. 104)

Practical theology's eschatological discourse sublates or "takes up" the positivist discourse of fundamental theology. Transcendental constructs of the conditions of possibility of phenomenology's datum (the "limit-of") become more and more adequate as transformative praxis clarifies the unthought of the reflecting theologian. In return, clarified consciousness (consciousness freed from distortions) provides fundamental-theological discourse with greater authority over practices, inasmuch as the truth of its object is more readily apparent to every responsible inquirer. Where Foucault's studied casualness leads him to see the movement between description of empiricities and critique of foundations as a vacillation between truth's two sites, Tracy's anthropological seriousness allows him to see the same oscillation as an *Aufhebung* of systematic description and critique culminating in the reunification of truth and the return of representation. Where Foucault sees "man" as the condition of the possibility of the perpetual reconciliation of the cogito and the unthought, the empirical and the transcendental, and the origin's retreat and return, Tracy sees the authentic self progressively clarifying its unthought, representing its transcendental foundations, and, through transformative praxis, advancing toward the day when the self's origin, present now as the world in front of classic texts and "glimpsed" in limit situations, will be the world of everyday experience. Marx, Freud, and Nietzsche, on whom the authentic self relies, all have set in motion dialectics of liberation and domination, genuine conversation and systematically distorted communication, freedom and alienation, critical and instrumental reason. And so we find ourselves in a situation, still confused, struggling for some final liberation that is always deferred. (*AI*, 351)

It is possible that Tracy would agree with the location of his theological anthropology within the parameters of the Modern episteme, and agree with my argument that the authentic self follows the same "double" trajectories of reflection as Foucault's "man."[20] However, he might reply that this says nothing against continuing the Modern project of authentic liberation as our best hope for the future. Can we say with assurance that one day the critique of language and society will not end in an enlightened population and an authentic Christian world order? And, in the meantime, adhering to the secular morality of knowledge ensures that conversation will not sink deeper into the "swamp of privateness" that threatens the legitimate public good of consensual decision making. Though anthropology may be an historical construct, it and its morality of knowledge are nonetheless the best options available for responsible reflection and change.

A careful response is in order. First, one cannot say with certainty that the kind of liberation Tracy has in mind will not one day come about. Foucault's work tells us, however, that the liberation of mind and society in the West has been pursued since the nineteenth century always in conjunction with the human sciences. The management of life and the administration of bodies through techniques of the self and domination have accompanied the project of emancipating women, children, and men since the idea of "liberation" was first proposed after the collapse of the Classic episteme. Transformative praxis builds on and expands the scientific study of human beings for its success. Before theology (or any discourse) takes up the cause of such praxis, it should consider its own historico-critical roots, including its alliance with certain discursive dividing practices and normalizing technologies.

As I argued in Chapter 4, however, revisionist theology endorses existing dividing practices by assuming prevailing norms ("rubrics") for the production of true statements in any public. The idea of authentic self-transcendence is not helpful for criticizing these practices since it is identified with reflection according to these same norms (it is "disciplined"). The genealogy of dividing practices implies the surrender of the "authentic self"'s sovereignty and the relativization of anthropological discourse to the

---

[20] Though prima facie he is opposed to the perpetuation of the Modern episteme: "We will learn to overcome our needs for the anthropocentrism of historical consciousness, our entrapment in an episteme which should be allowed to die" (*AI*, 361). He then cites Foucault's genealogical method as a means of overcoming this entrapment.

emergence of "man." Unless or until revisionist theology moves from anthropology to the historico-critical analysis of "man," it will remain a humanism in the service of unrecognized technologies, endorsing the latters' divisions in the name of liberation. This implies that the Modern project is the best hope of some for the future, but necessarily at the expense of others, just as the becoming exact of the human sciences would presuppose the legitimation of certain knowledges and the subjugation of competitors.

Because true discourse is always successfully invested in power relations, Tracy's attack on reflection conducted outside the secular morality of knowledge must be viewed genealogically. Those on various "reservations of the spirit" should not be condemned out of hand; some, like Foucault, are trying to make the formation of a future "we" possible. The blackmail of the Enlightenment must be refused. The response of thinking in the modern ethos is not to endorse every "swamp of privateness" nor wage war against every effect of biopower. *Debemus distinguere*, as Tracy says (*AI*, 77). But the modern ethos denies that the public realm is a space free of power or that thinking according to publically available norms is a guarantee that truth is impartial. Foucault's method of historico-criticism in conjunction with local action is informed by a morality of knowledge which respects consensus as a critical principle, but not as the justification for delimiting the conditions for any rational discourse (not as a regulatory principle):

> Starting from the point where you say regulatory principle, you grant that it is indeed under its governance that the phenomenon has to be organized, within limits that may be defined by experience or context. I would say, rather, that it is perhaps a critical idea to maintain at all times: to ask oneself what proportion of nonconsensuality is implied in such a power relation, and whether that degree of nonconsensuality is necessary or not, and then one may question every power relation to that extent.[21]

Tracy's secular morality of knowledge, because it is based on the assumption that disciplined reflection leads to universally applicable rules, is unwilling to tolerate a high degree of nonconsensuality among speakers. It systematically refers claims to adjudication by institutionalized discourses. Foucault's morality of knowledge, informed by modern irony, submits the truth of all claims, including and perhaps especially those formed in human-scientific discourses, to the pragmatic test of utility for the self-tranformation of groups and individuals, in their local resistance to situations of oppression. The modern ethos accepts consensus as a critical principle in power relations. As an ironic ethos, however, the modern attitude does not accept consensus

---

[21] Michel Foucault, "Politics and Ethics: An Interview," in Paul Rabinow, ed., *The Foucault Reader* (New York: Pantheon, 1984) 379.

in situ as a foreshadowing of an ideal discourse situation beyond relations of power, nor does it permit consensus to function as a regulatory principle empowered by norms derived from the "nature" of discourse itself.

In summary, Tracy's theological anthropology and the secular morality of knowledge which support it share with Foucault's historico-critical transformation of the self and the modern ethos a commitment to the Enlightenment's "heroic" renunciation of ahistorical authorities. Revisionist theology, however, by maintaining the inevitable transcendence of the self from its concrete history, remains seriously committed to foundational metaphysics and its search for absolutes. Transformative praxis, far from being the opposite of this project, is in fact its completion. Revisionist fundamental and practical reflection move largely within the Modern episteme and remain implicitly committed to the liberation of "man" through the expansion of biopower and its human-scientific techniques.

Starting from the same Kantian point of departure, but arriving at a different position, the constructive theology of Gordon D. Kaufman is the subject of Chapters 7 and 8. Although a liberal Protestant perspective with deep roots in the Modern episteme, Kaufman's theology holds perhaps unexpected reserves for postanthropological thinking and acting. The demise of the neoorthodox standpoint, as Kaufman interprets it, provides my point of departure.

# 7

# The Situation of Contemporary Theology: Gordon Kaufman

Kaufman and Tracy share the premise that the contemporary theological scene is in disarray and that the solutions of neoorthodoxy are wholly inadequate. They likewise concur that reflection on the human as a self-transcending entity is the appropriate first step toward restoring order to theological discourse. However, the nature of human self-transcendence, in Kaufman's view, demands the application of a constructive rather than a hermeneutic method to the sources of theological reflection in language and culture. Kaufman's ideas on the anthropological basis of self-transcendence have changed from (1) an early view in *Relativism, Knowledge, and Faith* (1960) emphasizing the organic origin of consiousness in striving life and a concommitant adoption of the hermeneutics of *Verstehen*; to (2) a later view in the *Systematic Theology* (1968; rev. ed. 1978) and some essays in *God the Problem* (1972) stressing the autonomy of consciousness (the "inner self") from its body and linguistic media, and highlighting the subject's privilege of self-revelation for communication; to (3) a position in *An Essay on Theological Method* (1975; rev. ed. 1979) and his work since which returns to an emphasis on the organic and cultural context for consciousness, and appears to point toward the development of a theory of understanding consistent with his overall historicist orientation. Kaufman's initial position was developed against the background of the decline of Protestant neoorthodoxy in the late 1950s.

# Revelation and Relativism:
# Demise of the Neoorthodox Standpoint

In his 1960 publication, *Relativism, Knowledge, and Faith*, Gordon Kaufman addressed "the rootlessness and aimlessness of Western culture" (*RKF*, vii) which, he contended, had so influenced thinking in the academy, that "the capacity of the human mind actually to come to grips with the Real" was now "called into serious question" (*RKF*, viii). Relativism, "the doctrine that no absolutes exist," was paralyzing both philosophy and theology in their traditional attempts to articulate an understanding of the foundations of human existence.[1]

Three years earlier, Kaufman had observed that "interest in the philosophy of religion, quite strong some years ago, has diminished almost to a vanishing point in many theological circles."[2] This is testimony to the confidence of Protestant neoorthodox theologians that revelation (as they understood it) would continue to supply not only the object of theological reflection (scripture), but the faith and wisdom necessary to interpret it as well. The low fortunes of metaphysics in the academy only confirmed what neoorthodox thinkers believed in principle, that is, that unaided human reason was incapable of comprehending our true "nature and destiny" (Reinhold Niebuhr);[3] at best, reason could only point to its own inadequacies.

Revelation, by contrast, could remedy our partial knowledge of the common human situation precisely because revelation was self-confirming and complete unto itself.[4] Attempts to understand it differently only subordinated revelation to fallible human standards. As Karl Barth, speaking for a generation, had said:

---

[1] W.L. Reese, *Dictionary of Philosophy and Religion* (Atlantic Highlands, NJ: Humanities; Sussex, England: Harvester, 1980) 487. On the distinction between relativism and scepticism, see the editors' Introduction in Michael Krausz and Jack W. Meiland, eds., *Relativism: Cognitive and Moral* (Notre Dame/London: University of Notre Dame Press, 1982) 1–9.

[2] Gordon D. Kaufman, "Philosophy of Religion and Christian Theology," *JR* 37 (1957) 233.

[3] For Reinhold Niebuhr, true self-understanding depends on receiving God's "special revelation" of Godself as will and personality in Christ, and consequently as "the only possible ground of real individuality" among human beings: "To understand himself truly means to begin with a faith that he is understood from beyond himself, that he is known and loved of God and must find himself in terms of obedience to the divine will" (Niebuhr, *The Nature and Destiny of Man* [2 vols.; New York: Scribner's Sons, 1964] 1. 15).

[4] See Emil Brunner who states:

All that the Church proclaims and teaches is an attempt to express in human language the truth she has received. Hence the divine revelation alone is both the ground and the norm, as well as the content of her message. (*Revelation and Reason* [Philadelphia: Westminster, 1946] 3)

God's revelation has its reality and truth wholly and in every respect—
i.e., ontically and noetically—within itself. . . . Revelation is not real and
true from the standpoint of anything else, either in itself or for us. It is
so in itself, and for us through itself.[5]

Protestant theologians could afford to lose interest in the philosophy of
religion because they believed it to be not only superfluous to but dangerous
for Christian faith. By 1960, however, the picture had changed dramatically;
what Kaufman called "the problem of cognitive lostness" (ibid.) characteristic of contemporary self-understanding was no longer adequately
addressed by the neoorthodox solutions. Instead, it would become increasingly apparent that the neoorthodox were themselves "cognitively lost" in a
model of divine revelation that was neither coherent nor existentially satisfy-
ing.[6] Thus Kaufman could acknowledge the failure of neoorthodoxy to deal
conceptually with the challenge of relativism, a phenomenon of general cultural significance and not one limited to the speculations of metaphysical philosophers:

In its narrowness—more characteristic, perhaps, of his disciples than of
Barth himself—the contemporary theological temper appears to be an

---

[5] Karl Barth, *Doctrine of the Word of God* (Edinburgh: T. & T. Clark, 1936) 350. Quoted by
Kaufman, "Philosophy of Religion," 237.

[6] A good study of contemporary forms of reflection on revelation is Avery Dulles, *Models of
Revelation* (Garden City, NY: Doubleday, 1983). Dulles criticizes the neoorthodox model of
revelation ("revelation as dialectical presence") for its incoherent demand that what transcends
human forms of thought and linguistic forms can only be known in and through these very
modes:

The dialectical model raises insistently the problem of religious language. It seeks to
communicate by metaphor and paradox what lies beyond the reach of direct propositional
discourse, and thereby suggests that there are nonpropositional modes of cognition of crucial importance for theology. The rhetorical style of Barth and his associates (but especially Barth) is no mere ornament to their theology, but rather its very life and substance.
Only by means of dialectical language, these theologians hold, can one speak of the
divine without imprisoning it in human conceptual structures. . . . [But if] men and
women lack the capacity to receive the word of God, can there be revelation at all? And
if the word can be received, must it not be distinguishable from its own contradiction?
The simultaneous yes and no cannot be final. (pp. 96–97; see also 84–95, 115–28)

Other criticisms of the coherence of the neoorthodox model of revelation are found in Langdon
Gilkey, *Naming the Whirlwind* (New York: Bobbs-Merrill, 1969) 91–101; Harvey, *Historian*,
127–63; and David H. Kelsey, *The Uses of Scripture in Recent Theology* (Philadelphia: Fortress,
1975) 209. Gilkey (*Whirlwind*, 98–99, 101–4), like Kaufman (*RKF*, ix), accuses the neoorthodox theologians of an existentially untenable separation of church and world, which denies in
theory the relativity of religious claims which they, as thoughtful secular people, experienced in
fact.

almost hysterical flight from the subterranean awareness of a corrosive relativism, which is more than men can bear, to the security of a theological orthodoxy. Contemporary theology, also [i.e., with metaphysics] , is an expression of the typically modern radical doubt and anxiety about all of our knowledge. (*RKF*, ix)

# Understanding Relativism

*Clarification of the Concept*

Kaufman's attempts to think through the implications of modern relativism for Christian faith begin with his clarification of the concept of relativism itself. Kaufman argues that the experience of relativity in all areas of life, now so common, could not be brought to conceptual clarity so long as relativism remained somehow "external" to the position of the observer, who, in noting the manifest variety of beliefs as to what is good and true (often by appealing to "objective" human science), concludes that meaning and truth have only subjective validity (*RKF*, 5–14).

The conclusion's clear error, Kaufman shows, lies in its tacit assumption as a premise of the very assertion it claims to refute: that at least one statement has general validity, namely, the statement that meaning and truth have only subjective validity.[7] The external relativist cannot account for her or his own standpoint in making a claim to truth. As Kaufman observes, all

---

[7] Harvey (*Historian*, 205, 229–30) claims that "Hard Perspectivism" (external relativism in historical studies) has influenced much Protestant theology and New Testament scholarship of recent decades Neo-orthodox theologians and their historian counterparts argue that because historical judgments are selective and socio-culturally relative, truth is not attainable within the morality of historical knowledge; rather, the traditional morality, with its theological dialectic of historical and existential "questions" and revealed "answers," remains the appropriate morality for genuinely Christian reflection. This view, which pits history against truth, assumes that historical knowledge inevitably involves distortion of the way things "really happened," the way known to an ideal observer which faith names "God." But as Harvey points out, the Hard Perspectivist theory of history assumed by theologians like Alan Richardson only avoids the question of what standards are available to us as temporal knowers and doers:

> The issue is not whether historians are to be compared with an omniscient divine observer, but whether *within* the limits of human observation, which is necessarily selective, there are some standards for judging the degree of arbitrariness of selection and for adjudicating historical disputes (p. 209).

Kaufman, in his discussion of the task of theology, concurs, noting, "Our theological work has to be understood . . . entirely in terms of what we can do on the basis of what is available to us" (*ETM*, 3). What is not available to us, in Kaufman's opinion, is "raw, preconceptual, prelinguistic experience" (*ETM*, 6) of the divine, which might somehow amount to a conferral of the ideal observer's perspective on a person or community.

external "relativistic theories presuppose the very concept of objective validity which they allegedly destroy, and without such presupposition they lose all meaning" (*RKF*, 9).

Internal relativism, by contrast, does not deny the notion of objectively valid knowledge, and may therefore consistently assume it as a premise. It does argue that what passes for the objectively valid, the so-called facts of history, "are really functions of the point of view from which they are apprehended" (*RKF*, 19). The internal relativist understands that the perception of diversity does not imply the relativity of truth, only the relativity of the norms of evaluation the investigator assumes.

Kaufman argues that the concept of internal relativism "grows out of the investigator's attempt to 'get inside' the strange culture, or historical period, or person" (*RKF*, 15) by an act of sympathetic imagination, in order to overcome that strangeness by making the foreign perspective (at least momentarily) one's own. Internal relativism, as Kaufman presents it, relies for its coherence on the theory of understanding developed by Schleiermacher and Dilthey, and "rationalized" in the twentieth century by R. G. Collingwood, which makes successful understanding (*Verstehen*) contingent upon some kind of valid reenacting or reexperiencing (*nacherleben*) of the historical circumstances, experiences, or thought processes contributing to the production of the standpoint in question.[8] A valid reenactment is one in which the

---

[8] Cf. Friedrich Schleiermacher, *Hermeneutics: The Handwritten Manuscripts* (Missoula, MT.: Scholars, 1977), esp. 116–51 elucidating the "grammatical" and "technical" sides of interpretation, and 150–51 on the "comparative" and "divinatory" methods within understanding; Dilthey, *Dilthey: Selected Writings* (Cambridge: Cambridge University Press, 1976) 88–97, on the mental basis of the human sciences and the methods of *Verstehen*; idem, *Pattern and Meaning in History* (New York: Harper & Row, 1961) 64–168, esp. 113–32 on "The Understanding of Others and the Objective World"; R. G. Collingwood, *The Idea of History* (London: Oxford University Press, 1956) 205–334, esp. 282–302 on "History as Re-enactment of Past Experiences." On the use of *Verstehen* in the social sciences, see the bibliography of classic sources in Theodore Abel, "The Operation Called *Verstehen*," as well as the article itself, in Fred Dallmayr and Thomas McCarthy, eds., *Understanding and Social Inquiry* (Notre Dame/London: University of Notre Dame Press, 1977) 81–92, esp. 91 n. 6.

The interested reader is invited to consult the relevant primary material in Gadamer, *Truth and Method*, esp. 153–341, and the appendix, "Hermeneutics and Historicism," pp. 490–91 (the latter includes Gadamer's response to Italian theorist Emilio Betti); and Habermas, *Knowledge*, esp. 140–86, 301–17. The history of Western hermeneutic theory, with particular attention to the modern Continental tradition, is ably recounted in Richard E. Palmer, *Hermeneutics: Interpretation Theory in Schleiermacher, Dilthey, Heidegger, and Gadamer* (Evanston, IL: Northwestern University Press, 1969). A more ambitious work seeking to elucidate hermeneutics as "method, philosophy and critique" is Josef Bleicher, *Contemporary Hermeneutics* (London/Boston: Routledge and Kegan Paul, 1980). Finally, the study of John B. Thompson, *Critical Hermeneutics* (Cambridge: Cambridge University Press, 1981), represents the continuing trend toward dialogue between post-Gadamerian hermeneutics (in this case, the hermeneutic phenomenology of Paul Ricoeur) and the critical social theory of Habermas.

investigator succeeds in perceiving reality according to the norms of the previously odd perspective (ibid.); indeed, according to Kaufman, only a valid
reenactment constitutes genuine understanding:

> Only by thus getting inside the situation is it possible to see what in fact
> the other man saw, to understand with what questions and problems he
> was attempting to deal, and therefore to understand why he gave the
> answers to those questions which he actually gave. (*RKF*, 17)

The relativization of all objectively valid knowledge in terms of reexperien-
cable historical and psychological conditions, effectively exposes the naïveté
of external relativism toward the context of its own assumedly neutral standpoint. At the same time, however, the problem of the standpoint returns, like
the broom of the sorcerer's apprentice, as the number of possible valid stand-
points becomes limited only by, on the one hand, the sum of significant
events as determined by historical and human-scientific research; and, on the
other, by the power of the investigator's imagination to place her or him in
the situation of the original author or actor, thereby experiencing personally
the normativity of the norms of the perspective.

## True Relative Judgments

For Kaufman, as a theologian in the hermeneutic tradition of Schleiermacher and Dilthey, the problem of relativism is a natural consequence of
our ability to adopt multiple perspectives as our own, while nevertheless "in
pursuit of the truth":

> Relativism arises because we are able to be historians who can sym-
> pathetically appreciate and interpret the thought of men with standpoints
> different from our own . . . the problem of the standpoint comes to light
> as a significant problem only because we find ourselves already seeing
> the possibility of differing standpoints in the pursuit of truth. (*RKF*,
> 21–22)

The proliferation of radically different perspectives (Tracy's "buzzing,
blooming confusion"), all valid from the standpoint of the sympathetic interpreter, yet only some or one of which may ultimately be "true," raises two
important and related questions for Kaufman's theology:

> (a) How can we understand this fact that Truth Itself appears different
> when seen from different points of view? and (b) Is there any perspective
> which *really* reveals the Truth and in terms of which others, therefore,
> can be evaluated? (*RKF*, 19).

Kaufman's distinction between valid and true perspectives is much like Tracy's recognition that the meaning and meaningfulness of a cognitive claim must be distinguished from the claim's truth. For Tracy, the validity of a perspective is established if it allows the formation of statements which are internally coherent (meaning bearing) and reveal something about the speaker (are meaningful):

> A particular experience or language is "meaningful" when it discloses an authentic dimension of our experience as selves. It has "meaning" when its cognitive claims can be expressed conceptually with internal coherence. (*BRO*, 71)

A true "experience or language" is something altogether different: it is one whose "adequacy to experience" can be established in "transcendental or metaphysical analysis . . . by explicating how a particular concept (e.g., time, space, self, or God) functions as a fundamental 'belief' or 'condition of possibility' of all our experience" (ibid.).

It is clear that both Kaufman and Tracy reject the notion that every valid perspective is a true one. Kaufman's work in *Relativism, Knowledge, and Faith*, attempts to refute the assertion that the relativity of the conditions of truth's appearance implies the relativity of truth itself. Tracy, in *The Analogical Imagination*, and elsewhere, makes a similar argument in his appeal for the recognition of the public character of theological discourse, and for the rejection by theologians of the "swamp of privateness" into which the dogma of external relativism is leading them.

Convinced that claims to truth and meaning have only subjective validity for the person or class asserting them, the external relativist, we may infer, easily retires to "reservations of the spirit" where every valid position is true and pleasures of the mind are harmlessly pursued for their own sake (*AI*, 8–9). Not so for the responsible pluralist and internal relativist.

Gordon Kaufman's clear endorsement in his early work of the Schleiermacher/Dilthey tradition in hermeneutics suggests that he, too, accepts some version of the contemporary model of authentic self-transcendence. Kaufman's concern with establishing that every perspective is true when viewed from "within," is intended to prepare the way for his critique of the anthropological basis of knowledge (considered in Chapter 8; see also *RKF*, 27–86). Though by no means a complete epistemology, Kaufman's analysis attempts to establish that true judgments in history are possible when we are attentive to the norms of the present, so far as we can know them, and if we bear in mind that our judgments and norms are themselves always moving into the past and thus subject to revision in the future. As for the veracity of the norms themselves, vis-à-vis the norms of other times and perspectives, Kaufman appeals to the inevitable historicity of all thinking and the givenness of the criteria under which we evaluate at any present moment:

> We know, of course, that our work in turn will be judged and reinter-preted and changed by the work of others in the future, and we have no way of knowing what directions these reinterpretations will take; but we also know that this is the work that we must do *in terms of the norms which have been given to us.* (*RKF*, 122; my emphasis)

Thus, recalling Kaufman's earlier twofold problem we see that he repudi-ates the possibility of the One True Perspective, beyond human history, but does not for that reason reject the veracity of any responsible claim in the present. This does not imply, however, that the same model of truth is appli-cable to every claim about reality. When the referent of a statement is some object in the world, Kaufman maintains that truth lies in some correspon-dence of our idea with the "thing":

> The question of whether theological claims are *true* . . . as usually under-stood, presupposes what I have called the "perceptual model" of reality, where the correspondence of our ideas with the reals "out there" is a proper issue. It is appropriate to raise the question of truth in this form with regard to every object or quality in the world, for here we are con-cerned with the way in which one item in our conceptual scheme relates to and represents one item in what we call (also in our conceptual scheme) experience or the world. (*ETM*, 75)

Testing the truth of a claim about reality when the referent of the assertion lies "out there" in the world may require only experience and good judg-ment, or, at the limit, may demand the more refined tools of disciplined scientific analysis and criticism. For contemporary men and women (those who think within the norms of the present Western perspective), Kaufman believes that allegiance to the conclusions of science is a given, where matters of fact are involved (*GP*, 32–37).

Questions of value, however, cannot be decided by reference to

> the way things now are, but from the way they should be, the way man ought to move in order to remake them and to remake himself. . . . There must be a vision of man that goes beyond the facts and a vision of the world that transcends anything the sciences can describe, and these visions and values provide the bases for man's continuous active move-ment into the future. (*GP*, 33)

## Truth Tests for Higher-Order Concepts

Testing a value claim, unlike testing an empirical truth claim, means judging the assertion according to criteria, standards, and norms drawn from an ideal picture ("vision") of the world and the human. Kaufman believes that the image and concept of God presented in the Western religious and philosophical traditions complete this picture of the final framework of valuation:

> Whatever else the doctrine of God is about, it certainly is about that ultimate norm or standard in terms of which every given cultural situation or complex of facts, value, and meaning can be criticized, transcended, and transformed. (Ibid.).

As the doctrine of an ideal entity, the Christian understanding of God is no theory whose truth or falsity can be established either by subjective experience or subtle scientific investigation. This is why the correspondence notion of truth is an inapplicable model for the decision of theological claims: God, for Kaufman, is not a proper object or person or "Other" of experience. "God," and related higher-order concepts "world" and "self," have no referents in ordinary experience, but (as we shall see in Chapter 8) are built up from our encounters with external nature and the self-objectification of persons in language, as ever-more-comprehensive frameworks of meaning:

> The concepts of highest generality with which the metaphysician is principally concerned are all cases imaginatively constructed on the basis of models or metaphors drawn from ordinary experience but now used in quite extraordinary ways to develop an overall conceptual structure within which all else can be understood. (*TI*, 248)

These frameworks are, to the findings of science, interpretive grids: Foucaultian *dispositifs*. Theology, for instance, "will attempt to grasp the facts about human life as set out in [scientific studies of religion], together with the other social and human sciences, and give those facts a theological interpretation" (*GP*, 32). Such interpretation for Kaufman is no mere sentimentalizing of "hard data," but rather the completion of a cognitive "map" (perhaps by "drawing the boundaries" of the "terrain") which does "justice to certain features of experience in a way that mere phenomenological description can never achieve" (*GP*, 33).

If a correspondence model is inappropriate for determining the truth of a theological claim, what model should one employ? Kaufman clearly states that "only criteria of coherence and pragmatic usefulness to human life are relevant and applicable" in this regard (*ETM*, 75). A model of fitness of theological construct with authentically human goals and projects is (for

Kaufman) the only model available to those aware of the perspectival nature of their knowledge, who are nevertheless moving always into a future constructed in large part by their own efforts. Theological statements are constructs, not reflections, of an ideal state of human affairs which allow for the humane interpretation of presently available facts and circumstances. A theological statement is true insofar as it conduces to the realization of this state of affairs; that is, a theological perspective is true if it

> holds within it greater likelihood than any other for opening up the future into which humankind is moving . . . making available new possibilities, raising new hopes, enabling men and women to move to new levels of humanness and humaneness, instead of closing off options and restricting or inhibiting growth into a fuller humanity. (*ETM*, 75)

The verification of theological assertions, similarly,

> will be found in the degree to which individuals and communities—as they attempt to order their existence "under God"—actually find new life, genuine fulfillment, their own humanity (i.e., what has traditionally been called "salvation"). (*ETM*, 76)

Our inability as historical beings to "check" our conceptions of self, world, and God with things "out there" leads Kaufman to the following conclusion:

> Thus a theological construct may be regarded as true—in the only sense of "true" properly applicable here—if it in fact leads to fruitful life, in the broadest and fullest and most comprehensive sense possible. . . . The only test we can apply is to see how satisfactorily these ideas do the intellectual and cultural work for which they have been constructed. (Ibid.)

"The criteria for assessing theological claims," Kaufman states, "turn out in the last analysis . . . to be pragmatic and humanistic" (ibid.; see also *GP*, 98 – 109).

The foregoing has been a general description of an appropriate model of truth for criticizing claims concerning higher-order concepts. I have not tried to show why Kaufman believes three such concepts—"self," "world," and "God"—cannot have referents in experience;[9] nor what precisely distinguishes the three; nor how they are related in Kaufman's idea of the

---

[9] Other higher-order concepts for the whole of reality, e.g., include "being," "nature," "events," and "experience" (*TI*, 248). The concepts "nature," "being," and "life," Kaufman elsewhere speculates, could possibly assume the functions of "God" if that symbol became inadequate (*ETM*, 17).

theological enterprise. I have only attempted to indicate that the problem of relativism, for Kaufman, cannot be settled by appeal to some dimension or object of experience itself (which is intrinsically perspectival), but must look instead for its possible solution to certain ideal, fundamentally humane entities that conceptually enframe some or all perspectives: the subject's own variety of otherwise disparate experiences ("self"); the unified totality of all possible perspectives ("world"); and that which "limits and relativizes" (*ETM*, 46) the world and our perspectives on it ("God"; *TI*, 63–67, 242–49). The truth of a metaphysical or theological proposition rests, Kaufman claims, in its utility for more fully organizing, under higher-order concepts like these, our various activities (memories, plans, facts, values, etc.; see, e.g., *RKF*, 115–16, *TI*, 255–57).

To summarize: internal relativism reveals that the validity of a perspective is a function of its intrinsic norms. These same norms provide in any particular perspective the criteria for the determination of the truth of an assertion. For contemporary Western people, at least, the truth of matters of fact is subject to the methods and conclusions of science. The truth of theological claims, as claims about an ideal state of human affairs, depends on the fitness of the assertions to act as an interpretive grid for situations ("facts") in the present, so that present situations and facts can be transformed by the value of humaneness into a better future.[10] A true theological statement, for Kaufman, adapts reality—both facts and values—to reality's ideal conditions better than competing claims do.

We will now turn to Kaufman's analysis of "God" to see why he believes theological construction to be contemporary theology's proper task; how this scheme is distinct from experiential and interpretive projects; and why he thinks theological construction is responsible to publically available norms.

---

[10] It may be objected that I misrepresent Kaufman in taking him to say that theological claims are claims about an ideal state of human affairs, since he himself defines the theological task as reflection on the concept of God (*ETM*,16 and passim). This objection would be true if Kaufman held theology to have but two moments: the construction of "world" and "God" (*ETM*, 43–58). However, I am justified in ascribing to Kaufman the belief that theology properly makes claims about an ideal human realm because he clearly regards theology's *terminus ad quem* to be the reformulation of "world," "so as to 'fit' intelligibly with the God who is thought to be its ultimate ground and limit" (*ETM*, 59). The addition of this "third moment of construction" completes the theological operation. Since it is to this end that all contemporary theology should aim (when it realizes its constructive nature), I believe my characterization of Kaufman's view of theology's "proper business" to be a fair one.

# Theology as Construction

*The "Real God" beyond Relativism*

Kaufman believes that the purpose of higher-order concepts in the discourses of metaphysics and theology is the rationalization of experience, so as to enable and facilitate the humane transformation of our words and actions themselves (*TI*, 278). In the instance of "God," the concept refers to an ideal entity which is beyond all perspectives but is nevertheless related to every perspective. How this is so can be briefly described.

First, because "God" refers to the absolutely transcendent, its referent alone is beyond the conditions of relative knowledge. If God is somehow accessible to us, this point of reference can perform unique critical tasks pertaining to the arbitration of finite truth and value claims:

> Men are condemned to fatally nihilistic relativisms by their perspectival condition, or to imperialisms that impudently judge all other perspectives in terms derived simply from their own, if there is no point of reference beyond all perspectival meanings and values that relativizes them all. Such an ultimate point of reference, transcending every finite position and thus making it possible to judge and criticize them all, is what the word "God" denotes. (*GP*, 33–34)

Second, whether or not God is so available to us, we are compelled to acknowledge the necessity of postulating God to account for the synthetic nature of human experience:

> This idea of an ultimate reference point (whether conceived as "God" or in some other way) is no optional or dispensable one. All experience involves the unification of plurality and thus presupposes (at least implicitly) some ultimate ground. (*ETM*, 12)

The range of this experience is not limited to speculative or moral knowledge, but extends to every domain of our involvement with reality: "The term 'God,' then, is typically taken to stand for or name the ultimate point of reference or orientation for all life, action, devotion, reflection" (*ETM*, 13).

Though in themselves the attributes of God which place God beyond relativism (aseity, absoluteness, sovereignty, etc.) serve only to accentuate the transcendence of the deity, considered from the perspective of a critique of human experience, these same marks of God reveal a distinct purposiveness toward the finite. The concept "God," as Kaufman understands it, describes an entity with humane intentions toward finite reality, but is not itself a part of this reality: "The genius of the word 'God' is that it unites the relativizing and the humanizing motifs and holds them together in one concept'' (*ETM*, 56).

If the transcendence of God is a condition of the possibility of God's humanization of the finite, in no way can this transcendence be compromised by theologians. Kaufman clearly rejects ''religious experience'' which would claim a prelinguistic intuition, sensation, or insight into the divine as a possible basis for theological reflection (*ETM*, 4–8). As ultimate reality, God is never a potential experience, object or person of experience:

> The real God always transcends and escapes our grasp; whenever we suppose that God has become directly available to us or is in some way (even intellectually) disposable by us, we can be certain it is an idol with which we have to do and not God. (*ETM*, 52)

God is properly conceived of as the Ultimate Limit of our experiences. Talk about God begins when we reflect on ''certain features of our experience'' which ''force us up against the limit(s) of all possible experience'' (*GP*, 49). All experience includes, inevitably, opposition to the striving of the self which is manifested in the self as a sense of limitation. Limitations are organic, physical, personal, or normative (*GP*, 56). The self abstracts from its particular experiences of limitation and gradually builds a concept of a final limitation, corresponding to its idea of itself as an intrinsically limited, or finite, self (*GP*, 58, n. 15). Without this self-construction, achieved gradually through reflection on immediate experiences of limitation, Kaufman emphasizes that we would never have an awareness of ourselves as radically contingent beings:

> All that we ever experience directly are particular events of suffering, death (of others), joy, peace, and so forth. It is only in *reflection upon these* and the attempt to *understand ourselves in the light of these happenings* that we become aware of our limitedness on all sides. . . . this ''experience'' of radical contingency is not an *immediate* awareness of restriction . . . it depends rather upon a generalization from such occasional immediate experiences of limitation to the total situation of the self. (*GP*, 53)

Kaufman holds that peak experiences and boundary situations do not immediately relate the human to its ground ''God,'' *pace* Tracy, but only serve as occasions, albeit important ones, for doing the kind of complex organizing that yields images or pictures of the self in relation to its Ultimate Limit:

> Thus, the so-called experience of finitude or contingency, however powerful the emotions that accompany and deepen and reinforce it, has

an intellectual root, and it is possible only because man is a reflective being. (Ibid.)

"Limit means *limit*" (*GP*, 50): the real God always transcends our awareness. God should not be thought of as an experiencable "limit-of" our experiences.

Neither should the transcendence of God be conceived on the model of a goal or terminus of finite human transcendence. Since we have ruled out the possibility of attaining insight into the divine self or plan at any given moment, our own constant and progressive efforts to rationalize events should not be mistaken for learning more about the referent of "God," that is, Godself. With Barth and against proponents of natural theology, Kaufman rejects any suggestion that the striving of the human mind or spirit to transcend its present state is directed toward a synopsis or perspective on reality which, at the limit, would be identical with the God's Eye View itself:

> With teleological transcendence the fittingness or correspondence of the transcendent goal to the striving of the finite self is always implied, and with it a certain proportionality between the experienced finite order and the Infinite. (*GP*, 80–81)

The absolute transcendence attributed to God is not a possible future for finite striving; this is the case for both humanity's collective rationalization of experience (history) and for the individual's transcendence of limits. Because there cannot be a final synonymity of the concept of God and the idea of the human, the question of relativism does not await its answer in a resolution of the "real" and "available" God.

The "real God," or object of theological discourse, is inaccessible to human reason and sensitivity. If and when we speak of God it must be through those linguistic forms which make the God-concept "available" for its proper critical and regulatory tasks. The "available God," as Kaufman terms it, comes to us primarily in the monotheistic religious traditions. As such, it is part and parcel with all historical knowledge and thus subject to its constraints. The "real God," on the other hand, as the ultimately transcendent, is by definition not present in the words and symbols of the traditions. Even when "God" performs humanizing functions, it remains the concept of the ground of experience, not some being *in* experience or *all* experiences taken together, that is, "history" (*GP*, 82–115, esp. 84–100).

## The "Available God" for Theology

The foregoing reveals that God is not available for theological reflection in at least two ways. Epistemologically, "God" is a higher-order concept which performs interpretive functions for experience, but cannot itself be instanciated in experience. Analytically, "God" refers to the ultimate point of reference for human life, beyond relativism, and thus not available to the historically conditioned categories of finite consciousness. The first distinction separates "God" from all empirical concepts and places it among "self," "world," "being," "nature," et al. The second raises "God" above all the preceding notions in so far as these ideas do not refer to the ultimately Real, the final point of orientation.

Given the limits set down or implied by the above, it is not surprising that Kaufman understands theology to begin in the more mundane and circumscribed realm of language, and "ordinary language" at that. Kaufman strongly argues that theological and strictly religious language is parasitical on the events, meanings, and terms of everyday life. These happenings and their significations are not bound to one social locale, or "public" (Tracy), but occur within and across many and varied contexts. As Kaufman observes, "Theological terms and concepts are rooted in the wide experience and history of a whole culture, or a mixture of cultures" (*ETM*, 3).

Consequently, no one public is a privileged interpreter of the theological vocabulary, even though scripture is the chief source of so-called religious language, and the church has traditionally assumed itself to be scripture's authoritative and sufficient interpreter. Arguing that the "entire vocabulary of the church—including such central terms as God, man, church, reconciliation, prayer, faith—consists of ordinary words from the everyday language of people" (ibid.), Kaufman rejects appeals to "particular traditions and special communities of interpretation" (ibid.) in determining theology's point of departure.

The distinctiveness of Kaufman's approach may be brought out by comparing it with Tracy's modus operandi in systematics.[11] The latter begins by

[11] Tracy accuses Kaufman of assuming without argument that "church traditions are by definition particularist" (*AI*, 92, n. 77) in their interpretation of tradition and its scripture. In contrast, Tracy claims to argue that traditions and texts can possess a universal appeal which need not be compromised by a specifically ecclesial hermeneutic (*AI*, 68). Tracy's objection is particularly directed to *ETM*, 8, where Kaufman appears to identify "special technical meanings" with meanings decreed by "the authority of scripture or church pronouncement," and the meaning of "ordinary language" with that of the "common language in the societies and cultures where church and scripture are found." Kaufman assumes that discourse in the church is conducted according to the traditional morality of knowledge. Tracy clearly believes church

arguing for the specificity of the discourse conducted in one region, the church, and then proceeds "outward," as it were, to convince the reader that this discourse is truly "public" (potentially meaningful and true for any competent communicator). Kaufman, conversely, begins by postulating a discourse common to all competent communicators in a language ("ordinary-language users"), and so presumably the most genuinely "public" discourse, and then moving "inward," into that language to construct a specifically theological discourse using certain key terms of the public vocabulary as "raw materials." That the majority of these words (like "God," "soul," "world," etc.) also form the root metaphors of Tracy's specifically ecclesial public has no special importance for Kaufman so far as his methodological principles are concerned. It is potentially useful or fruitful that "the theological vocabulary is an organic whole" (*ETM*, 9) of secondary and tertiary terms explaining and interpreting "God," and that this unified network should coincide with the discourse spoken in Tracy's church-public; but neither of these facts, for Kaufman, tells us anything about how they should be interpreted. Nor does any part of this vocabulary whole—not word, sentence, or text—contain an immanent principle of interpretation. The truth of a theological claim remains its fitness for human service, not in any occult significance which clever exegesis of, or faithful attendance to, a sacred text can disclose. For Kaufman, the church-public is not a privileged interpreter of its traditional sources; nor do the scriptures interpret themselves:

> Doubtless both the Bible and the creeds are relevant and important for understanding the image/concept of God and for judging what are proper, and what improper, uses or formulations of that symbol, but it is their utility for getting at the image/concept of God that gives the Bible and the creeds their importance for theology, not the other way around. (*TI*, 265)

Kaufman's clear rejection of textual hermeneutics as the proper task of theology does not imply his denial of the importance of scriptural interpretation for making present the "available God": he intends only to subordinate this explicitly hermeneutic work to a preeminent operation he calls "construction." Thus he defines the nature of theology as follows: "The proper business of theology (*theos-logos*) is the analysis, criticism, and reconstruction of the image/concept of God" (ibid.). This view of theology has been distinguished from its rivals by Kaufman himself in his analysis of the three

---

discourse can take place in accordance with genuinely secular (public) norms, and firmly believes that the onus is on Kaufman to show that it cannot.

orders of past and present theology. It is to Kaufman's own location of his theological work that I turn for my next set of observations.

## Constructing toward God

Kaufman understands first-order theology to be any theology whose practitioners believe themselves to be charged with the task of creating a picture of God, humanity, and the world which is as accurate as possible to the way these things are in themselves (*ETM*, 37). It is representational theology in the strict sense of attempting to provide, primarily for a community of devotees, exact descriptions of the objects of its discourse.

Theology of this kind "originated in the myth-making activities of primitive men and women" in their search to find "orientation for life" (ibid.). These primitive peoples did not clearly distinguish between themselves and the world, and so could not recognize the largely constructive nature of their thinking. Rather, they believed that the heightened sense of order their myths and symbols , rituals and theologies, gave to their lives was in fact due to the presence of God among them; it became the task of theological reflection to understand that presence and communicate its implications for the community. First-order theology has a long history in the West, a history ended in some quarters of academia and society by the Enlightenment and Kant's turn to the subject. Theological discourse in the church has been less affected, and much conversation in both Protestant and Roman Catholic communities remains first order in its theological assumptions.

Second-order theology proceeds "when awareness arises that theological concepts are fundamentally imaginative constructs rather than abstractions or generalizations or deductions from percepts" (ibid.). Theologians working at this level recognize, as a matter of principle and method, that they do not have access to the referents of their discourse, that the words "God," "soul," "human," and the rest of the theological vocabulary do not admit of instanciation in experience; thus, no theology can claim to describe these things more accurately than another.

Given this, the question of appropriate criteria for reflection assumes paramount importance, since without standards, continued conversation about God is at best subjectively valid. For Kaufman, such criteria must be framed on the basis of a revised anthropology, a constructive one acknowledging the contingency of the validity and truth of the statements produced on its foundations. For the philosophical theologian, establishing this anthropology, which is both thoroughly "historicist" and capable of addressing traditional theological concerns, is a prerequisite for attending to the more abstruse, technical vocabulary of the church:

> The theologian will now [in the second order] be engaged in exploring the character and details of one or more of the great theological schemas known to him or her, attempting to see what functions they perform, seeking to understand what significance or value for human life they may have, trying to grasp why they have been created, and whether, or in what respects, they ought to be retained. (*ETM*, 38)

The experience of contingency informing the work of second-order theologians is shared by their nonprofessional contemporaries. This shared cultural experience of many possible valid perspectives precedes second-order theology; or, as Kaufman states, it is "in this pluralistic and relativistic consciousness" that such reflection "becomes a possibility" (ibid.).

Kaufman believes most theological work today is second order. The challenge for the discipline is to move beyond the "chaos of conflicting claims and criteria" (*ETM*, 39) endemic to second-order reflection, while retaining methodologically its "analytic and descriptive functions" (*ETM*, 38) in religious symbol systems and language. That toward which theology should move, in Kaufman's view, is the conscious construction of the concept "God" and related ideas and images.

The attempt "deliberately to formulate theological conceptions and to create theological symbols" (*ETM*, 39) should henceforth take precedence over all strictly hermeneutic, analytic and descriptive projects in theology. The purpose of "constructing toward God" (*TI*, 12), as Kaufman now calls theology's task, is to enable contemporary people "once again to see their world, and themselves in that world, as ultimately under a purposeful and humane order" (*ETM*, 39). Theology practiced in this fashion and for this purpose would be third-order theology.

Kaufman's own scheme for the construction of "God" calls for the logically successive articulation of meaningful visions of the whole of reality ("world"); that which transcends and unifies reality ("God"); and reality transformed by the wholly transcendent ("world under God"). The order of construction reflects Kaufman's theory of the three moments of theological construction (*ETM*, 43–73).

In the first moment, analysis of "world" reveals it to be a higher-order concept representing the idea of nothing less than "the whole of reality" (*ETM*, 44). "Whole" refers to "the unified structure of parts . . . that which enables us to think this multiplicity as a unity" (ibid.). Unlike those unified structures we experience in everyday life ("things"), the referent of "world" is never directly accessible to us. "World" is a regulative, not constitutive, idea for our relations with things and people. It provides the ideational context for conceiving of these entities as bearing real relations with one another. Unified structures (empirical wholes) are not in the world like marbles in a bag: the idea of the world, Kaufman claims, is just the idea of that "by means of which we order and hold together the multifarious dimensions of experience in a unified whole" (ibid.). Discourse about "the world" is a *dispositif* for these multifarious dimensions.

Recalling the two ways in which "God" is, on Kaufman's analysis, unavailable for reflection, we may make a similar point concerning "world." Epistemologically, "world" is a higher-order concept performing key functions for experience, but cannot itself be instanciated in experience. Analytically, "world" refers to an entity (usually nonpersonal) which is the penultimate point of reference for human life, the delimiting context for all human acts, and so not available in any one  act of historically conditioned reflection.[12] The second point is expressed by Kaufman on an analogy with our experience of horizons:

> We never, in fact, know reality as a whole, nor can we clearly conceive what we might mean by that. The whole (the world) is a limiting idea, a forever receding (and approaching) horizon which appears to surround us but which we can never reach. (*ETM*, 45)

Kaufman emphasizes that the construction of all concepts in the theological vocabulary (including "world") is not a scholastic exercise. When, at the first moment, metaphysics sets out to describe the world, it must follow the criterion of accounting for all aspects and dimensions of experience. Metaphysics

> is no mere speculative game; it is an attempt to articulate an intuition or understanding of what, finally, is real. . . . It is in and through the metaphysical moment underlying theological construction . . . that contact with our sense of what is real and genuine and true is made. (*ETM*, 47–48)

The second moment of construction generates the concept of God. Though this concept is unnecessary to a purely naturalistic view of "world," to a monotheistic view (a tradition shaped in and by the language of

---

[12] I said above that Kaufman's analysis places the referent of "God" outside history, "beyond relativism." Is that of "world" also "beyond relativism?" On the one hand, relativism appears as a phenomenon within world history, in many forms, since the Greek sceptics and sophists. Its resolution today in favor of order would be another "world event." However, in another sense, the debate about relativism is a debate on the orderliness of reality itself; on whether or not what Heidegger called the "worldhood of the world" is a contingency of modern thinking. (Early Heidegger, at least, clearly thought it was not.) As such, the debate concerns the reality of the referent of metaphysical discourse: have we, all of us, a world in common or not? This debate continues the West's systematic dissolutión, or "deconstruction," of its chief higher-order concepts.

monotheism) the concept "God," Kaufman argues, is indispensable. In the West, the world is thought to achieve its meaning only in contradistinction to something lying beyond it, which functions for the world as its ground. "God" refers to that which relativizes the concept of the world, "thus destroying its absoluteness and finality" (*ETM*, 45). At the same time, Western metaphors conceive of God's relation to the world as radically asymmetrical, with God as the world's creator and conserver, the world's "final cause." Kaufman's analysis reveals that although materially God's role as creator and ground of the world makes God logically prior to the world, formally it is the concept of "world" which precedes "God," since God is only available to us insofar as "God" performs critical and nomic functions on the world; if "world" is not adequately constructed, there can be nothing to be relativized and grounded. This is why in third-order theology, the order of theological construction assigns construction of "world" before "God."

In the second moment, imaginative construction of "God" observes the criterion of ultimate relativization of the world. Already, however, analysis of Western religious language reveals a comportment predicated on the referent of "God" which is decidedly personal and compassionate. Thus, construction of the ultimate relativizer obeys, as a second criterion, the requirement of humanization:

> The fundamental model or "root metaphor" on the basis of which the concept of God is constructed and unified must make intelligible the ascription of moral, intellectual and other humane concerns to him—at least sufficiently to enable God to be the ultimate point of reference for our full human life. (*ETM*, 55)

The criterion of humanization causes us to focus our attention on those linguistic resources which symbolize both our hope for a more humane existence and our faith in the correspondence of this hope to a tendency or thrust toward humanization on the part of reality itself:

> "God" is the personifying symbol of that cosmic activity which has created our humanity and continues to press for its full realization . . . ["God"] represents with great vividness and power the fact that we are created, sustained, and fulfilled as human and humane, not by our efforts alone, but from beyond ourselves, from resources in the ultimate nature of things. (*TI*, 50–51)

Ironically, for the realization of this humanization to come about, we must look beyond ourselves in devotion to that which we are not and cannot become.[13] The criterion of relativization remains a necessary condition for valid theological construction, since, when coupled with that of humanization, it allows for the imagining of images which subordinate our wills while perfecting them. Absoluteness and humanization exist as motifs in tension in the concept of God (*ETM*, 56).

The two criteria described above (relativization and humanization) are joined by a third: presence. The goal of imaginative construction in theology is "to present the Real with which humans have to do":

> If a theological construct does not convey a sense of the hardness and firmness of the real, but seems a mere speculative exercise, it fails to be representing God in any way that he can be acknowledged as the one to be worshipped and served. A God who cannot be grasped as the center of orientation for life is not God at all: such theological construction is a failure. (*ETM*, 58)

By placing the criterion of presence alongside those of relativization and humanization (*TI*, 272), Kaufman suggests that the concept of God's presence is to function in construction in a fashion analogous to the aforementioned two concepts; that is, in a regulative not constitutive manner for our experiences. This concept Kaufman has previously described as the idea of oneself living in an ultimately "purposeful and humane order" (*ETM*, 39). Constructing the concept of God's presence, therefore, returns our attention to the world, conceived of both as the abstract whole of reality, and as our present symbolic universe.

The third and final moment of theological construction reconceives the world, as constructed in moment one, both formally and materially. Formally, our construction of "God" at moment three denies "world" its previous coherence, as the concept of the whole of reality, and affirms a new definition of the concept in relation to "God." As Kaufman states:

> The world is no longer to be conceived simply as the autonomous and self-determining whole of Reality . . . the world is now at best the whole of *finite* reality, of creation; and it must be conceived as relativized in all respects . . . by the ultimate Reality, God, which is to be distinguished from it. (*ETM*, 59)

Materially, the reconstruction of "world" is the deconstruction (by available tools of criticism) and rebuilding of our words and images of the world. Here

---

[13] "We need a center of devotion outside the self, a center powerful enough to draw the self out of its own narcissism, if our self-centeredness and anthropocenteredness are to be overcome. The symbol 'God' can provide such a focus" (*TI*, 187).

the criterion of humanization appears to come to the fore, as the theologian, drawing from the full range of linguistic and imagistic resources present in culture, "thinks the negative" in the status quo, and creates an imaginative picture of this faulted world transformed by the concept of God.[14] It is at this, the third moment of construction, that introduction of "theological terms and concepts" is warranted, insofar as these symbols facilitate our "attempt to grasp and interpret experience and the world now no longer simply phenomenologically but theologically" (*ETM*, 64).

The goal or end of theological construction is a new symbolic world which is not only conceptually integrated (coherent) and adequate to our concepts of the ultimately relativizing and humanizing (meaningful), but a world in which the referent of these concepts—God—is present in the lives of the community's members (true). Ideally, this community is coextensive with humanity itself; the reform of the community is therefore the reconstruction of all particular cultures:

> As the truly absolute and humane One becomes the ultimate point of reference in terms of which all human life and experience is understood, all the institutions and practices and beliefs of the culture necessarily become exposed to a theological judgement on their idolatry and their inhumanity. In this way God no longer remains merely the God of the tradition but becomes the *living God* for persons living in that culture. (*TI*, 278)

## Imaginative Construction and the Modern Ethos

Kaufman, like Tracy, begins by specifying pluralism as a theological problem (the problem of relativism) and renouncing irrational, would-be authorities (neoorthodoxy) as legitimate theological solutions. Both Kaufman and Tracy invoke the public character of theological discourse as a warrant for continuing its use in contemporary conversation. I will first consider Kaufman's conception of relativism and then his understanding of theological discourse.

Foucault's archaeology of Modern "man" shows relativism to be a necessary consequence of philosophical anthropology. "Man" knows nothing of himself apart from his historical-cultural situation. His self-knowledge is

---

[14] By associating relativization with formal third-moment construction and humanization with material reconstruction, I am suggesting a merely logical relation between the members of each pair. In the actual doing of third-moment theology, the imagination varies constructs of our material world in relation to the idea of the absolute, and the idea of the ultimately humane with our notion of the world as fundamentally related to God.

positive. But he experiences his situation as norm governed, as responsible to foundations in reason. Kaufman appreciates the Modern dilemma:

> To conceive of thinking as a function only of universally true norms is to make the rationalistic error; to conceive of it as a function only of the concrete historical and psychological situation is to make the error of external relativism. (*RKF*, 20)

Kaufman's solution of internal relativism has merit in its emphasis on the historicity of systems of knowledge, as well as its usefulness for deconstructing transcendental claims about human nature:

> If the only significant thing that we can say about man's nature is that he has history, then the "nature" of man is a purely formal notion. . . . The most one could ever hope to discover would be what Collingwood has called a "relative essence" of man, an essence from one's point of view. No claims could be made that the "nature" which has been uncovered had permanent validity. (*RKF*, 128)

The "nature" addressed in contemporary reflection on the human would be correlative with the mental structures of those engaged in that same reflection, and these structures could be placed historically alongside other pictures of human being:

> If human consciousness is really in history, then the most that can be hoped from an analysis of mind by a modern Western thinker is that he might succeed in laying bare the structure of the mind of modern Western man, but it would be impossible to infer from this how far the conclusions held for man as such. (Ibid.)

Laying bare the structures of Western mind, where "mind" is conceived to include discursive practices dividing reality, is consistent with Foucault's project in *The Order of Things*. So, too, is the self-consciousness of the investigator as himself or herself involved in the historical structures observed: the recognition of the nonidentity of the "modern Western thinker" and "man as such" is preserved consistently by both Kaufman and Foucault.

However, Kaufman is willing, while Foucault is not, to defend a common basis *for this nonidentity* in certain shared features of experience, including a "biological basis" to existence and in large measure a "physical environment" (*RKF*, 129). The point of arguing for this formally common biological-environmental basis (to be discussed in more detail in Chapter 8) is to ground the emergence of consciousness in the striving of the organism (*RKF*, 30). What distinguishes humans from other entities "is the structure of consciousness and spirit that emerges out of the biological foundations and in interaction with the physical environment" (*RKF*, 129). Presumably, if this consciousness exhibits similar patterns of choice it is because the individual organisms doing the choosing have adapted in similar ways, not because underlying these behaviors are transcendental predispositions to speaking, working, or living. This dependence of consciousness and thus of culture, on the successful adaptation of the organism is a constant for Kaufman, and, at the theoretical level, ensures that no description of specific mental structures can be identified with a transcendental or "deep" reconstruction of general anthropological systems: "man as such" remains out of reach. Significantly, Foucault distinguishes between an historical archive peculiar to the West and common human nature only in order to dismiss the latter as a no-longer-useful fiction of Modern reflection, and its attempt to reconcile the two once and for all. Kaufman appears to retain the distinction as a meaningful one, while paring down "man as such" to a formal propensity for self-transcendence, evident in the organism's evolution of consciousness and (in maturity) its "quest for formulation and understanding of an ultimate point of reference" (*ETM*, 17). When Kaufman claims we can never know the human *in se*, he is talking about an inability to grasp spirit or consciousness through a description or analysis of the culturally specific constructs of mind. Kaufman avoids a recapitulation of the Modern project to the extent that he recognizes that even a formal description of the human as a self-transcending being who makes his or her world—a constructive agent—does not provide transhistorical knowledge, just another historical portrait of features of shared experience. Throughout his career, Kaufman has expressed his commitment to the historicist orientation which informs the following, and which clearly recognizes the historicity of all discourse, even that concerning historical human nature:

> The most significant thing that we can say about man's nature, then, is that it is such that man can have a history; and all understanding of man, *even the understanding of this fact about his nature*, will be a kind of historical understanding. (*RKF*, 129; my emphasis)

The present chapter suggests three areas, however, in which this commitment to the relativity of experience and knowledge to particular historical arrangements is compromised to some degree.

The first is Kaufman's embrace of the hermeneutics of *Verstehen*. He believes that understanding is only possible by "getting inside the situation" (*RKF*, 17) through the investigator's ability "sympathetically to enter into the situation which he is studying"; like an actor, "imaginatively reliving the feelings and values of another time and place" (*RKF*, 16). The transcendent nature of the imagination allows the inquirer to put him or herself in the place of others, and only through the imagination's activity can the inquirer be certain that the portrayal developed is adequate to its object.

> It is, of course, evident that the more sharply the perspective being investigated differs from one's own, the more difficult it is to apprehend it with genuine sympathy . . . it is also true that only insofar as such a sympathetic analysis and understanding is achieved do we adequately apprehend and portray the life of other peoples, whether we be psychologists, anthropologists, historians, or philosophers. (Ibid.)

The problem with this theory of understanding is that the investigator's standpoint in an historical set of circumstances is acknowledged as but a springboard for sympathetic reenactment of a different set of events: we transcend (from *transcendere*, "to climb across") our unique situation in order to grasp that of another. Foucault's historical-critical analyses of Western practices argue to the contrary that the formation of a standpoint is the precise location of an individual within discernible relations of power. Understanding and consensus are predicated on shared technologies and the parameters for self-transformation they enable. Understanding is not the imaginative reexperiencing of another's life, but the deployment of *dispositifs*, which may or may not correspond to the social practices and reflective accounts available to the foreign position. Thus, the understanding of people and events achieved by psychologists, historians, theologians, and anthropologists (and by us with their help) does not come about by leaving one standpoint for another, but by performing genealogically specific techniques of discursive formation according to the operative norms of their respective disciplines.

This genealogical objection to the hermeneutics of *Verstehen* does not deny the reality nor the ethical significance of performing acts of understanding or sympathy. It does ask that these acts remain subject to the constraints of conversation in culture when addressed at the theoretical level, rather than attributed to an anthropological capacity for self-transcendence. The morality of genealogical knowledge prohibits claims to understanding based on the transcendence of "man," and instead asks the reader to compare Dilthey's "triumph" of empathy with Delleuze's observation on "the indignity of speaking for others." Can there be an indignity in claiming to see as others see? Kaufman's theory of understanding compromises the historicity of both knower and known when it follows the anthropological presuppositions of romanticist hermeneutics (which he has never explicitly disavowed).

Kaufman's understanding of construction is a second area in which the historicity of language and culture risks compromise. On the one hand, he clearly places the imagination in a necessary context of linguistic materials bearing meanings and values, thus emphasizing the potentially local character of theological construction and its reliance on existing dividing practices for its available resources. The context of construction, its dependence on an archive or effective history to support the theologian's choices of (re)symbolization, is explicitly acknowledged in passages such as the following:

> The theologian's task of constructing a meaningful and humane world is in part the task of articulating and explicating a world already in certain respects defined in and by the culture in its religious traditions, its (conscious and unconscious) myths, its rituals and taboos, its linguistic classifications; that is, it is always based on the prior human constructive activity which produced and shaped the culture. (*ETM*, 33)

On the other hand, by failing to qualify the acceptability of romanticist hermeneutics, the constructive imagination's relationship to its materials can appear strongly unidirectional:

> Theology must conceive its work more like building a house: using materials given in experience it is in fact *constructing a world* the fundamental design of which is not found in the materials themselves but is employed to give them a significant order and meaning. (*ETM*, 28)

In the above, the mind has a formative power which the materials do not; like a builder, the mind picks and chooses according to an ideal plan, the materials are "available"; the mind gives order and meaning, the materials of culture receive this significance in new constructions of higher-order concepts.

For the modern ethos, nothing is simply "material" for the mind's projection of meaning. The "fundamental design" of one's world is given to the self by background practices organizing reality according to contingent divisions of sanity and madness, the speakable and the prohibited, competent and unqualified speakers, et al. (*AK*, 219–27). Indeed, Kaufman's work has consistently emphasized the contingency of experience. Religious experience,

> (like the rest of experience) is always a construction or composite, heavily dependent for its form and qualities on the learned terms and concepts which give it particular flavor and shape . . . it is in terms of these connections and valuations and interpretations that we focus our attention in experience, divide it up the way we do, and see in it what we can. (*ETM*, 6)

A thoroughly historicist analysis of experience, like the above, is congruent with the modern ethos and at odds with the hermeneutics of *Verstehen* and *Nacherleben*.

Kaufman's assumption of a synthesizing, or "constructing" conscious-ness remains pregenealogical to the extent that thinking stands over against the materials of culture, transcending these materials in order to rearrange them according to norms drawn from concepts reflecting universal, anthropo-logical interests. Foucault's modern ethos does not argue against construc-tion nor the materiality of discourse. Awareness that theological discourse is, like all discourse, interested, local, strategic, and of "lowly origins" must qualify future claims that theology speaks about universal interests and tran-scendental foundations, in a manner which is impartial and dialogical; from a history tracing the inexorable development of insight out of primitive ani-mism, to polytheism, and forward to monotheism and its illumination of anthropological structures.[15]

For example, the "hidden creativity" referred to below should be under-stood genealogically, as the action of individuals upon individuals, within technological boundaries for specific, local purposes, before the concept of creativity can be reconstructed by postanthropological discourse:

> There is a hidden creativity at work in the historicocultural process, and it is this which has given us the basic social and cultural structures which have actually created and continue to sustain human existence, as well as those qualities of life which we most deeply cherish. (*TNA*, 41)

When the link between creativity and technologies is not made at the start, the negative effects of biopower (like the nuclear situation Kaufman addresses) seem foreign to the constructive powers of the mind. The possi-bility of nuclear holocaust then appears as the illumination of a "paradox" into which contemporary human striving has fallen. The prospect of nuclear annihilation, Kaufman says,

> forces us to confront forthrightly the paradox of our finitude and our power, of our knowledge and our ultimate unknowing. Whereas in ear-lier generations that mystery [of our common human existence] seemed in a sense something imposed upon us from outside, something rooted in human lack of knowledge, in human weakness, today it is our own enor-mous knowledge and power which, paradoxically, we do not know how to control or properly use. (*TNA*,11)

Because "man" is both the cogito and the unthought, the mystery of his existence today is indeed revealed in the dangerous disparity between an

---

[15] See *TI*, 99 – 122 on the anthropological elaboration of "radical monotheism." Kaufman develops the analysis presented in H. Richard Niebuhr, *Radical Monotheism and Western Cul-ture* (New York: Harper & Brothers, 1960).

essential and unrestricted knowing capacity, on the one hand, and the deployment of this capacity into the unthought through the technologies of instrumental reason. The repetition of the cogito and the unthought is perpetuated not merely by the unsatisifed curiosity of depth analysts, but by a "will to know" embodied in anthropocentric practices of varying obviousness and complexity. When Kaufman, writing against anthropocentrism, attacks nationalism, the arms race, the objectification and technical exploitation of nature, and the social hegemonies of race and gender, he is arguing implicitly against the concrete arrangements of biopower the Modern episteme has sanctioned.

His theological recommendations for social reconstruction, however, remain Modern to the extent that they assume the double of the origin's retreat and return. The following is the third area in which the historicity of construction is slighted. Kaufman's reflection on "God" is at times a Foucaultian "eschatological" discourse, realizing "man"'s truth in history as the origin of his limited freedom, creativity, justice, and other virtues:

> By devoting themselves to the God who transcends both humanity and the world, humans increasingly (over time) can discipline themselves into morally responsible agents with powers of freedom and self-determination similar to God's. (*TI*, 112)

For neither Tracy nor Kaufman is the return of the origin finally to be equated with a dramatic inbreaking of "man"'s destiny into time (though Tracy's dialectic of limit experience and critique gives such inbreaking a place in Modern self-liberation). The origin is promised as the culmination of life, labor, and language, when finite experience and reflection have worked together, in the third moment of theological construction, to make the available God the real God's presence.

This will happen when our constructions of "God" have the effect of referring to "what is finally Real," to "that in terms of which we can confidently orient our lives," to what can be "grasped as the center of orientation for life" (*ETM*, 58). "Grasped" existentially, no doubt, but elusive to linguistic representation. The return of "man"'s origin coincides with the return of representation. But since representation of God is for Kaufman impossible, the origin's return is indefinitely postponed and approached by constructive reflection.

> It is important to recognize that every concept or image of God which we employ is our construct, and it suffers from whatever limitations this implies; but it is our best attempt to construct a conception of what is

finally Real, of that in terms of which we can confidently orient our lives.[16]

In short, the Real cannot be grasped within the parameters of Modern thinking without "man" ceasing to be "man." But for him to become something else, for example, the fallen soul addressed by orthodox and neoorthodox revelation, or the pure cogito of Classical reflection, is impermissible according to the secular morality of knowledge. Kaufman's analysis of the anthropocentrism informing the nuclear age, and his most recent thinking on language, representation, and being suggest that the doubles of post-Enlightenment theological anthropology are beginning to lose their hold on his imagination.[17] To the modern ethos and the ironic morality of knowledge, any move away from either representation or an analytic of finitude is potentially a move toward historical criticism and local resistance to oppressive practices, and is, for that reason, to be welcomed. The historicist orientation of Kaufman's thinking should, I have argued, lead him to reconsider the three areas of (1) romanticist hermeneutics, (2) constructive activity and its relation to an archive, and (3) the usefulness of a theological criterion of God's presence. Viewed through the grid of Foucault's analyses, the imagination does not *move across* symbols to grasp a foreign standpoint; *act upon* its archive to confer meaning; nor, finally, attempt to *complete* the archive by reconstructing elements within it.

---

[16] *ETM*, 58. The origin's retreat before the advances of biblical scholars is also the theologian's concern, since tradition "mediates" God's presence:

> There is, however, a dialectical tension between the tradition that has formed us and given us our conception of God and the *ultimacy* of this point of reference, of which we have become aware through the tradition. As theologians we necessarily dig ever deeper into our tradition that we might better grasp the God that is mediated through it. . . . The theologian must necessarily and continuously drink deeply from the Bible and the best of biblical scholarship . . . even while learning to take up a critical stance over against all of these in the name of that very God of whom they also spoke. (Gordon D. Kaufman, "Theology as a Public Vocation," in Theodore Jennings, Jr., ed., *The Vocation of the Theologian* [Philadelphia: Fortress, 1985] 61–62)

[17] Kaufman seems to be in the process of relativizing his own anthropological "foundationalism" by Nagarjuna's "two truths" doctrine. Whether this results in yet another dialectical twist in the origin double remains to be seen. Gordon D. Kaufman, " 'Two Truths' and Foundationalism," unpublished paper, 8 January 1985.

# 8

# Constructive Theology
# and Self-Transcendence

Kaufman's earliest reflections on philosophical anthropology were indebted
to a model of the self as subject of experience and knowledge. Although
never explicitly abandoned, his work after 1968 and the *Systematic Theology*
relies more heavily on a model of the self as agent, aspects of which were
already evident in *Relativism, Knowledge, and Faith*. The reason for
Kaufman's shift of anthropological models, as well as the structure of the
models themselves, will be evident I hope from the following discussion.

## The Self as Subject

### *Origin and Structure of Consciousness*

Kaufman understands the genesis of individual consciousness to occur in a
bipolar relationship between the nascent subject and the external world. The
organism itself

> is fundamentally dynamic; it drives forward and extends itself into the
> external world more or less spontaneously and naturally until it meets
> with obstacles or limitations which cause sensations of pain. With-
> drawal occurs spontaneously with the occurrence of a feeling of pain;
> attraction, with pleasure. .... The important point here is that our cogni-
> tive processes are enmeshed and intertwined from the beginning with the
> feelings and drives of the organism. (*RKF*, 30)

The experience of limitation, a consequence of frustrated intentions, is the experience on the basis of which the subject comes to awareness of some Other which thwarts these intentions, the character of the drives themselves, and the subject itself as the source of these urges. It is because of experience's essential bipolarity that the external world assumes its equally fundamental appearance of reality:

> The overwhelming conviction we have of the reality of the external world arises from the fact that our consciousness of the world is rooted in the direct and unavoidable encounter of our wills and that which restricts them. . . . We encounter the object only in its opposition to, and limitation of, our strivings. (*RKF*, 32, 34)

Kaufman's account of the ontogeny of consciousness emphasizes the role of frustrated desire in the development of personal identity. The significance of satisfied urges for this same development is discussed by Kaufman several years later in the context of an essay addressing the phenomenon of interpersonal attachment. Here Kaufman acknowledges the foundational role of successful attachment, especially in childhood, for genuine human existence:

> Particular attachments among human beings . . . are not merely expressions of our conscious interests or even our unconscious desires: they constitute the very structure of our existence to the very deepest levels of our being. Our selfhood is incorrigibly social. (*TI*, 59)

Kaufman goes on to emphasize the importance of the quality of the objective world the striving self encounters. Reality must be more than a source of frustration if the subject is to develop a healthy personality (*TI*, 59–60): it must be a trustworthy base of support for the subject's tentative formation of its conceptual identity (*TI*, 63–67).

Nevertheless, the process leading to selfhood is one of individuation of the subject from its early attachment figures (parents). The subject-object polarity remains for Kaufman the normative relation (psychologically and epistemologically) for the self and its world. The movement from attachment to autonomy is required not only by the physical maturation of the organism, but by (1) the inevitable failure of trusted figures to satisfy needs in every instance; and (2) the logic of the development of consciousness. Kaufman's anthropology brings these two conditions together.

First, the operation of consciousness requires the subject to distinguish from out of a total field of sensations one particular aspect of experience. This operation implies "an act of attention that first lifts the level of bare *Erleben* [the sensory field] into the consciousness of the polarity of subject and object" (*RKF*, 40). Along with attention, the act of consciousness presumes a faculty of imagination to ''hold'' the fleeting sensa before the mind and to ''construct'' them into a unitary mental entity:

> Through the dual activity of attention and imagination they [the sensa] become a complex product, a sensum conjoined and fused with the memory of previous sensa by the constructive power of the imagination. The level of consciousness, then, at which we first make any distinctions whatsoever, involves constructiveness on the part of the subject. (Ibid.)

The role of the constructive imagination for experience is key for Kaufman, since only through imagination can we move from perception to thought, and on (ever more inclusively) to thought about *thought* (i.e., reflection on concepts). The logic of consciousness admits of levels or stages leading from mere perception to self-consciousness to reflection on concepts of the most general reference (being itself). These ''numerous levels of consciousness,'' Kaufman states, ''emerge out of, and are superimposed on, the previous levels in ever increasing complexity'' (ibid.) through the combined work of attention, imagination, and memory.

The movement away from ''overly binding relationships with other human beings'' is, for Kaufman, ''an inevitable consequence simply of growing consciousness'' (*TI*, 62). Just as one grows away from physical dependency on others, so, with the construction of one's own ideas, does the subject achieve increasing cognitive autonomy from the constructive mental activity of other selves. At the same time, however, because imagination creates its objects in the linguistic media (words, images) of the subject's culture, the subject optimally never gains complete freedom from the thoughts and corresponding reality referents of others (*RKF*, 51–52 contrasting genius and maladjustment).

The logic of self-transcendence described schematically above is realized in the organism's striving to achieve mature selfhood. What Tillich terms ''ontological anxiety'' is, for Kaufman, an essential part of this selfhood. Ontological anxiety is a state of being distinct from the fear experienced by the child or adult who fails to sustain adequate attachments at critical moments in its life, and is therefore unable to enter into mature interpersonal relationships (*TI*, 61). Ontological anxiety, claims Kaufman,

> is an inevitable concomitant of our awareness of the fragility of the network of relations and attachments in which we humans stand, and its absence would testify not to our healthiness or wholeness but to our lack of sensitivity to what it is to be human, to be finite ... we should not expect it to be overcome by better methods of childrearing or more adequate psycho-therapy ... or dissolved by any combination or mode of human attachments. (*TI*, 62)

The subject's anxiety in the face of its own finitude is directly related to the constructive nature of its self-experience, and this in two ways.

First, we recall from the preceding chapter that the subject is never the object of its own experience, but is only available to reflection mediately through its construction of concepts and images of self-reference. We do not "know" ourselves first and then assign the word "I" as a placeholder for the locus of this "experience," as we might an empirical concept for a sensorily absent object.

Rather, "I" is "an indispensable element of the original consciousness of self" (*TI*, 65), whose functional acquisition in the life of a child is a significant achievement. Kaufman's thesis, that "symbolic elements—images, concepts—are constitutive for every instance of human self-consciousness" (*TI*, 66) implies the denial of the counterthesis that some self-consciousness is not constituted by linguistic elements, but proceeds by direct intuition or revelation of the subjectively real, by or to the reflecting self (*ETM*, 5–6).

Limiting the subject's knowledge of itself to what it can construct out of language, however, places the self irrevocably within that social "network of relations and attachments" (*TI*, 62) whose fragility signals the intrinsic finitude of self, and awakens within it an awareness of its own possibility of nonbeing. The constructive nature of self-experience makes ontological anxiety an implication of the knowing process itself.

Second, because self-knowledge is not only constructive but imaginative as well, the subject can extend itself mentally backward and forward in time. The referent of the "I" constructed is not only "this present speaking subject," but is always at the same time

> that whole complex of memories of past experience through which I have gone and which has shaped me into what I now am; on the other hand to say "I" is to identify this present reality with that somewhat dim and unstructured future into which I am moving, sketched as it is in my plans and projects, my hopes and fears. (*TI*, 64)

The futurity of the subject allows it to project its own death as an intrinsic possibility of its life. This awareness gives rise to ontological anxiety. The content of imagination as well as the constructive nature of self-experience thus leads the subject to an appreciation of its finitude.

To summarize: self-transcendence for Kaufman is a constructive response to the subject's experience of limitation. It has its roots in the adaptiveness of the organism to its environment, and addresses human needs for order and comprehensive understanding. To satisfy the latter, the imagination constructs higher-order concepts of ever-greater inclusiveness in order to organize its experiences more effectively for ongoing life tasks. The subject's experience of ontological anxiety is characteristic of mature selfhood. Onto-logical anxiety is the fear of nonbeing subsequent to the recognition of one's finitude. Correlative to the concept of ontological anxiety is the concept of God, as the idea of the only adequate foundation for human life so under-stood.[1]

By introducing the concept of God to the logic of self-transcendence as its terminal concept, however, the issue of intersubjective relations is raised. If the image of God is to play an ultimately foundational role in human life, how is this role to be understood epistemologically, and how do finite rela-tionships serve as its model?

## Intersubjectivity

The genesis of intersubjectivity between two individuals is, for Kaufman, the subject's sympathetic recognition of itself in another. Making a logical distinction between inner experience and external, observable expression, Kaufman maintains that for the developing consciousness there is "a kind of *intrinsic* connection between the outer state and the inner experience" which results in the spontaneous manifestations of "certain facial expressions, tears, etc." whose appearance before another consciousness "tends to arouse within us, through spontaneous sympathy, the appropriate feelings" (*RKF*, 54).

These "certain expressions" function symbolically to the nurturing adult as signs of an emerging individual: a person. The sympathetic understanding (*Verstehen*) of the child's state may be of an immediacy suggesting such facial expressions to be "natural symbols," but they are symbols neverthe-less. Because the adult responds to these gestures in a manner categorically distinct from his or her response to nonpersons, the child, in turn, experiences the objective world as composed of things and other wills. Intersubjectivity is an original category of the child's experience of reality. The child's experience of itself as self depends in part on attaining the power of self-ascription (learning to say "I"), which presupposes the child's ability to

---

[1] Kaufman calls the idea of God "the idea of an absolutely adequate attachment figure" (*TI*, 67): parental, creative, reliable, compassionate, just, etc. So conceived, God "provides the anchor for a relationship which can overcome that ontological anxiety which naturally and inevi-tably emerges in the course of our growing into full self-consciousness" (*TI*, 74). If ontological anxiety is a natural and inevitable consequence of human life, how can it be "overcome" by a "relationship" which is not fatal to either (a) the subject's finitude, or (b) the subject's clear per-ception of its finitude? See Tillich's discussion of "the courage of confidence" in Paul Tillich, *The Courage to Be* (New Haven/London: Yale University Press, 1952) 155–56, 160–63. Tillich's anthropology allows for a personal encounter with the source of the overcoming of anx-iety.

recognize persons who have first recognized him or her as a person, and so supplied the child with the linguistic resources and appropriate performative contexts necessary for construction of self-consciousness (*TI*, 64 and *ST*, 334). To summarize:

> We come to self-consciousness in relation to other persons of whom we also become conscious at the same time, while we would not come to consciousness at all if we were confronted by a world of mere objects. In Buber's language, I can become an *I* only in relation to a *thou*. (*RKF*, 56)

From the foregoing sketch of the development of intersubjectivity, it appears that the rise of self-consciousness and consciousness of the Other (both by the child and the adult) is largely a process of ever-more-sophisticated cognitive constitution: the construction of the infant as a person by the adult; the child's construction of a world of persons and nonpersons; the child's construction of itself. Yet the origin of intersubjectivity can also be stated as a dialectic of discovery :

> The discovery that the other has communicated to me by means of his external expressions and that the other understands my internal feelings through my external expressions is simultaneously the discovery of self and other. (Ibid.)

The difference between the two descriptions can be thought of as perspectival: the order of intersubjective being is most usefully stated in terms of constructive activity; the order of intersubjective knowledge should be articulated in the language of discovery (see *ETM*, 4 on the confusion of these orders in theology, and its consequences, and *GP*, 169–70, n. 13 on the objectivity of constructs).

The idea that the discovery of self and world implies the subject's awareness of a distinction between an inner feeling and its outer expressions, and the subject's willingness to predicate of another person this same sort of awareness, led Kaufman to a sharp differentiation of the self from its body and other phenomenal media of expression:

> In our interaction with other persons we presuppose a reality (the active center of the self) *beyond* that which we immediately perceive, a reality encountered by us and known to us not simply in physiologically based perception (though that of course is also involved) but in and through the language that we jointly speak. (*GP*, 64)

The "deciding, acting, purposing center of the self" (*GP*, 63) is the constructive subject, the subject who speaks the word "I" constitutive of self-hood (*TI*, 63).[2]

Kaufman's employment of the model of the self as subject was ramified for intersubjective communication as follows. The subject is known to others only through an act of self-revelation, in which the active center hurls its intentions toward another such center. On this view, language and body both function as media for the self's communication of its decisions, actions, and purposes.[3] Kaufman explains:

> In speaking to someone, we "throw" meanings, as it were (we do not simply make noises) out beyond the circle of our own world, to a personal center transcending our direct experience and not open to our view, but which we believe capable of apprehending our meaning. Only the other's body is visible to us, and thus within our world in the sense of being directly accessible to our senses, not the dynamic self with whom we are seeking to communicate, though we usually think of that self as somehow "in" the body confronting us. (*GP*, 74)

---

[2] In a later discussion of self-awareness, Kaufman argues that the self is not known to itself through comparison with objects (including mental objects like self-images?), but through an "essential" relationship with itself:

> In self-awareness the self is related essentially to itself, not to something else with which . . . it is being compared. . . . There is only one very complex reality, the self, turning back on itself and relating itself to itself. To be self-conscious is not to be conscious of something other (though that is also always involved) but rather to be conscious of the very self that is conscious. (*TI*, 63)

[3] Under the model of the self as subject, the body and the external world are both opposed to the activity of the dynamic self. The self works persuasively on the body to effect its communication with the outside world (*GP*, 64–65, 74, 181, n. 8). The model of the self as agent, as emphasized by Kaufman in his later work, tends to combine the dynamic self and body into a single entity which acts coercively on external reality. David R. Griffin argues the following thesis:

> When Kaufman is stating theoretically what analogy should be used for thinking about God, he generally speaks of the human self as distinct from its bodily behavior. However, when he actually employs the human person as an analogue for God's activity, it is the total psychophysical organism that comes into play. (Griffin, "Gordon Kaufman's Theology: Some Questions," *JAAR* 41 [1973] 558)

Griffin thinks that only the former conception, distinguishing self from body, can allow Kaufman the opportunity to "develop a fairly consistent position." However, cf. F. Michael McLain's conclusion, in an essay devoted to Kaufman's views ("On Theological Models," *HTR* 62 [1969] 155–87), that only when the acting person is construed as an embodied subjectivity can it serve as an analogue for God's action in the world. Kaufman's response to McLain can be found at *GP*, xiii–xviii.

Correlatively, the other self is entitled to remain "concealed" to us as an autonomous active center (a "dynamic self") unless and until it chooses to "reveal" its intentions. Indeed, it is this very feature of selfhood—that the self of the other is originally beyond our reach—that originally gave Kaufman his preeminent example of transcendence:

> The other self can, if it chooses, refuse to reveal himself to us, remaining almost completely out of our reach even though his body is directly at hand. . . . In this experience-of-inaccessibility-except-in-moments-of-revelation we are provided with a model for the peculiar meaning of our word "transcendence."[4]

Beneath the surface of language, indeed, below all phenomenal expressions, the dynamic self, the active center of the individual, remains concealed, related essentially only to itself.

Recall that it was not always so: intersubjectivity was an original category of the emerging self's experience. Only in relation to a "Thou" did the subject become an "I." In adulthood, however, "growing consciousness" achieves its goal of establishing "independence from overly binding relationships" (*TI*, 62). In fact, the mature self can gain "its own integrity and become truly free" only in so far as it subordinates its "finite attachment" (*TI*, 74) to "that highest reality which is above and behind and under them all" (*TI*, 75), namely, God.

> Attachment to God, through relativizing all other attachments, can free the self from idolatrous bondage to them. God, thus, is finally the only appropriate counterpart to the self-conscious self. "I" and "God," both known to us only in image or idea, are polar realities which establish and sustain and reinforce each other: a strong "I," a strong and self-confident sense of self not overcome by ontological anxiety . . . is made possible and sustained by a firm confidence in and reliance upon God. (Ibid.)

## Objection to the Model of the Self as Subject

Kaufman's anthropology as developed within the model of the self as subject has been criticized at length by F. Michael McLain.[5] We recall that at this time Kaufman held that divine transcendence should be understood on analogy with the self's transcendence in personal revelation. As the active

---

[4] *GP*, 74–75; see also *ST*, 35: "It is because the active center of the self transcends my private world completely that his accessibility to me depends finally on his own act of self-disclosure."

[5] McLain, "Theological Models."

center of the self transcends its phenomenal modes of appearance, so does God transcend our human history through which God is known (*GP*, 152–53, 160–70 for the analogy). McLain, taking over an argument of P. F. Strawson,[6] observes that

> the force of the analogy hinges upon a clear and convincing distinction, in our meetings with other persons, between the "inner" and the "outer," the "unobservable" and the "observable," the "revealed" and the "hidden," "bodily appearances" and the transcendent "subject," "openness" and "pretense," and so on.[7]

Distinguishing a "real self" from its revealed "self-expressions" is a habit of thought and speech we frequently rely on, particularly when we believe our communication with others or even ourselves to be distorted. However (and this is McLain's and Strawson's point), our recognition of self and others as persons is neither our recognition of bodies that talk nor of subjects that signify. Personal knowledge including self-knowledge, is, Strawson maintains, knowledge of

> a type of entity such that *both* predicates ascribing states of consciousness *and* predicates ascribing corporeal characteristics, a physical situation etc. are equally applicable to a single individual of that single type. . . . The concept of a person is not to be analyzed as that of an animated body or of an embodied anima.[8]

Strawson's thesis holds, in brief, that

> one can ascribe states of consciousness to oneself only if one can ascribe them to others. One can ascribe them to others only if one can identify other subjects of experience. And one cannot identify others if one can identify them *only* as subjects of experience, possessors of states of consciousness.[9]

Our recognition of other persons is not, *pace* Descartes, the result of comparing other's behavior with a knowledge of ourselves as subjects with bodies, and then proceeding inferentially to a knowledge of the other's subjectivity.[10] For such reasoning presumes that we can know what it is to be a

6 *Individuals* (London: Methuen, 1959) 102–3.

7 McLain, "Theological Models," 160.

8 See note 6 above.

9 Ibid., 100.

10 In his early discussion of the ontogeny of consciousness, Kaufman denies that personal knowledge is, at least for young children, inferential. Regarding infants' awareness:

person in our own case before we know what it is to be a person at all, that is, before we learn to predicate personal action (talking, thinking, laughing, etc.) and states of being (such as feeling depressed or happy) of other entities. To ascribe these personal predicates to oneself, one must be able to ascribe them to others, and since we have no knoweldge of other individuals without encountering them corporally, learning to ascribe personal predicates to any entity is always learning to ascribe them to an embodied reality. Thus, mastering the concept "person" requires us to learn by concrete examples, even (or especially) in learning about ourselves.

Strawson's argument concludes that personal knowledge is not knowledge of a revealed self, but of an entity with physical and social presence which is at the same time a subject of experience. When corporality is treated only or primarily as a medium of self-revelation, as a sign of subjectivity, such treatment is an abstraction from our epistemologically more basic experience of the Other qua person.[11]

For Strawson and McLain, then, the concept of person is a logically primitive notion, "logically prior to that of an individual consciousness."[12] As McLain observes:

> Our primitive notion of the self is that of an embodied reality; the public and observable side of the self, so far from being merely adventitiously related to a hidden subject, is intrinsic to the very concept of a person. And if the objective situation of the person, its observable states and acts, is the origin of logically adequate criteria for the ascription of

---

Such an inference could be made only if we were fully conscious both of ourselves as persons with feelings and of the connection between inner feelings and bodily processes, e.g., tears. But at the level of development of consciousness at which this awareness begins to appear, we are no more conscious of our own natures in this regard than we are of others'. (*RKF*, 54)

Kaufman believes early knowledge of other persons is not inferential, but sympathetic. In adulthood, however, the healthy autonomy of the self is demonstrated in its ability to use its phenomenal "side" as both a medium of expression and an enclosure for the "dynamic self." On McLain's view, Kaufman's understanding of authentic selfhood is an unwarranted abstraction from our actual relations with others.

[11] When Kaufman says "Our knowledge of persons is more fundamental—genetically, existentially, and ontologically—than our thing-knowledge, the latter being an abstraction from and specification of the former" (*ST*, 35, n. 22), he understands "person" to be synonymous with "active center of the self." It is the Strawson/McLain point that "person" includes the idea of an entity of which both material and immaterial actions and states can be predicated. They would hold that Kaufman's conception of the person as the immaterial substratum of such acts and states reduces the individual to an object of thing knowledge ("the active self") just as much, in the opposite direction, as those who would defend the physicalist position to which Kaufman is so much opposed.

[12] Strawson, *Individuals*, 103.

mental predicates . . . then it is not the case that persons are only, or even primarily, accessible in self-disclosure.[13]

He concludes:

> Thus the self cannot be construed, after the interpersonal model [here the model of the self as subject] , as a radically transcendent reality, which is knowable and known only in personal disclosure and encounter.[14]

Kaufman's response to McLain's criticisms both acknowledges the validity of McLain's "principal critical point . . . that neither a dualistic nor a one-sidedly subjectivistic conception of the self is tenable" (*GP*, xix), and reiterates his position that the self has "two sides," one phenomenal, the other "hidden" and potentially "transcendent." Kaufman reasserts his view that "the self has a certain privacy and in its innermost recesses even a measure of inaccessibility, apart from its own deliberate acts of communication" (*GP*, xvii). Although willing to admit that some of his prior anthropological analyses tended to be "one-sidedly subjectivistic" in their emphasis on the dynamic self as the real self, Kaufman is unwilling to accept McLain's conclusion that his "earlier discussions of transcendence and of the revelatory character of the knowledge of God are to be called seriously into question" (*GP*, xiv).

Kaufman never abandons the dualistic anthropology which McLain and others have called "residually Cartesian."[15] Instead, he has tried to reformulate the "two sides" distinction in terms of a model of human agency. The side of the person always removed from observation, retains its privileges of essential self-relation, reflection, and free self-revelation, but now Kaufman wants to direct our attention away from the distinction between the deep self and its modes of expression, and toward one function of the self as a whole: its ability to form and realize intentions in the observable world, particularly in the realm of language. By emphasizing the purposiveness of the inner self, Kaufman had hoped to make more intelligible the idea of God as one who is both intrinsically absent from observation (like the self as subject) but nonetheless active in the phenomenal world (like the self as agent). Thus, after considering McLain's objections, Kaufman states:

> It is on the basis of this model of the hiddenness and transcendence intrinsic to selfhood and the consequent revelatory character of our

---

[13] McLain, "Theological Models," 166.

[14] Ibid., 167.

[15] Ibid., 162. Cf. the remarks on Kaufman's "dualistic assumption" in Don Wiebe, "On Kaufman's Problem God," *RelS* 10 (1974) 197; and David R. Griffin, "Gordon Kaufman's Theology: Some Questions," *JAAR* 41 (1973) 558.

knowledge of other selves that, as I argue, a meaningful doctrine of God as agent can be constructed. (*GP*, xviii)

# The Self as Agent

## *Instrumental and Moral Agency*

An act is "a specific event brought about by an agent" (*GP*, 126). It is opposed to both "mere activity" (random motion) and the immanent realization of an innate end (the "act" of plant growth). In every case in which an act takes place, "there must be an *agent* who performs the act, a reality in which is lodged the teleological intention to be realized through it" (*GP*, 126–27). As an event, an act requires an orderliness and form distinguishing it from background occurrences; it is a unit of change. An act is initiated by an agent, however, and thus represents the actor's attempt to realize some future project which would not occur had the agent not intended it. Actions are the building blocks of culture:

> Thus, an act involves an element of creativity not characteristic of lower forms of life than man. The culmination of such (creative) acts produces the *historical* order, culture, a new order of being superimposed on the process of life and not to be simply identified with it. (*GP*, 126)

The intentionality of the agent sharply distinguishes acts from unintended natural events. The agent's intention is also responsible for distinguishing what Kaufman calls "master acts" from "subacts."

> Simple or particular acts are often phases of overarching complex acts—we will call these "master acts"—which unify and order various sorts of behavior and otherwise disconnected stretches of time. . . . It is the master act, rather than each simple act taken by itself, that renders any given piece of activity intelligible. (*GP*, 136)

Kaufman gives the example of building a house: the ideal entity of a constructed dwelling provides the raison d'être for hammering a nail into a board. Here the master act is building a house; the hammering and related behavior (related because part of the master act) constitute subacts in the realization of the organizing principle (ibid.). We do not ordinarily attend to each subact, though in principle we could (ourselves being the "author" of the act, no matter its relative insignificance).[16]

---

[16] Kaufman states a threshold criterion for genuine action in the following:

An act thus receives its necessary unity from the intention of the agent who seeks to perform it. It is always future directed and therefore an attempt to bring something new into being. In recent years, the model of the self as agent has assumed a central place in Kaufman's reflections. He argues:

> The one model of genuine autonomy or self-determination is the human self. In the self's cultural creativity and moral responsibility, we have an image of what genuine freedom or self-determination might be: an action from within which produces that which has never been before (creativity), an action which is taken deliberately and with conscious regard of its consequences for other beings in the field of action (moral responsibility). (*ETM*, 71, n. 19)

There is implicit in Kaufman's description of agency a distinction between what I shall call "instrumental" and "moral" acts. Instrumental agency is presumed in Kaufman's mundane examples of hammering a board, building a house, or waggling a finger. The act criteria of unity and intentionality are met in coming up with a viable plan to achieve a practical end. These instrumental acts are easily divided into master- and subacts; the image of the artisan at work prevails.[17] Finally, instrumental action meets the criterion of creativity insofar as the product of the deed is novel (it is not the culmination of an Aristotelian immanent teleology).

Moral action, however, must rely on standards besides those of unity, intentionality, and creativity. It requires a deliberate and "conscious regard" for an act's "consequences for other beings in the field of action" (ibid.). Here significant problems arise for any philosopher or theologian working in the post-Enlightenment tradition, bearing directly on the question of criteria

---

Even the simplest of acts, such as waggling my little finger, is teleologically ordered and takes time. It is an act (and not an involuntary movement) only if I am (at least implicitly) intentionally doing it (or something of which it is the consequence or side effect) and could have done otherwise. (*GP*, 181, n. 8)

[17] In the following, Kaufman constrasts the notion of God as "cosmic Magician and Miracleworker" with the idea of a being whose primary goal is to "bring *order into time*," by executing a grand plan through subordinate steps (subacts):

> An agent is not one who erratically and impulsively performs first one instantaneous act and then another, without either plan or goal. On the contrary, an agent posits objectives to be worked out in systematic and orderly fashion through time, his minor or subordinate acts being steps directed toward the realization of his ultimate ends. His power of agency, then, is his power to bring *order into time*. (*GP*, 183)

Conceived of along these lines, God is the instrumental agent par excellence. The question of the morality of God's subacts does not arise, since everything is, as Leibniz would say, "for the best." This leads to the apologia for apparent evil cited in n. 18, below.

for moral action: can a subact be evil if the master act is good?; [18] where do we find our criteria for ethical action?; where does creativity rank in the list of goods?; and, when is an agent's responsibility for an act mitigated (by lacking the requisite intention) and how is this to be determined—perhaps, as some have, by the human sciences?

## Anthropological Basis of Moral Agency

Because Kaufman's point of departure for thinking about moral agency is theological, his views are couched in religious language. He states clearly that an analysis of the concept of God must determine our understanding of the human (*TI*, 266). In Chapter 7, I elucidated Kaufman's opinion that "God" implies a ground of action which is at once ultimately transcendent, humane, and present. Concretely, the Christian moral agent should imitate Christ, as "the final or definitive revelation of God" (*TI*, 270). Other monotheistic traditions imaginatively represent God out of their textual and related resources. For Christians, Jesus' life, death, and resurrection provide a picture of God as "essentially suffering and forgiving love" (*TI*, 271).

The question of articulating ethical standards quickly "turns secular," however, as Kaufman admits the possibility that one day "the word 'God' will eventually die as a living and meaningful focus of attention and reflection" (*ETM*, 17). Kaufman's method allows for this transformation of our symbolic landscape by subordinating construction to the realization of humane souls not identifiable with the viability of any particular image or symbol, even "God." What one may call a major premise of Kaufman's thinking is expressed in the following:

> All religious institutions, practices, and ideas—including the idea of God—were made to serve human needs and to further our humanization (what has traditionally been called our "salvation"); humanity was not made for the sake of religious customs and ideas. (*TI*, 264)

From the assumption that religious language and images are intended to

---

[18] Kaufman appears to have believed at one time that if a master act is good, then the subacts required for its completion may only be apparently evil; i.e., they cause affects in other subjects which the subjects perceive as evil (pain of various kinds), but because they serve a higher, if undisclosed, purpose which is good, they are not inherently evil. He claims:

> We may not analyze the problem of evil in terms of disconnected atomic events or circumstances that we wish God had not allowed to happen: if God is indeed an effective agent and the world is the product and tharena of his activity, there are no such isolated and independent events. We must see all events in the context of God's purposes for the world and the way in which he is carrying them through. (*GP*, 184; see also 193–200)

perform humanizing functions, it follows that if any item from our religious vocabulary ceases to serve these needs, others, ought to be adopted if humanization of culture is to continue:

> A continuing full indigenization of all theological metaphors, models, and concepts is both appropriate and necessary, no matter how far this departs form biblical or traditional conceptions. ... Thus, Christian theology is completely free—indeed, theology is under the imperative—to become fully indigenous in every respect in each culture in which Christian believers live and work, so long as the Principle of God's Absoluteness and the Principle of God's Humaneness are maintained. (*TI*, 277–79)

In developing our standards of moral action, then, one is not bound to the preservation of and commentary upon particular, material elements of the Christian tradition (or any other), but to formal notions of the ultimately humane which an analysis of "God" reveals. Anthropology remains subordinate to theological reflection:

> It is sometimes said that theology is primarily anthropology, an interpretation of the nature of the human, and that therefore the first task in theology is to develop a conception of the human. But this once again is putting the cart before the horse. Though we certainly cannot develop an interpretation of God without simultaneously working out an understanding of our human condition ... the primary business of theology is to work out an understanding not of humanity but rather of that supreme focus for human service and devotion, God. *And our understanding of what humanity really is will have to be secondary to and derivative from what we conclude God to be.* (*TI*, 266; my emphasis)

The final sentence of the above suggests theology to be a deductive enterprise: we "conclude" that God is best pictured in a certain way, then this conclusion acts as a major premise from which we "derive" our "secondary" understanding of "what humanity really is." The theocentric orientation of this claim must be contrasted with a different essay written three years after the above, in which Kaufman expounds the dialectical nature of constructive activity and its reflective location in a Christian fourfold categorical scheme (*TI*, 99–122). There, Kaufman argues that contemporary theologians should attempt "to interpret modern experience and knowledge in terms of a worldview structured by the four principal categories, God, world, humanity, and Christ" (*TI*, 121). He emphasizes that these categories are themselves subject to change, and (regarding God, world, and humanity) the reconstruction of any one will necessarily affect the rest:

> The terms of the monotheistic categorical scheme are not really detachable from each other in such a way that we can decisively modify one or two without affecting the third; any change in one of these categories reverberates throughout the whole scheme, transforming and reshaping the entire perspective. (*TI*, 119)

And again, in contradistinction to the position of Barth, "that all our thinking about God and the human is to be *derived* from Christ," Kaufman maintains:

> On the contrary, I am holding here that the Christian worldview is structured by four fundamental categories, each with its own intrinsic meaning and thus a certain independence from the others, yet dialectically interconnected and interdependent with each of the others. (*TI*, 289, n. 5)

The derivation of anthropology from theological findings is a point reiterated in Kaufman's very recent work, which proposes construction of the two concepts, "God" and "Christ": "A theological understanding of humanity must ultimately be dependent upon and in some respects derivative form what we conclude about God and Christ" (*TNA*, 23). The methodological priority of theocentric and Christocentric reflection cannot be identified with a priorism of Barth to the extent that Kaufman successfully defends two related theses: first, that theological reflection is construction of images and concepts, not interpretation of divine revelation; and second, that the constructions of these particular two concepts, "God" and "Christ," are intrinsically humane, and so have relevance beyond the traditional religious communities in which they have been used. Kaufman, in *An Essay on Theological Method*, and since, has argued at length for the first thesis, and been successful in relativizing Christo- and theocentric reflection to the limits of particular symbol systems and the imaginative powers of the symbolizers. The second thesis, that construction of "God" and "Christ" has general import, has been established in principle by Kaufman's ongoing recognition of the dialectical character of theological thinking about not only God and Christ, but human existence as well: "We certainly cannot attain understanding of the meanings and uses of our two fundamental symbols without simultaneously working out a conception of certain features of human existence" (ibid.). Thus, Kaufman can urge that the three concepts of God, Christ, and human existence must be treated as dialectically interdependent for their sense and meaningfulness. The second thesis remains unestablished, however, beyond its principled claim to the dialectical interrelation of theologically significant concepts, inasmuch as Kaufman has not developed an anthropology which would substantiate not only his claim that humans are constructive agents (thesis one), but his claim that "God" and "Christ" are fundamentally humane (thesis two).[19]

Kaufman picks out certain biblical "depictions" of God as preferable to others. He sees the "characteristically Christian metaphors" which deemphasize "God's arbitrary imperial power" (*TI*, 271) as desirable theological resources. He thus likes God depicted as "suffering and forgiving love," as "loving, gracious, forgiving, faithful, a 'father' " (ibid.). He does not advocate constructing "God" as "lord, king, mighty warrior, and judge" (ibid.), nor as the traditional bestower of providence (*TNA*, 30–46, esp. 45). One may agree with him or not. But implicit in his option for the first set is his *feeling* that they are more worthy than the latter to symbolize or "image" the concept of "that which fulfills and completes our humanity" (*ETM*, 56). Articulating why some symbols are better candidates than others for theological construction is just to say why some "conform" to a certain idea of what it is to be genuinely human better than some others. Making this evaluation and then articulating this idea is what I understand to be anthropology.

Even the judgment that God is best described as absolutely transcendent expresses the theologian's preference for this attribute from among many alternatives and does so on the basis of the same theologian's sense of what it is finally to be human. This does not imply that either the preference for transcendence apropos God or the sense of transcendence's appropriateness for human being is arbitrary with respect to social practices: both preference and sense represent the continuing strength of one significant self-ascription—transcendence—in and for the theologian's linguistic community (culture). But this does not mean that the formal notion of God as Absolute Limit or Relativizer is "eternal" and cannot change with the social practices of the theologian and her or his community.[20]

---

[19] "For Christian theologians ... God is to be thought of as loving, forgiving, redemptive reality—as moral reality, concerned with the personal being and the personal fulfillment of human beings. Jesus is a criterion or model in terms of which we are to construct our idea of God" (*TI*, 117; see also 270).

[20] Kevin Sharpe questions the status of Kaufman's formal principle of God's absolute limiting ability in the following:

> If we are to accept this logical function of the word 'God' as the basis for theology, something we have derived from the use of the word in ordinary language, what room is there for change (especially change instigated and guided by theology) in the use and meaning of the word? ... Does Kaufman feel there is something eternal about the concept of God which he has isolated as this logical function (something perhaps hard to prove?) ... is theology forever tied to Kaufman's perception of a use of the word "God"? (Sharpe, "Theological Method and Gordon Kaufman," *RelS* 15 [1979] 178–79)

I think Kaufman does believe that God's absolute transcendence is a sine qua non for future theology and that he would be willing to admit that his belief is based on a conceptual analysis of "God" guided by his personal intuition of what it is to be genuinely human. Cf. his remarks on a possible "absolute demise of theology" as an event if and only if "human consciousness ...

In summary, Kaufman's methodology reflects a tension between a theocentric orientation, which derives an anthropology from pictures of "God" and "Christ," and a dialectical understanding of theological reflection, emphasizing the interrelatedness of "God," "Christ," and "human existence," in the constructive operation itself. Although Kaufman has argued persuasively that theological thinking is construction, not Foucaultian "commentary" on the important symbols of a religious tradition, he has not produced to date the anthropological portrait—which need not be a "serious" critique of foundations—that would support his position that the dialectically related concepts of God and Christ (related to each other and to the idea of human existence) are concepts of normative humanity which can be ethically reconstrcuted to serve common human needs today. It is not enough for Kaufman to show by analysis that "God" and "Christ" (and "human existence") have traditionally been used in discourse to address a supposedly universal audience. If these concepts are to be used once their cultural relativity and relations with power have been recognized, Kaufman must argue for the possibility of conceptual reconstructions which both retain a universal addressee ("provide overall orientation for human life," *TNA*, 26) and acknowledge

> that all Christian God-talk, and everything associated with it . . . belongs to a specific worldview, a specific interpretation of human existence, created by the imagination in one particular historical stream of human culture to provide orientation in life for those living in that culture. (*TNA*, 24)

Providing moral agency with a basis in a dialectically constructed vision of God, Christ, and human existence depends on such an elucidation of common human interest themselves in dialectical relation with the material (archive) of construction. What are these interests? How are they represented in the existing archive of religious language, primarily in "God" and "Christ"? How, finally, is this archive of Christian effective history related to the present situation of the constructive theologian, his or her genealogically specific relations with power? Kaufman has offered answers to the second question through his analyses of the principal concepts of the Christian tradition. The task remains of linking these analyses with a portrait of common human interests, on the one hand, and with genealogical self-criticism, on the

---

no longer attempted to see the meaning of human experience in some unified way. . . . Reflection on the ultimate point of reference for all life and thought and reality must surely go on in some form so long as human life persists" (*ETM*, 17). The latter is a point to be argued, not assumed, since we often say and do things we would call "humane" when we are not thinking about "the meaning of human experience," or even thinking at all.

other.[21] Specifying an anthropology can rely on the investigative and critical techniques of the human sciences. Such is the tack taken by Tracy in his fundamental-theological analysis of the deep self, in which these would-be sciences, guided by the secular morality of knowledge, specify authoritatively the norms for genuinely human conduct. The direction of Kaufman's thinking, however, has been away from an acceptance of the human sciences' authority for theological reflection, toward the assertion of theological construction's autonomy from both the sciences of "man" and the tutelage of traditional religious authorities.

## Theological Construction and the Human Sciences

I noted in Chapter 7 that Kaufman saw the human sciences playing a preparatory role for subsequent theological interpretation (*GP*, 32). In response to my suggestion that a version of the fact/value distinction was operative in his work of the late 1960s – early 1970s, Kaufman has said,

> In the period when I was writing my *Systematic Theology* (which was the same time when many of the essays in *God the Problem* were produced) positivism still seemed to be in its heyday to many of us, the fact/value distinction was of course taken for granted to be valid by the positivists. Though I think I never fully accepted that distinction, it probably seemed much more plausible at that time than it has more recently, and I suspect that that accounts for the difference that you have detected between that earlier text and my more recent remarks.[22]

These "more recent remarks" include the following:

> All thinking about human existence is "self-involved" and thus shaped by presuppositions of many different sorts, some hidden, some more obvious. . . . It is always subject, that is to say, to criticism and correction from other perspectives using different methodologies and giving rise to different sorts of insights and understandings. . . . This means that as theologians we cannot simply "take over" conclusions from social sciences and build our theological work on those conclusions. . . . We as theologians . . . must finally be the judges of what is of significance here; we should never give social scientists or philosophers a kind of blank check on any problem which seems to us of theological importance. They are not in a position to judge that, and they haven't worked out

---

[21] Kaufman's willingness to make such self-criticism is evident in his acknowledgment of the androcentric nature of his early work (see *ST*, xx; *ETM*, xii; and *TNA*, xi).

[22] Gordon D. Kaufman, letter to the author, 19 February 1985.

their positions in terms of what we might regard as important theological concerns, so it would be a mistake ever simply to "take over" their work or their conclusions. . . . Though insights from the human sciences will certainly inform our thinking about God, all of this thinking will finally have to be ordered by the conception of God which we put together, if indeed God is truly to be regarded as "the ultimate point of reference" for all of our work.[23]

Clearly, Kaufman expects philosophy and the human sciences to play subordinate roles to theological reflection on "God." As Kaufman addresses the need in his program for an anthropological position, however, the authority of the human sciences in the construction of this position may become problematic. If his analysis of "God" revealed God to be only the Ultimate Relativizer, beyond all significance for human self-understanding, Kaufman could with the coherence of neoorthodoxy claim that thinking about God undercuts all merely human critique, while supplying our reflection on the mundane with a point of reference. But once he depicts God as the Ultimate Humanizer, and that this depiction legitimately guides and informs theological reflection, Kaufman must develop not only an anthropology, but must relate his understanding of the human to the claims of the disciplines appropriate to the study of human phenomena.

Granted that they have not "worked out their positions" vis-à-vis "what we might regard as important theological concerns," can Kaufman offer a position making claims about human life (a portrait constructed in relation to those of God and Christ) which does not build upon just those findings of the human sciences and philosophy which best represent, according to the methodological criteria appropriate to each discipline, the state of contemporary knowledge about the human and hence *humaneness*? To whom, finally, is the constructive theologian's reflection on a humane God responsible? If to a community of interpreters whose consensus on the human varies from that of the human scientists, by what right does it vary? "Human existence" may indeed be "self-involved," but for theological anthropology this does not imply that the project of a thorough critique of human behavior—speech, productivity, communication, desire—is not a sound one, a scientific one, whose incremental progress toward self-clarification may yet prove the legitimate measure of that theology's own movement toward an adequate understanding of the human. This, at least, is the assumption of Tracy's theological anthropology.

[23] Gordon D. Kaufman, letter to the author, 3 January 1985. Note the theological relativization of history, religious studies, and philosophy in Gordon D. Kaufman, "Theology as a Public Vocation," in Theodore Jennings, Jr., ed., *The Vocation of the Theologian* (Philadelphia: Fortress, 1985) 49–56.

For it is Tracy's great hope that theology can account for the "negative" in experience by making, first, a thorough study of the facts of "our actual economic, political, cultural, and social situations" (*BRO*, 246) with the application of empirical social-scientific techniques (*AI*, 75), followed by, second, a diagnosis of inhumanity immanent in these same situations, with the theoretical assistance of psychoanalysis, ideology critique, and possibly a critique of communicative competence (*AI*, 146–47, n. 80). As I have interpreted Tracy, the more we transform situations of systematic distortion into occasions of clear thinking and interaction, the more we can trust the phenomenology of lived experience and hermeneutics of classics to reveal the (undisguised) truth of the authentic self's foundations. Theology of praxis redeems the coherence, validity, and truth of fundamental theology's potentially distorted claims. Making this transformation possible are supposedly undistorted critical theories and interest-free techniques of the human sciences, the tools of Modern "liberation."

To the extent that Kaufman has not offered a full-blown anthropology, grounding his preference for an Ultimate Relativizer in some interpretation of "common human experience and language," he remains less "postmodern" than Tracy, and the results of his conceptual analysis of "God" seem arbitrary to the contemporary transcendental imagination and its love of foundations. This is so despite this attempt to set out pictures of the human modeled on subjectivity and agency. The model of the self as subject failed in part because it could not account for relationship as a fundamental category of personal experience. The subject transcended its body and its language, both of which played instrumental, mediational roles in the subject's volitional attempts to "throw meanings" to other subjects, equally remote from their bodies and language. That we do not originally experience ourselves or other persons as subjects with bodies was argued at length by McLain, following Strawson.

The model of the self as agent seeks to correct this strong distinction of subject and object by emphasizing the subject's capability to plan and execute projects. When instrumental acts are distinguished from moral ones, though, I argued that constructive theology's commitment to the dialectical transformation of "God," "Christ," and "human existence," exists in tension with a potentially deductive theocentrism, to the extent that Kaufman has not developed an anthropological justification for the Christian categorial scheme.

In developing this anthropology, Kaufman will not hold theology responsible to the conclusions of the human sciences. By so doing, he differentiates his methdology from Tracy's revisionist endorsement of critical theories and empirical social science as legitimate theological authorities. The challenge for Kaufman at this time appears to be the construction of an anthropology, enabling claims about common human life to be justified, but which does not require theology to treat with Modern "seriousness" the discourses which have, since their beginnings, taken as their rightful responsibility the analysis and critique of human thought and action.

For the modern ethos, however, the heroic renunciation of both revelation and anthropology is consistent with the critical spirit and immanent historical consciousness of the Enlightenment. Giving up traditional seriousness for ironic concern for the present is consistent with Kaufman's historicist orientation. Having put the authority of revealed norms behind him, it would be appropriate for him to put the authority of anthropological and conceptual norms behind him as well. The ingenious resolution of the nuclear threat, which Kaufman has singled out as a source of shared distress, will define its own conditions of possibility.

# Conclusion

Kaufman's analysis of the three orders of theological reflection can serve as a first interpretive grid for evaluating Tracy's revisionist program (*ETM*, 37–39). Foucault's critique of first-order thinking will serve as a second. I have attempted in this dissertation to show how the anthropological subject of Tracy's theological discourse strives toward authentic self-knowledge by disciplined reflection on the religious dimension of its life. This reflection begins with the phenomenological description of the limit character of uncommon experiences (positive and negative) as well as questions about the origin of morality and inquiry. This stage of Tracy's thinking may properly be described as "first-order theology," to use Kaufman's phrase, since Tracy is holding that the theologian as existential phenomenologist "is to set forth as adequately as possible a picture of God, humankind and the world *as they are*, as though they were objects over against us which in some way could be described" (*ETM*, 37). Because reality in its most significant manifestations has been adequately described by phenomenology, the second, transcendental moment of revisionist fundamental theology can proceed to articulate the conditions of the possibility of limit experiences and limit language. Transcendental theory thereby justifies theoretically the validly described appearances (self-manifestations) of the "limit-of" experience and language, which it names "God."

However, two related objections, one theoretical, the other practical, were raised against Tracy's methodology. The first I developed in a comparative analysis of Tracy's program with Heidegger's analytic of *Dasein*. I argued that the authentic self could reflect in fidelity to the logic of inquiry and still arrive at a "limit-of" suffering which could not be called "God." Tracy, I suggested, admitted the limits of phenomenology for theological discourse, when in 1981 he disavowed "the route of the negative realities" as a distinct path to "religious questions."

Tracy admitted this not, however, as a concession to the *theoretical* incoherence of a transcendental justification of two mutually exclusive pieces of evidence ("the limit-of is trustworthy" versus "the limit-of is absurd"), but as a concession to the *practical* inadequacy of his particular phenomenology to represent the depth experiences and language of the oppressed. This second objection, raised by certain Latin American theologians, does not question whether *some* reflective operations can describe and justify cognitively a gracious "limit-of" suffering (and to this extent accepts Tracy's fundamental methodology on its own terms), only that the oppressed themselves are the proper subjects of these reflective acts by virtue of the intensity of their suffering.

Nevertheless, Tracy is unwilling to concede that North American thinkers cannot make authentic claims about the nature of the injustice done to people in sociologically very dissimilar situations. Intensity will not have the last word, even if it has the first.[1]

Tracy therefore moves cautiously from what Kaufman calls a "second-order" appreciation of the sociological relativity of any theological claim to a nascent "third-order" position. This position, programatically presented in the context of his discussion of practical theology, is potentially third order because it strives to move through relativity to normative reflection. But unlike Kaufman's proposed pragmatic norms (and here is where the two differ markedly), Tracy looks yet deeper into the authentic self for norms of economic relations, personality, and possibly communication. These norms he systematically incorporates into theological reflection in the form of the valid conclusions of critical theory (which, in turn, have been tested against the results of valid analyses by empirical social science). Practical theology strives to be third-order theology when it methodologically recognizes the

---

[1] Foucault's work enables us to see the tension between oppression interpreted by biblical portraits and oppression criticized by praxis theologies as a struggle between local knowledges and normalizing discourses. See Lee Cormie, "The Hermeneutical Privilege of the Oppressed: Liberation Theologies, Biblical Faith, and Marxist Sociology of Knowledge," *Proceedings of the Catholic Theological Society of America* 33 (1978) 155–81, who advocates the authority in theology of both the biblically based portrait of early Israelite and early Christian suffering, and Marxist social-scientific analyses for the overcoming of oppression. Cf. the attempt to develop a theological method integrating the two, in Juan Luis Segundo, *The Liberation of Theology* (Maryknoll: Orbis, 1976); and the insurrection of black hermeneutics, in James H. Cone, *God of the Oppressed* (New York: Seabury, 1975). Cf. Sharon D. Welch, *Communities of Resistance and Solidarity* (Maryknoll: Orbis, 1985), a feminist theology of liberation that integrates Foucault's analysis of subjugated knowledges, esp. pp. 23–31 including discussion of the "epistemological privilege of the oppressed."

relativity of its theoretical constructs to the situation of the theologian, and nevertheless proceeds to reform both traditional secular and religious language and the social contexts in which they are spoken, according to anthropologically immanent norms of social interaction.

Tracy's call for the transformation of language and situation by theology echoes Kaufman's demand that third-order reflection

> now take control (so far as possible) of our theological activity and attempt deliberately to construct our concepts and images of God and the world; and then we must seek to see human existence in terms of these symbolical constructions. (*ETM*, 38)

But it is less certain that Tracy would agree "that all theological positions are rooted fundamentally in imaginative construction" (ibid.). Third-order reflection for Tracy seems to involve the efficient not constitutive use of the imagination to "see" similarities (analogies) and nonidentities *in the nature of things*. In an emancipating, critically sophisticated fundamental theology, the imagination grasps more adequately than before how things really are, while in language the symbolic representation of reality in the transcendental "moment" more nearly mirrors that state of affairs. The space between words and things narrows with each turn of the reflective spiral, as the critical and constructive imaginations work together to bring language and reality back into "that obvious correspondence between logos and being" which was "finally dissolved" with the end of Hegelian philosophy.[2] Although he criticizes the naïveté of his earlier fundamental theology by subjecting it in principle to the hermeneutics of suspicion performed in practical theology, by continuing to accept the legitimacy of foundations as a distinct theological subdiscipline Tracy's conception of theology remains within the orbit of first-order reflection. If the "truth claims" of foundations (and systematics) remain "operative" in any critical sublation, a fortiori so must their models, and the model of truth in fundamental theology is "truth-as-adequacy-to-experience" (*AI*, 96, n. 104).

My conclusion that critical, disciplined reflection on the authentically human is actually first-order reflection is supported by the work of Michel Foucault. Foucault's historico-criticism of anthropology argues that accord-

---

[2] Gadamer, *Truth and Method*, 195. Foucault sees the Modern episteme similarly, as the point in Western thinking when a "spontaneous grid for the knowledge of things" was lost:

> The threshold between Classicism and modernity (though the terms themselves have no importance—let us say between our prehistory and what is still contemporary) had been definitively crossed when words ceased to intersect with representations and provide a spontaneous grid for the knowledge of things. (*OT*, 304)

ing to the conditions of their possibility, the human sciences have tried vainly since their beginnings to set forth an adequate picture of "man" as he is in himself. These conditions are based on the assumption that "man" can become clear about himself in the way that natural science becomes clear about the physical world. The human sciences try to grasp "man"'s metaphysical foundations through an analytic of his positive knowledge and experience. I have shown how contemporary philosophy of the human sciences supports this project (Habermas) and variously opposes it (Rorty, Taylor, and Dreyfus). Taylor, Dreyfus, and Foucault have argued that social practices create the frame within which reflecting individuals sort relevant from irrelevant features of their experience. Because these practices change, what counts as positive knowledge of the human also changes. The result is that the human sciences cannot provide an adequate picture of "man"; their critiques of life, labor, and language will be, as Dreyfus argues, necessarily incomplete and unpredictive. The attitude which supports the sciences of "man" and the search for anthropological foundations is "traditional seriousness" (Dreyfus and Rabinow). Traditional seriousness in the service of philosophical anthropology is first-order reflection.

For revisionist theology the consequences of traditional seriousness are both futile and dangerous. They are futile in that the phenomenology and critique of common human experience and language, in association with the human sciences, moves within the Modern double of the cogito and the unthought. The interpretation of the Christian fact, also in conjunction with reconstructive techniques, anticipates the return of the origin. Finally, sublating fundamental theology to theology of praxis, the critique of foundation's transcendental constructs (adequate to the appearances of the self's "limit-of") is the perpetual resolution of "man"'s most meaningful experiences into an ever more comprehensive and enlightened transcendental portrait. A theological "positivism" (performed in foundations) alternates with a theological "eschatology" (performed in practical reflection), as the truth of Tracy's unitary theological discourse shifts from the object to the discourse and back.

The consequences are dangerous in that the liberation of the authentic self relies on power relations invested in social practices and formations of disciplined reflection which are systematically elided by the revisionist's explicitly transcendental point of departure. Foucault's genealogies of Western techniques of domination and the self show that the human sciences presume and promote normalizing dividing practices, which work to create the disciplined individual consistent with "biopower." The secular morality of knowledge binds Tracy to the conclusions and techniques of the human sciences, as the responsible forms of Modern inquiry, and thus binds revisionist theology to the expansion of biopower. Conceivably, a critical perspective on biopower could be incorporated into theological thinking, but this would presume adopting a critical perspective on the secular morality of knowledge itself, (e.g., moving to an "ironic" morality like Foucault's) and, moreover, criticizing rather than presuming the transcendence of "man" and the legitimacy of "authentic self-liberation." A theology criticizing the secular morality of knowledge and its anthropological subject/object would not, however, be recognizably revisionist.

It might be recognizably constructive. In 1960 Kaufman stated: "The question of the standpoint thus can be answered only, if at all, by pushing *through* relativism to see where in fact one is standing when one apprehends the relativity of different perspectives" (*RKF*, 21). Pushing through relativism, Foucault has argued, means pushing through the Modern anthropology to designate historical critically one's standpoint in determined and determining discourses and relations of power, and acting in response to situations of shared distress to transform these practices and so transform ourselves. Unfortunately, Kaufman's own initial answer to the problem of the standpoint was to push "through" relativism to advocate the construction of a theory of knowledge

> which can account for both its normative character and for its being bound to the concrete historical and psychological situation of the thinker. . . . Such a theory . . . would be *more comprehensive* than previous theories, thus expanding our knowledge and deepening our insight into the knowing process." (*RKF*, 23)

This project of grounding internal relativism in a theory of knowledge adequate to diverse sociocultural perspectives must appear Modern to the archaeological imagination. The hermeneutics of *Nacherleben* and *Verstehen* ignore the historicity of understanding in order to write the history of the past in terms of the present (the subject's own "transcended" and thus unacknowledged standpoint). The higher-order concepts function to ground the subject's experience of multiple positive perspectives by acting as the principles of their unification and transcendence in and by a self, world, and God. As the ultimate postulate of finite self-transcendence and freedom, "God" is a Modern concept, introduced by Kant (*ETM*, 24–25). Reflection on the concept of God is likewise Modern when it takes the form of constructing "toward" this anthropologically ideal entity. The reason is as follows.

In the preceding chapter I argued that the Principle of God's Humaneness left Kaufman's theology with the task of defining the human in terms of its ideal features (the attributes of God) and defining the Ultimately Humane by reflection on instances of finite humaneness. The truth of constructive discourse lies both in examples of "authentically human" behavior and in discourse *about* the authentically human, as construction nears that toward which reflection is directed ("God"). Constructive theology is both empirical, relying on cases of self-sacrificing love, responsibility, nonviolence, and transcendence for the truth of its discourse, and critical, depending upon the humaneness of the concept of God to justify any particular construction's truth. As Foucault's analysis of the empirico-transcendental double has shown, however, "a discourse attempting to be both empirical and critical cannot but be both positivist and eschatological; man appears within it as a truth both reduced and promised. Precritical naïveté holds undivided rule" (*OT*, 320). What is "precritical" about Kaufman's theological anthropology is its theoretical relation between the imagination, on the one hand, and the "materials" of language and culture on the other. The imagination can be directed toward "God" as its unthought, origin, or transcendental foundation when the reflecting theologian believes that the imagination is not properly "at home" in its genealogically specific environment. It is "precritical" to think that the imagination *transcends* power relations immanent in discourse and social practices. The *transformative* imagination advocated by Foucault is a thing of this world, which does not see its ideal function to consist in constructing (anthropological) pictures of an ultimate relativizer, beyond the specific concerns to which the transformative imagination is always already dedicated.

Having criticized the leading anthropological assumptions of constructive theology, however, at least three of its principal components remain potentially useful for thinking in a postanthropological ethos. These components are not lacking in Tracy's revisionist position, but their organization there around the formation of authentic self-knowledge, as I have analyzed it, limits their appeal for any postanthropological discourse.

First, Kaufman endorses construction and the self's responsibility for creatively transforming its linguistic and social world. Kaufman's call for third-order thinking has been hailed by theological deconstructionists and others as an important criterion for future work.[3] Foucault's many projects show that construction must think within power relations, not strive to go beyond them. His work also multiplies the targets of reconstructive activity, by demonstrating the capillary arrangement of power in contemporary society and its investment in anthropologically "liberating" discourses.

---

[3] Cf. Charles E. Winquist, "Body, Text, and Imagination," in idem, et al., *Deconstruction and Theology* (New York: Crossroad, 1982) 50–51; and the three papers of the AAR/Arts, Literature and Religion Section written in response to imaginative construction: J. Alfred Martin, Jr., "The Significance of Aesthetics for Theology as Imaginative Construction," *JAAR* 50 (1982) 81–85; Giles Gunn, "On the Relation between Theology and Art in the Work of Gordon D. Kaufman," *JAAR* 50 (1982) 87–91; and Walter H. Capps, "Theology as Art Form," *JAAR* 50 (1982) 93–96.

After Foucault, however, there is more for the constructive theologian to be responsible for, but fewer to whom the theologian is to be responsible. The size of the constructing theologian's community is defined by the numbers of those sharing his or her distress, not by the "community" of intelligent, reasonable, responsible persons. The theologian assists others in their struggles, but does not claim to speak for them.

Second, constructive theology offers a critical principle for interrogating the truth claims of any discipline. If the concept of God could be deconstructed to perform in discourse as the concept of difference, it could function as the raison d'être of genealogical "suspicion" and imaginative self-transformation.[4] For Foucault, the validity of a critical principle is warranted by the genealogist's perception of difference in manifest unity. In the Modern age of normalizing discourses and technologies, one must question every claim to identity, continuity, and depth significance, as potentially a denial of truth's affiliation with power. The transformative imagination criticizes the appearance of identities, genealogically restoring their existing matrix of power relations and tracing their emergence from "lowly origins." In so doing, it does not transcend its own "origins" or empowered relations. (If it attempted to do so, it would cease to be ironic and would resume traditional seriousness.) It risks construction within these interests for the sake of those who have them.

The responsible criticism and transformation of language and practices is additionally served by constructive theology's pragmatic criterion of truth. The truth of an assertion is not its adequacy to common human experience, but its usefulness in pointing out the difference between particular experiences (its value for criticism) and its usefulness in transforming reality according to concrete needs and interests (its value for construction). By rejecting representation as a goal for constructing higher-order concepts, Kaufman opens the door to transforming the self and its realm of concerns according to pragmatic criteria of true discourse. In short, construction, criticism, and pragmatism are the components of Kaufman's program which I believe would be useful for thinking in the modern ethos.

Whether, after renouncing supernatural and anthropological foundations, this thinking would call itself "theology," or assume a new identity, or no name at all, is an important question only to the "Modern soul," which relies

---

[4] That genealogy and construction imply each other, once the hermeneutics of suspicion has been accepted as "a part of what it means to think theologically," is an extension of the thesis developed in Charles Winquist, "Theology, Deconstruction, and Ritual Process," *Zygon* 18 (1983) 309. Winquist claims, "The construction of limit concepts is a continual deconstruction of fixed frontiers" (ibid.).

on the deployment of serious discourse to establish its deep truth. I must agree with Foucault, however, when he observes, "The irony of this deployment is in having us believe that our 'liberation' hangs in the balance" (*HS*, 159).